WHAT MATTERS MOST

WHAT MATTERS MOST

THE GET YOUR SHIT TOGETHER GUIDE TO WILLS, MONEY, INSURANCE, AND LIFE'S "WHAT-IFS"

Chanel Reynolds

HARPER WAVE
An Imprint of HarperCollinsPublishers

WHAT MATTERS MOST. Copyright © 2019 by Chanel Reynolds. All rights reserved. Printed in the United States of America. No part of this book may be used or reproduced in any manner whatsoever without written permission except in the case of brief quotations embodied in critical articles and reviews. For information, address HarperCollins Publishers, 195 Broadway, New York, NY 10007.

HarperCollins books may be purchased for educational, business, or sales promotional use. For information, please email the Special Markets Department at SPsales@harpercollins.com.

FIRST EDITION

Images courtesy of HorenkO/Shutterstock, Inc; Andriano/Shutterstock, Inc.; deardiz/Shutterstock, Inc. and ILYA AKINSHIN/Shutterstock, Inc.

Library of Congress Cataloging-in-Publication Data has been applied for.

ISBN 978-0-06-268943-6

19 20 21 22 23 LSC 10 9 8 7 6 5 4 3 2 1

For Gabriel and Lyric

Keep the snarl open and loose at all times and *do not pull on the end;* permit it to unfold itself. As the process is continued the end gradually emerges. No snarl is too complicated to be solved by this method; only patience is required.

Clifford Ashley, *The Ashley Book of Knots*

Contents

PART III: ALWAYS

A Note to the Reader

never wanted to have to write this book. And yet, even though I find myself here completely by accident—here we are. So, friend, a couple of quick things.

No, I am not a lawyer, financial planner, or insurance agent. Other than this book, I'm not here to sell you anything, just to tell you what I learned over the last nine years.

Yes, it's a little embarrassing to share my lowest moments after one of my biggest fears came true, the mistakes I made, and how wrong I got it. However, if it really is the truth that sets us free, here is every inch of it. My hope is that this path becomes a little easier for you if (or when) you find yourself (or someone you love) walking down this road. Besides, if it weren't all too true, you can bet *I would have made myself look much, much better.* Struggle isn't pretty, so we might as well just get honest about it.

And being honest is exactly what getting your shit together means in this book. Serious topics require real-life language and talking like humans. *I don't have my shit together* were the actual words I said standing five feet away from my husband, who wasn't waking up from a coma. Giving all or none of the fucks or swearing up a marketing trend was never the point. I was entirely terrified. That's all.

In fact, because my memory was, let's be clear, not exactly reliable on occasion, I triple-checked facts, toured the hospital, and interviewed dozens of people who were there in order to describe as accurately as I can what really happened. But the only story I'm telling is my own, as I experienced and remember it. Excavating and mapping friends' memories and asking what the kids remember revealed that we were often in the same room but completely in our own heads, our brains interpreting wildly different meanings, feeling entirely opposite emotions.

However, what we all remember is, everything really sucked after José died. For a long time. But even during the moments when I felt like I might die, too, I knew that I wanted to live, be happy again, and come out the other end alive and whole. There is hard stuff in here, but you *can* absolutely get your shit together. You can do this. We all can.

We don't drown by falling into the water. We drown by staying there.

WHAT MATTERS MOST

Introduction

n July 2009, my husband, José, was riding his bike down Lake Washington Boulevard in Seattle when he was struck by a van and killed. It took a week for him to die. I did not choose for him to die, but I had to choose to let him go.

Three and a half years later, I launched a website called Get Your Shit Together. It wasn't fancy, but it tackled all of the legal and financial things I wish I had done before José's accident and I wish I'd known in the weeks and months afterward. The seed had been planted as I sat next to José in the ICU wondering, *What if he doesn't wake up? Can I keep the house? What is probate? How much insurance do we have? What is the password to his phone?*

I'd turned to my friend and said, "Oh my god, I don't have my shit together. At all."

As the days went by, the questions multiplied and my fears snowballed.

If I don't have my shit together, what about everyone else in this hospital, and those people with young kids sleeping in the waiting room? And all of their families? And people in every other hospital?

There were so many forehead-slap moments during my tumble down the rabbit hole after José died, but I could feel this one forming a permanent bruise: the fall might have been shorter, the landing a bit softer, and the uncertainty perhaps less terrifying, if we had completed a few more of the basics ahead of time, like updating our insurance and having an emergency fund. Turns out, this stuff is actually pretty easy to get done once you know where to start. Through the advice, tips, and "handy lists" on the Get Your Shit Together website, I hoped to use what I'd learned to help as many people as possible get prepared before something terrible happened, so they wouldn't have to slog the same path I had.

It worked.

In fact, it really worked. I launched the site on a Monday night, and in twenty-four hours, thousands of folks had visited. By the end of the week, it was featured in Ron Lieber's Your Money column, and my face was on the front page of the Business section in the *New York Times*. Apparently, a lot of people read it. The online article stayed at the top of the "most read" and "most shared" lists for days. Traffic to the site spiked so quickly, the server almost crashed. Tina Brown called me.

Within days, strangers hugged me in the dairy section of the grocery store and told me their secrets. A few weeks later, I was on *CBS This Morning* chatting with Gayle King. Before the month was out, a much larger company with deep pockets offered to buy me out. I turned them down. Invitations to speak at conferences all over the country poured in and within a year my first, very simple two-page checklist was downloaded over a million times. I was beside-myself excited, but how happy can you get when you're being celebrated for the hard lessons you learned after your husband's death and essentially getting your ass handed to you? It got, um, complicated.

But I no longer felt alone in the struggle. In fact, my inbox flooded with thousands of emails from strangers, from Australia to Abu Dhabi. Many said over and over how bad they felt about putting off doing their wills for so many years, how worried they were for themselves, their kids, or their families because nothing had been organized or sorted out. Others knew *exactly* what I had gone through, or some adjacent level of hell, and were relieved to hear that they weren't alone, and maybe not crazy after all.

My sister's husband has been diagnosed with terminal can-
cer and they have very little in the way of planning taken
care of.

I worry, worry, worry about what might happen to our chil-
dren if one or (god forbid) both of us died. The idea of my
children going into the care of the state paralyzes me with fear.
Okay, there it is. Fear because of the past, and fear of the fu-
ture. We're a bit stuck here.

My elderly parents . . . spent the last four months fighting to
get online access to their banks, to find paperwork for accounts
and policies started 30+ years ago. Nothing is organized and
it's taken many phone calls and faxed power of attorney letters
to start to get a handle on their finances.

About half of the people who wrote to me were grateful for the
kick in the pants to actually get their shit together. The website gave
them just enough info and pointed them in the right direction. A few
simple steps had an incredible impact.

On the last day of maternity leave last week, we had our wills
and power of attorneys notarized and witnessed! I also got us
term life insurance to help cover the costs of the girls and even
some college.

After I watched a family friend go through a sudden death that
no one was prepared for . . . I went through and laid out as
much of what I want to have happen as I could.

To know that no matter what happens to me, or how our final
interaction with each other goes (assuming we don't go out at
the same time) the last thing my wife and family will remember
me by are the letters that I took the time to write.

Another group of letters knocked me on my ass. These were from people hurting, hard, right now.

My husband recently died in our home unexpectedly with my children here . . . There was no insurance. It's a scary situation.

My adult daughter is currently in an induced coma.

A week ago, a friend of mine very suddenly lost her husband and finds herself a single mother of two.

They were looking for help, advice, any kind of lifeline or beacon in the fog, even from a complete stranger who just told the whole world she hadn't gotten a lot of it right herself.

How do I pay her bills? And if she dies, which is always a possibility, how do I handle that if no will is found?

Our neighbor's husband just died of a massive heart attack and she needs to get organized quickly because finances are going to be very tight.

This one just gutted me. I could have written it myself only a few years before:

This is going to be short as I am now sitting in a hospital room with my husband . . . I am in the same boat . . . I have no passwords, documents, etc. We don't know what the future brings us. We don't even know if he will wake up. I went to your site, but am too exhausted to look.

But it was this question, and a handful of letters with the same question that really sucker-punched me:

Do you have any examples of how people use this site after-the-fact?

Um, nope. I did not.

Once again, I could have had a red spot on my forehead for the number of times I wanted to slap myself. Not for one stupid second did it dawn on me that in my hopes to help people take care of this stuff *before*, I would find a whole lot of people, like me, living in a world of hurt *after*.

As good as I felt about launching Get Your Shit Together, all of the advice, tips, and "handy lists" on the site were helping many of the 50 percent of Americans who still had time to get their shit together before something happened. But there were also those for whom the shit had already hit the fan. And the site wasn't doing much of anything for them.

After the outpouring of responses, I realized what I'd touched on was bigger than I'd ever imagined. Reading email after email from strangers around the world, asking for help and advice, convinced me there was still so much more I could do to help folks avoid unnecessary sadness and very avoidable confusion before *and* after disaster strikes. However, as much as my Midwestern upbringing was trying to tell me to toughen up and just work harder, after a year or two of trying, I had to admit I couldn't do it alone.

We're in the Same Boat

As early as those first days in the hospital, my friends squeezed my hand, saying, "We don't have any of this stuff done, either." If I had a dollar for every time over the years someone whispered to me, cold terror in their eyes, "You could be me," I could have purchased helicopters for each member of my extended family by now. I can throw out pages of stats, but these should do:

- Over half of the adults in the US don't have a will.
- Seven out of ten have not written down their end-of-life wishes.
- Out of all the twenty-year-olds today, over one in four will become disabled before retirement.
- About 40 percent of adults in America can't cover a $400 emergency, and 25 percent have no retirement savings at all.

Every study seems to report that pretty much no one is saving enough for retirement. We're living longer but are generally sicker. However, we've been fire-hosed with stats for so long, they don't really seem to "move the needle," as folks like to say. But a few things do. Like stories of personal, searing loss. The truth is, we could all use a hand to guide and help us along.

So, when I was approached by a few Seattle start-up veterans who each had a personal story of near miss or sudden death or parents with shifting health, I decided to team up with them and create a new site and a company where "we" help people get shit done. With this book, I want to tell my whole story of what happened and everything I had to go through to learn (the hard way) what critical things were on the "what I wish I would have done" list in the first place. I believe the action items and checklists are the tasks we need to do, but our stories are what opens the door and gets us in the room. We, not the documents or to-dos, are the entry point.

How I Got My Shit Together

So it's all here, all of it. I've included practical advice, checklists, must-dos, and detailed guides—and what really happened, alongside what I had to do and go through to come out the other side. With the help of this book, you can get your shit together based on what your life looks like and what is most important to you. I won't presume to know how you can best take care of yourself or your family, kids, house, pets, bills, mortgage, grocery shopping, housecleaning, carpools, finances, or forgiveness. Everyone is different, yes, but if you accomplish a handful of basic tasks, I guarantee the benefits can be profound. I'll walk you through them.

- Jot down a few important personal details and passwords.
- Assign or update your beneficiaries.
- Update (or finally get) the right insurance policies.
- Finish your will, living will, and power-of-attorney documents.
- Plan for at least six months of expenses in a savings fund.
- Save for a long and lovely retirement or an emergency tomorrow.
- Prioritize the urgent items from the not-so-important.

And I'll answer questions, including

- What happens if I can't find the will or any legal documents?
- How do I make sure beneficiaries and heirs are clearly outlined?
- What happens when someone dies without a will?
- What if my best friend's husband just died and I don't know what to say?
- How do I choose guardians (and temporary guardians) for my kids and pets?
- Who should be my executor or health-care representative and what do they do?
- What's the safest way to share my account information and passwords?

And, of course,

- What do I do about our sex toys and all the porn?

You may already be thinking, *Oh god, I don't know the password to my partner's phone,* or, *Shit, is my ex still listed as the beneficiary on my life insurance?!* Maybe that last one got your attention. I've got good news: you've got options.

Language Matters

Do you know how much your vagina is worth? Your partner's ability to walk? Your mother's vision? Your own life? My latte almost got laughed out through my nose the first time I heard the term the insurance industry uses, being "made whole," to define what it means (or how much they owe you) when they cut you a check to make up for your loss.

I've now given hundreds of talks where we workshop, role-play, and get really direct about naming and writing down end-of-life wishes. People use real words that reflect real life, including their fears and feelings.

The phrase "get your shit together" rings true. It's real. And human. This is how we actually feel and talk about this stuff, whether you're at the kitchen counter over a pile of bills trying to figure out how to pay for summer camp or if your parents can still manage on their own, or squeezing your partner's hand while on the phone listening to your doctor share the lab results. Talking about the things that scare or worry us in the most honest way we can is so powerful—but, oddly, the colloquial sometimes rubs people the wrong way.

I'd assume that, given the fact that the insurance, legal, financial, funeral, and cloud-storage industries are making hundreds of billions of dollars off American consumers each year—yes, I said *hundreds of billions of dollars annually*—they'd be better at, you know, talking to us like real people. The barista down the street knows how to spell my name and sometimes writes a cute #5 next to it. The insurance company? My husband's name was José, but as soon as he died, they only referred to him as "the decedent."

The legal folks? Among all of the positive feedback and "You

go, girl" support I received at the launch of the Get Your Shit Together website, I needed only my fingers to count the number of
"You suck" or "I hate your bangs" letters I got, but there was one
comment that made me wish I could shoot lasers out of my eyes.
It came from a lawyer who took issue with my website's name and
its "coarseness of communication" because "the whole process de-
serves more dignity."

To this I call bullshit.

When the housing bubble burst and people lost their homes, *or everything*, did they say, "Well, darn, we really should have looked into
our debt/spend ratio and loan options more closely"? When all those
people lost their entire retirement savings because of Enron's collapse,
did they say, "Oh my heavens, we really should have diversified our
investments to minimize risk"? I don't think so. I'll bet, "Oh shit,
honey, we're totally fucked for retirement now," is a *lot* closer to what
was said at the dinner table. There is no dignity in ripping people off
and getting rich in the process.

Dignity is a word often used to shut people up or to gaslight them.
Let's stick with honesty.

Save your clutched pearls for Sunday brunch; we're building a
movement so more of us will be less screwed when something happens.

In fact, this tighty-whitey sanitized language—like "passing on"
instead of just saying "died"—is part of the problem, along with
the reams of opaque laws with undecipherable language to spell out
the policies we pay for, and the no-accountability, non-fiduciary,
jacked-up fees that siphon hundreds of millions off our retirement
plans. This is what makes us throw up our hands and not even want
to deal with any of it. Consider:

- Do you think Americans aren't saving well because we don't
  know where the bank is?
- I am pretty sure the reason over 50 percent of us don't have
  our wills done is *not* because there aren't enough lawyers.

Getting Shit Done

So, yeah, we're going to go at this a little differently, with real words and human language about actual people that has room for feelings and space for what scares us. And we'll just do our best a day, or a page, at a time.

You can't be certain that Future You won't decide to spend every penny on a one-way ticket to Mars instead of giving it all to charity someday. And I will argue that's a good thing. It means you're thinking about what's important now, while the stakes are low—so you aren't panicked and problem-solving critical stuff for the first time when you are at your lowest and the stakes are much, much higher. But Present-Day You can make sure Future You isn't screwed over by getting started. A 90 percent perfect will that is done and signed is far better than none at all (almost always better, the lawyers would say).

I know. You're busy. I hear your sighs and see the eye-rolls. I get it. Gen Xers (raises hand) today are a huge sandwich generation of extremely stressed people: work, kids, car pools, dishes, laundry, errands, bills, and no time or money. Add our aging Boomer parents who don't have their shit together either, and it's a perfect storm of suffering simmering just offshore—swelling and heading in our collective direction.

Trying to brace for a wave that huge makes pretty much everyone want to binge-watch Netflix or rearrange the sock drawer instead. But there *is* a big wave just over the horizon, and it is coming straight for us. We need to stop avoiding it as if we can just have a dance party on the beach taking selfies and giving the wave the finger.

If you can make it to the dentist, get your oil changed, have your annual exam, pull your kid's retainer out of the garbage disposal with your bare hands, or survive one of those Brazilian waxes, getting your will done will be a fucking cakewalk.

Many legal and financial professionals incorrectly assume that "people don't want to talk about death." In fact, we think and worry about it all the time. We are almost always relieved when we can talk about it instead of anxiously wringing our hands together in the dark long after we should be sleeping. *What Matters Most* takes away the fear and overwhelm of estate planning and shows you where to start.

I get it. I've been there. And I've got some answers to your questions ready.

Hoping for the Best Is Not a Plan

I've spent twenty-five years managing big, new-technology projects, and every inch of my brain has been working nonstop for the last nine years figuring out how we, collectively, can get our shit together. I've researched, conducted surveys, talked to experts, and listened to stories from thousands of people across the country after workshops and in coffee shops, and I've consolidated all of that information in this book. There will be something in here, if not many things, that you or someone you know may really need. It could make a huge difference.

When life gets hard, everything else around you should get softer. Sadly, that is rarely the case for most of us, as losing someone often means losing income, financial security, or our home. It may also force bankruptcy. How much of this suffering can we ease? What are the items we can put into the "optional" pile? There *are* ways to make that a smaller, lighter pile.

As Ron Lieber wrote in his *New York Times* article about my story, "Sometimes, we just need to meet the person in personal finance." This letter tells a story that could be mine, yours, a friend's, or a coworker's.

A very dear friend lost her husband to a sudden heart attack. In a moment of levity and lightness in the dark, scrambled days immediately following his death, she calmly and proudly brought out a folder to show us how organized (and loving) her husband had been to get all of his shit together in one place, having followed your website's checklist after the birth of their twin daughters 15 months prior.

Nine years after José died, almost to the exact day, our community lost another person in a very similar accident, leaving a spouse and young children behind. Even after almost a decade, doing this work is still hard on me. News like this makes my chest tight, and I'm anxious for days. *And,* through a mutual friend I received this note from the surviving spouse just *days* after the accident:

Chanel, you are the sole reason I made Alex keep a notebook containing every damned username and password. I'm sure there are many times I will run up against a brick wall with things, but I'm in fairly good shape, all thanks to you.

So, friends, in a world where so much is out of our control, let's take care of the stuff we can change.

PART I Before

Breathe, you are alive.

—THÍCH NHÁT HẠNH

Life Goes Sideways

I f your world is going to fall entirely apart in one second, having a martini in your hand at a dear friend's BBQ on a perfect summer evening in Seattle isn't the worst place I can think of to "get the phone call."

Actually, I missed the call. It was an apocalyptic voicemail that told me my whole life had just gone sideways.

You know that feeling when adrenaline kicks in and you time-travel across the kitchen to grab your toddler's hand before he touches a hot stove, or you pull someone back from the curb an eighth of a second before they step in front of speeding car? In the car, my nervous system warp-speed skipped straight to DEFCON 5, making it hard to think straight at the same time my adrenaline was going nuclear. I would have wrestled a bear to get to my husband, José, but I didn't know exactly where he was. The voicemail said the ambulance took him but didn't say to which hospital.

OK, Chanel. Hands at ten and two o'clock.

Your son, Gabe, is safe with friends.

Your job right now is to drive the car.

What time did you leave the house? How long has it been?

Stop far enough from other cars to still see the car's tires in front of you.

Put your headset on so you can drive and make calls . . . oh god.

Don't die on the way to the hospital to see if your husband is alive.

Is he dead?

Call the big hospital.

"Harborview Medical Center. Can I help you?" said the emotionless voice of a hospital operator who had said these words a thousand times.

"Hi, I'm calling to confirm if you have my husband, José Hernando. He was in a bike accident?"

"Name again?" she asked.

"His name is Hernando, José Hernando. H-e-r-n-a-n-d-o. Not Hernandez, Hernando, with a silent *H*."

I'd been married to a Latino living in Seattle long enough; this was a well-practiced clarification.

"Hold a moment," she replied.

Then, "Just a minute please." Her voice was no longer flat.

Quickly, a new voice got on. "Are you calling for Mr. Hernando?"

"Yes, is he there?" I asked.

"We have him." Then she asked, "Is this the wife?"

"This is Chanel, his wife. Who is this?" I answered, trying to breathe.

"I am your social worker," she replied.

My heart skipped a beat. *Did she just say "social worker"?* An old friend who was a social worker herself always said, "You get the social worker when you're pretty much fucked."

Oh fuck.

Pause. Whatever-her-name-is took an about-to-say-something in-breath.

My tone drops. "Listen," I said, cutting her off. "Do everything possible to keep him alive until I get there."

Without even thinking, I said, "We have insurance."

"Oh, don't worry about that; we're not that kind of hospital," she replied.

"But we have it, the good kind, just so you know," I added.

Mile Markers

Halfway to the hospital I realized I needed to pull it together.

I needed help. Reinforcements. Because once I got there, it occurred to me I'd have to just . . . be there.

At the traffic light near Seattle's landmark Elephant Car Wash, I called my favorites list from the top down—the equivalent of shooting up flares and hoping someone sees the distress message.

Erin Galvin, my very close friend and a social worker who'd attended my son's birth and was listed as the emergency contact at Gabe's school and swimming lessons, was first. I left a voicemail. Not sure what to say, I told her José had been in an accident and I was on my way to Harborview, adding, "I think it's really bad" before hanging up.

Next. Curtis and Brad. We'd had dinner with them at least once a week since our kids were babies, but they were out of town with friends. I'd call them later.

Jen, José's dear friend and "spiritual sister," was after that. Straight to voicemail.

"Jen, I think you're already out camping for the weekend, but just in case, I wanted to let you know. José's been in an accident. I don't know anything more yet. Call when you can."

I called my mom next. Here I was, thirty-nine years old with a house, kid, dog, and adult life, but when this shit hits the fan, you just kinda want your mom there. She could fly out, stay with us for a few days, and take care of Gabe. Which meant she could also help take care of me.

"*Hiiiiiiii*, honey," she answered.

The overly exuberant voice threw me.

"Let me get your father on the other phone so . . ."

"Mom, no, wait. Stop. José was in an accident. I don't know how bad yet. I'm on my way to the hospital, but it sounds bad. I'm going to need some help. Mom . . . Mom . . . I . . . I gotta go. Driving."

I was leaving José's mother for last. Honestly, I was stalling, skipping over her name to avoid having to say her youngest child was taken to the ER at the hospital where the medevac helicopters go.

I paused, finger hovering.

José's name was next on the list. . . . *What if?*

I pressed CALL and voicemail picked up right away. Too quickly.

"Hi, you've reached José. . . . Please leave a message."

I'd heard the dip-swing in his voice a million times when leaving last-minute grocery store requests or when-are-you-gonna-be-home-from-work messages, but hearing it then sucked all the air out of the car. Tears, so hot they stung, poured down my cheeks.

"Um. Babe?" I choked on the words.

Please, please, please be alive when I get there.

I pulled up to the massive, old building and looked up at the big sign next to the Emergency arrows. PROVIDENCE, it said. Oh holy fuck, I'd driven to the *wrong hospital.*

I stared at my car's gearshift for a long moment, unable to move it from PARK back into DRIVE. I couldn't, or wouldn't, move.

Then I closed my eyes and attempted some sort of temperature check on the universe. Didn't work.

So, I leaned forward in my seat and squinted over the car dashboard toward the horizon over Puget Sound, past the rooftops, west, because that's where one is supposed to look, as if answers were written in the sky to tell me where he was, how he was.

Is he dead? Can I feel it? Shouldn't I be able to?

My *calm-the-fuck-down-you-can-do-this* voice was getting harder to hear. There was a low, slow wail rising up into my throat like the tornado warning alarm I remembered from Minnesota summers.

I'M WASTING TIME! WHAT IF I MISS HIM? WHAT IF HE'S DYING RIGHT THIS SECOND?

Chanel, sweetie, as far as problems go right now, this is one you can solve. Call the hospital back. Ask for the address and cross streets. Then, you drive there.

I recognized I was in shock: my calming voice when shit really goes wrong is the Midwestern accent of my childhood. Think *ding*, "This is the captain speaking," in the voice of Frances McDormand in the movie *Fargo*:

All righty, then, so we've just run into a little bumpy patch here, so we're going to take it nice and easy here the next few minutes to get to the hospital in one piece. Just real easy now. You see? All ya hafta do is drive the car down the road now, OK?

I pulled up in front of the correct hospital and swerved into a thirty-minute loading zone as a white medical-supply truck pulled out. I jumped out of the car, followed the red Emergency signs through the entrance door, and ran down the hallway only to skid to a halt at the entrance to the ER waiting room, like some silly cartoon character flailing on ice. An invisible, visceral force field prevented me from walking one more step. My intestines lodged in the back of my throat with the same ferocious nausea I'd felt only during the worst of my first-trimester morning sickness.

I don't want to go in there.

We're not supposed to be here.

The double doors were wedged open so without even entering I could see into the room and the few dozen people in rows of chairs waiting. One man held bandages to the side of his head, and a teenager a few aisles away struggled to hold a giant blue icepack on his elbow. Each person, including the handful of staff holding clipboards or at the heavy-glass windowed desks, appeared to have been washed too many times on the heavy-duty cycle. Everyone appeared as if faded into monochrome. Their faces expressed what I'd imagined a demilitarized zone looks like after learning there are no more transports coming.

When I got my feet back underneath me, I forced myself to march through the doors, past the take-a-number ticket stand, and straight to the intake window, where I blurted out, "I am supposed to come straight up here. The social worker told me she'd be waiting for me. Not to wait."

Both the drab hospital admin with the demeanor of the aggressively tired or underemployed and the client she was assisting, a woman vibrating to some jacked-up frequency with a concave mouth and eyes, stopped talking to stare at me with slight bows of the head and eyes full of pity.

"Are you the wife? She's waiting for you," the intake admin reassured me as she reached for the phone.

"The wife is here," she whispered into the receiver, no longer meeting my eyes.

I didn't hate the social worker right away, whatever her name was. As I was walk-running down the hallway, I looked back at her wondering why she wasn't moving more quickly. For a half second I assumed she couldn't physically keep up, but the look on her face said she wasn't pushing to keep up; she'd stopped on purpose.

She just fucking stood there, watching me sprint down the hall, even though she knew where José was located in the ER and I didn't have a clue. All I wanted was to get to him as quickly as possible. Her eyes scanned the walls and ceiling as if the right words were around there somewhere but she had misplaced them. She opened her mouth and started to talk.

Oh god, she's trying to have a fucking intervention with me.

"Your husband, Chanel, José. He's very . . . he's very sick," she stuttered.

I was a solid few yards ahead of her and forced myself not to claw her eyes out or light her on fire to get her to stop talking and start moving again.

Oh Jesus, she's using some Social Worker 101 "break news gently" technique or something. Is she new?

And sick? Did she just say he was sick?

"He is not *sick*. He's *hurt*. I get it and I don't want to talk to you so just bring me to my husband! WHERE IS HE?!"

I was no longer not yelling.

She pointed around the corner to an open door and I never saw her again.

Out-of-Body Basics

I had an eerie feeling when I walked into the room and saw José for the first time. There he was on the bed, in a hospital gown, IVs and tubes everywhere, but besides the ventilator thrumming away with a noise about as pleasant as Darth Vader trying to make out with you, it was oddly quiet. There was only one other person in the room, a nurse, and he looked relieved to see me. And sad to see me. When he asked if I was the wife, I barely nodded. Pulled across the room as if by a magnet, I snapped to the left side of the bed and before even reaching him somehow inhaled and choked out a sob that came from somewhere light does not get.

The thing about keening is that it feels like you are actually dying. Tears exploded out of my face, and I sprayed snot and spit when I was able to push out an exhale. Long stringy slobber dangled out of my mouth as I leaned over him, bent in a ninety-degree angle with my arms stretched across his chest. I became a million screaming suffocated cells.

I must have been like that for at least twenty minutes, but finally I started to breathe halfway normally again. The noises, like a herd of velociraptors being slowly crushed to death by a mountain, had stopped coming out of me.

The nurse put the Kleenex box near me, as he must have sensed I would come around and look up at some point. That little bit of kindness was so sweet. It was a small thing, but he was telling me that I wasn't alone in here. I noticed that he'd put the box on José's chest, as if it wasn't weird to just put stuff on people as if they were furniture or just convenient places to put things. But that may be something folks who work in the ER don't have the luxury to think about. The nurse walked past me and said he'd let the doctor know I was here.

Then I really saw him. I stroked his dark hair and noticed the thin hospital gown. His face looked fixed; he wasn't moving, and he was pale. The eight-inch line of Frankenstein stitches down his neck and shoulder looked clean but so puffy. That was the one thing that looked specifically wrong. Even so, I could tell that everything was so not right. His chest rose and fell with jerks, a harsh surrogate for breathing. The little pieces of dried blood from his hair had rubbed off and started to soften and turn red in the palm of my hand. Later, I learned that his body tore the passenger-side mirror off the van.

The curtain rings scrape-swooshed open and the beginning of a constant flow of people started coming in and out. A lot of people. And they all looked right at me, or through me, and everyone seemed to talk to everyone else all at once. Thankfully, this was when Erin arrived.

Erin had been at a movie and drove over immediately after getting my voicemail. She placed her steadying hands on both my shoulders and I was relieved she was there. Of course I had no idea she'd already located and called the head nurse of the shift on staff and speed-counseled her husband, Josh, one of José's closest friends, who was sobbing in the hallway outside, to "pull it together before you go in there."

The ER doc rushed into the room. "You're the wife? They just told me you were here."

I stood in front of him with my hand on the end of the bed near José's feet, and Erin stood just behind me.

He introduced himself as the attending physician; the way he so casually took over the room, or maybe just the white coat, seemed to say he was in charge. To keep myself in my body and help me pay attention to what he was starting to say, I blinked harder and squinted a bit. I hoped it would help me translate the sounds coming out of his mouth into a string of letters with meaning. It was a fight to think or hear clearly, to keep my brain from melting through my eye sockets onto the floor.

"The paramedics were shocked to find a pulse," he said. "They were sure he was a DOA . . . cardiac . . . intubated . . . first aid happened to be on scene."

More word-sounding noise.

X-rays were being held up and compared like some spot-the-difference search in a magazine, but I could barely tell what part of José's body I was looking at.

They thought he was a DOA?

"Um, OK—you've never seen anyone in all your years in the ER survive an injury like this," I repeated.

While the doctor was pointing to where the spine and skull connect in another X-ray, I stared at his lips, preparing myself to catch all of his next words, squinting to focus.

I wonder if he knows he has really nice-looking lips?

"Well, if we can get him stable, then there's maybe a 50-50 chance," he said.

One fifty percent he lives and . . . what? Walks again? Lives in a wheelchair? Is paralyzed from the waist down? At least he could compete in the Special Olympics. . . . What about from the neck down? No movement at all? Like Christopher Reeve? Biting that straw-thing to move the chair around? But can he talk? Play chess? Say hello? Know who I am? Blink out a novel with one eye?

"When you say 50-50, do you mean you can fix his neck?" I asked.

"Let me say that again. *If* we can even get him stable enough for surgery, there is maybe a 50-50 chance he makes it off the table. We just don't know; we can't say," he said, meticulously choosing his words.

"I've never seen anyone sustain this kind of injury this long before," he continued, looking at José.

Is he looking into José's body, a bit confounded, imagining the X-rays of his neck?

"Chanel, you realize he can still die at any second, right? Chanel?" His eyes locked onto mine. His gaze was completely calm.

I squinted back, trying to track what the ER doc was saying. *Blink. Blink.* My brain said "huh?" while my head nodded "yes." The hospital smell was making me woozy. All the pings and bings of the machines, the jerky rise and fall of José's chest, the tubes, all the voices and medical terms—everything started swirling around me, like the head rush that comes with those black starry dots and tunnel vision

that appear before you pass out. I looked down at the floor, then back
to the hospital bed and the rise and fall of the ventilator.

"He can still die . . . Chanel?" the ER doc repeated, still staring
at me.

The yelling and moaning coming from the other patient just a few
feet away got louder.

I turned from the metronomic rise-fall of José's chest to look back
at the ER doc's face.

"Chanel?" he asked again, holding my gaze.

*Some guy is losing his shit or dying behind a bedsheet-thin curtain
a few feet away and it's like white noise to him.*

The doc's eyebrows, deepening with concern, appeared farther and
farther away.

*Isn't it odd that right now I am paying attention to how lovely his
lips are?*

"So C1 through C4 is damaged or, you said, crushed? Tell me
about the surgery. How do we get him into surgery?" I somehow
managed to ask.

The low moaning from the next bed continued.

"Sir, Sirrrrrrr. I am going to need ya to put your penis away again
or we're gonna hafta put those handcuffs back on, okayyyyy?" the
nurse instructed in a voice of unflinching sternness. She was clearly
beyond irritated.

"You're a bitch cunt . . . *mumble-mumble* . . . argh-auuuggh!"
shouted our friend next door.

The doctor left to check on the latest tests and consult with the surgeon and head neurologist. I pointed at the curtain where it sounded
like the hospital staff were "assisting" our belligerent roommate next
door and looked back to Erin for an eternal few silent seconds before
saying, "I can't believe you used to work here." She'd been a social
worker in the ER at Harborview and had probably counseled families
in this very same room.

She nodded in the way you do when there is no good answer, or
none really at all.

"Hey sweetie, where is Gabe right now? Can Josh go pick him up for you?" she asked.

"He's at my friend Sunshine's. You remember her from the baby shower? I told him it was a surprise sleepover. He wasn't convinced and looked a little freaked out, but he's safe and is totally taken care of for the night. I didn't know what I'd find when I got here. I didn't want him to see . . . this."

"Of course. How smart of you to figure that out so fast. OK, so is there anyone we need to call?"

I showed her my phone and pointed to the list of folks I'd called or left a voicemail. "My mom is getting on an early flight. I talked to José's mom and she's coming. She's going to call his brother and sister. I suppose we should call Connie once we know what's happening so she can talk to Lyric?"

José's ex, Connie, should decide what and when to tell their middle school–age daughter, my stepdaughter, Lyric. She was at summer camp out on the San Juan Islands and was a full day of travel away.

"I saw Connie in the hall and already talked to her. She went back home. I told her I'd update her," Erin assured me.

"Wait, she's here? She left? How did she know to come here?" I asked.

"I'm not entirely sure, but it sounds like someone from José's bike team was at the accident and started calling people to find you. He went straight to your house but when you weren't there, he started knocking on all your neighbors' doors to see if anyone had your number. I guess a woman a block away named Maia knows you and had your number, and she called Connie, too. Do we need to call anyone else?"

"Well, I suppose I should let our friends know that Gabe probably won't make it to the birthday party tomorrow."

I thought this was very important.

After a long few seconds, she said, "OK, how about I call them for you later. For now, how about family? Any of the Hernandos?"

"Oh yeah. I don't have their phone numbers saved in my contacts but they gave me this when I first got here."

I held up José's phone, surprised it'd been in my hand the whole time. Someone had given it to me. Was it the nurse?

"They couldn't open it. I tried a few times, but I don't know the password, so it keeps locking me out."

"How about we give this to Josh to figure out. And, can I carry your phone for you?"

"But what if someone calls?"

"I'll answer it for you. I'll just make a few calls for you and give it back."

My hands did not want to let go of the phone. But I did.

I've heard many people say they hit the jackpot because their sister-in-law is an attorney, or someone's close friend is a doctor, or a real estate agent, or a locksmith, and that person magically bailed them out of an otherwise catastrophic event with one phone call. I see your doctor or attorney and raise you social workers with every chip I've got. Erin understood how the ER worked and how to navigate what ends up being an unfathomably giant system. If we'd been in *The Hunger Games*, Erin would be the player with the bow and arrow you'd want as your ally.

Somewhere between minutes and an eternity later, the surgeon had been located and was on his way. Meanwhile the doctors gathered a team of people, a special gurney, and a surgery table with straps that could somehow hold José steady while flipping him over. This way, his back faced up so the surgeon could "get in there" and "see what was happening." Trying to describe José's injuries, the ER doc made a hand motion like popping a cork out of a champagne bottle. I didn't know what it meant but I knew it wasn't good.

José was alive, but I saw how the doctors, nurses, cardiologists, neurologists, pulmonologists, and specialists who streamed through his room looked at him. Their heads shook back and forth with a mix of respect and despair, and hung lower, in what looked like shame, the longer they looked.

The Long Dark Night

The surgery waiting room was in the freezing basement and promptly became the war room. José's mom, Pat, and sister, Shelley, arrived in the ER just as he was being prepped for surgery. His brother, the oldest of the three, Robert, was close behind. I'd only half paid attention as I heard other folks had arrived or called well into the night. As I sat there, shivering in my lime-green sundress, with my purple bra poking out from under the thin straps, and flip-flops, I had a sense that outside of the room friends and family were scrambling to get to the hospital and make arrangements to stay for a while. But José's dad and the whole Hernando side of the family still hadn't been reached. Our wedding was the first time José's parents had been forced to be in the same location at the same time in over twenty years.

Sunshine was sending me regular updates that Gabe was fine. My mom was flying in at noon. Our friend Jen had gotten my voicemail and was en route from Yosemite back to San Francisco and would get the soonest flight up to Seattle.

Knowing Gabe was OK and my mom was coming was all I could really retain. Erin was able to triage and field phone calls, send updates, and coordinate the logistics for people just arriving. She'd assured me Josh was trying to find contact information for the Hernandos.

I stared at the double doors to the operating room, knowing that if the doctor came back too soon, it meant José hadn't made it. Before going into surgery, he stopped by to say he'd do everything he could, and the longer he was in there the better it was going. So, no news was good news, apparently. And all we could do was sit there and wait. Sit, and wait, and stare at the door.

Hours later, neither Erin nor Josh had been able to locate contact information for any of José's family, even by calling Information, so she handed the phones, mine and José's, back to me. His father's side of the family didn't know what had happened, and it had been hours since I'd arrived. The only way I could think of to reach them was through social media. It made me cringe to think of posting some-thing so public, but I was desperate. There wasn't any cell-phone cov-erage in the waiting area, so I took the elevator a few floors upstairs, sat against the wall of some hallway, and posted a status update on my Facebook page: "Hernando family please call me. . . ." A less-than-ideal way to get news that something is likely very wrong, but getting no news was worse. And it worked.

The East Coast cousins were the first to see the Facebook post. They called the Chicago cousin, who called their mom, José's aunt Marcia, who called Aunt Martha, who lived just an hour south of Seattle. Martha had called around to the hospitals, found out which one we were at, and was on her way before I even knew my call for help had been seen. I was relieved to learn the Hernandos knew, but it occurred to me that now *everyone else we know* knew, too.

Back in the freezing basement with the uncomfortable chairs cov-ered in medical-office-pastel cloth patterns that somehow looked gray, I waited out the night. A woman who looked a lot like the one at the desk in the ER kept fast-walking in and out of the waiting room to make phone calls via the free landline they had on the table for patients' families to use. She was obviously pissed about a missed hookup with what I assumed was her dealer and was getting pretty twitchy about it. A new social worker introduced herself, as we were now officially on the night shift. But then I didn't see her again.

Someone must have noticed I was cold, because Erin handed me a sweater I immediately put on and pulled over my chin and nose to rest just under my eyes as I stared at the door. I didn't sleep. I'd jerk my head back up after drifting or dozing off long enough for the worry-panic-screaming free-flow to swirl louder. It's not that my life flashed before my eyes but rather that I watched giant pieces of it calve off like hunks of an iceberg then rush at me in a wall of waves that smashed the past, present, and future into a squall hitting from every direction.

It was morning by the time the doctor finally appeared at the door. José was still alive. He pulled his surgical cap from his head and held it in his hands. Someone grabbed him a chair and placed it in the middle of the waiting room. We circled around him as if he were our camp counselor or preschool teacher. I think I asked him a lot of questions, and his responses, or lack of them, seemed to offer some hope. But the only real answer he seemed to have was, "Now we wait and see."

A new hospital shift was starting. Someone brought me a coffee. Sunshine texted me a picture of Gabe with a not-so-convincing smile, but he was at the beach with his arms around Sunshine's golden retriever with an impressive Cheeto stain across his shirt, so he was safe and being taken care of. It would take a number of hours for post-op to move José to the ICU. This would be a very good time to go home for a little bit, said everyone. At least to take a shower and change. I knew I had to sleep, or at least close my eyes, but that's when the thoughts swell up and come for you.

Guide:
When Life Goes Sideways

How long is forever? Sometimes, just one second.

—OFTEN ATTRIBUTED TO LEWIS CARROLL

I t's nearly impossible to look back on those first hours at the hospital and tell myself I was lucky. In fact, it didn't dawn on me until much later how lucky I was. In one or two ways, at least. Because during the worst possible moment of my life, nothing else went wrong—and it easily could have.

What if I wasn't at a friend's house where I could leave Gabe and run off overnight, knowing he was safe? What would have happened if I'd moved to a new town without friends or family living nearby and had to face that first night at the hospital alone? Or alone and trying to console or comfort my child or children at the same time? What would I have done if we'd had both kids staying with us that weekend and they were at playdates across town from each other? As a single mom with parents who don't live in the same state, I was kept up at night by these what-if scenarios. It haunted me that there was something I could have done to plan for predictable problems, as simple as leaving out an emergency key or agreeing with a neighbor to be backup childcare for each other, but hadn't.

I have been forced to admit that while I can't stop accidents or natural disasters from happening (I haven't figured out how to control nature or build a time machine, yet), I can make sure that if my car breaks down and I'm stuck, someone else can pick up my son from school or go to the house, send the babysitter home, fix dinner, and handle bedtime for both kids. But everyone has a different list.

Emergency Planning

When the shit hits the fan and a real-life high-stakes, scary, or traumatic event happens (or even *almost* happens), your brain goes into hyperdrive. From an evolutionary perspective, this initial rush of adrenaline helped us humans get not eaten or fight off predators, and in moments of extreme emotional duress our bodies still react the same way.

This is the moment you see in movies where the alien ships have just arrived and parked over your city and everyone frantically runs around throwing food and supplies into backpacks, looting stores and hotwiring cars, while others completely shut down and grab thirteen pairs of clean underwear but no drinking water and start mowing the lawn.

In my case, I was upright most of the time, trying to project-manage the threat away, but many other moments I was swimming in the completely-overwhelmed-and-not-thinking-straight pool, as evidenced by staring longingly at the ER doctor's lips (seriously, what the hell?!) and thinking that RSVPing to a five-year-old's birthday party was super important.

Emergency Situations

First of all, these are normal responses to extreme situations. When you experience a traumatic event, like a terrible accident or natural disaster, your brain and body go into crisis mode. You may breathe rapidly and feel nauseated, dizzy, or weak. You might feel anxious, irritable, hyperactive, or numb. I repeat: these are all completely normal responses. Since you'll likely feel off-kilter and have difficulty concentrating in a high-stress situation, having a plan in place for what to do in an emergency will make it a lot easier on you in those first few hours.

Emergency Planning: Start with Three Things

I feel better having a few basic things prepared in case of an (or another) emergency. I'm not alien-invasion ready, but I am "uh-oh, shit's going down" ready. Keep it simple—remember, this is for emergencies. Now isn't the time for endless edge cases. The first two things will help you in just about any scenario (from zombie apocalypse to planning a surprise birthday party), and the third is your choice. What could you do that would make you less worried? For me, and hundreds of people I've talked to, just a few things make a big difference in turning the anxiety and worry noise down a few notches.

1. On your cell phone, create a list of emergency contacts in your Favorites list. In case anything happens, you will be able to quickly and easily contact your family and friends. Bonus: fill in the "in case of emergency" (ICE) info in your phone so that in case anything happens to you, your emergency contacts will be informed immediately. Most phones enable your emergency contact info to be accessed when your phone is locked.

Have you set up the default emergency settings on your phone? Have you looked for and downloaded an ICE app?

Can you print out a fill-in-the-blank wallet-size card to keep in your wallet?

2. Establish an "in case of emergency" plan with your immediate family, especially your children. For example, Gabe knows that he should go to our neighbor's house if he's in trouble or anything is wrong.

If you are at home, who is closest and can help?
If you are at work or another location, can you (or someone else) meet or pick up your children or family member?
If you can't reach your family or emergency contact, what do you do next, and what/who is your backup plan?
Is your plan written down or saved to your phone to help you remember?

3. Your choice! What is one thing that would let you breathe easier, knowing it was prepared in case of an emergency? Consider:

Do you have elderly parents who need assistance?
Do you have pets that would need to be cared for?
Do you or your family members need medication or specialized care?

I feel better knowing there are two spare keys available in case my son is locked out after school or if there is an emergency. One is in a lockbox outside of my house, and one is with my neighbor (who can also feed our cat, Freddy, in a pinch).

YOUR EMERGENCY CHECKLIST:
GET A STATE OF THE STATE

Getting a "State of the State" means getting enough informa-tion to have a big-picture understanding, or at least good-enough overview, of the actual situation.

More simply, most of us just want to know: *What the hell is actually happening?!*

When things go terribly wrong, even if everyone is OK, or a near-miss derails your day but not the rest of your life, it really does feel like falling down the rabbit hole. That fall sucks ex-ponentially more when you can do nothing other than hope to hit the ground soon. This checklist is more of an in-the-moment guide, a list of things to think about before you're falling or have already crash-landed.

WHEN YOU "GET THE CALL"

☐ Are you clear about what the situation is? Are you in a safe place?

☐ Is someone with you, or does someone know where you are or can come get you?

☐ Do you need help? Is there someone you can ask?

☐ Are your family/kids/parents OK and in a safe place right now?

☐ Ask yourself: What (or who) would be helpful?

GET YOUR BEARINGS

☐ Do you know, or can you ask, what might happen next?

☐ Does care for children or elderly need to be arranged?

☐ What questions do you have, and what details should you remember?

- Record conversations with your phone to check facts and details later.
- Write questions down so you won't forget them.

SEND UP A FLARE

- ❑ Call key family members.
- ❑ Have someone else make/manage the rest of the calls.
- ❑ Use (or ask for) the professional help that is offered/available.

REMEMBER! If your brain and body are not at regular functioning capacity because you've just been thrust into a nightmare scenario, that is likely the worst possible time to search for phone numbers, scramble for a backup plan, or do *any* kind of problem-solving. Take five minutes now to get a few things organized in advance, and save yourself (or your friends and family) what could be hours of stress and frustration down the road.

Waiting for the Dice to Roll

I t was late into Saturday morning, and being away from the hospital for just a few hours already felt like far too long. I hadn't gotten any calls in the few hours I'd been home, so he was still alive. I'd made the head nurse and surgeon promise to call me if anything changed, if he woke up, if he died. In just over twelve hours, I'd gone from fearing José was dead, to surprise that he was still alive, to worried he could die at any second, to having no clear idea what his chance of recovery was.

Was there a chance?

So much waiting.

It had been light out when I crawled into bed a few hours before. I might have slept a little, but I only remember staring at the ceiling hearing imaginary voices in conversation about the details of how a spine connects to the brain, as if two television news show anchors read from Wikipedia pages and debated their contents. Then the channel in my head would switch to a moment when José called me by a favorite nickname. Then it would change to a replay of the time we were out on a walk and I was irritated about wedding planning (or something) and after a minutes-long monologue of my growing list of grievances against him, he jokingly clutched his chest and fell down on the grass in an overly dramatic attempt to fake a heart attack so

I'd stop spiraling out and complaining. I smiled as I remembered how I *still* stood over him, unable to stop until we were both laughing at his rolling back and forth over-the-top acting and he pulled me onto the grass on top of him.

More channel flipping: The last time we'd had sex was two nights before the accident. Lyric's nickname was Nut-Nut. It took us a week after Gabriel was born to finally pick his name because we thought he would be a girl. Gabe thought José's new carbon-fiber bike was "carpet fiber" and was sad to see it was just a regular (very light, very expensive) bike and not an actual magical carpet that could go very fast.

Where did his bike go?

And so on (and so on) went the fire hose of sleep-deprived memories that appeared as relentless, fast flashes of images you see as you scream through thousands of cable stations. The stockpile of memories, some uncontrollable accounting of our lives together, had been unleashed inside my head and was on a continuous loop.

Beneath the memory show was a growing buzz of worry about the future.

What happens if José lives?

What happens if he dies?

I'd have to deal with these later. Right now, I was in the-ship-is-sinking defense mode. Trying to think and talk clearly took as much effort as running through waist-deep pudding or disarming a bomb, so I didn't want to waste any energy reorganizing the deck chairs if I could keep the ship from going down.

I couldn't control if José lived or died. The only thing I could control was how well I handled the present situation. How well I could *do this*, I told myself. But hell, really, I didn't even know what "this" was or what I'd be facing. I didn't even know what I didn't know.

Get up, Chanel. Get up.

My mom would be picked up from the airport around noon and Sunshine would bring Gabe back home to spend the day with his grandma. I had to get back to the hospital. Standing in our closet, I couldn't shake the feeling that trying to figure out what to wear, including the perfect shoes, was somehow important. I thought of

Gabe's big, surprised eyes as I left him at Sunshine's house the night before. I almost took him with me to the hospital but was worried he'd be too scared. What if his dad was dead when we got there? What should a five-year-old see?

As I brushed my hair, I tried to relax and unhunch my upper body, which looked like it had tried to coil up into a tight ball. My shoulders dropped enough to stop brushing the bottoms of my ears. I stood an inch or two straighter as I slipped on a pair of expensive jeans and the nice work shoes instead of the comfortable pregnancy clogs, yoga pants, and T-shirt I would have worn any other weekend. I may have been "the wife," but at the very least I would be the "intelligent yet wildly likeable, not overlooked pushed around or otherwise about to let her husband be fucked with or ignored" wife. Now it was up to me to do everything possible to keep all of us alive—whatever that looked like.

I remembered José's words years ago when something addressed to a "Joseph" Hernando came in the mail. "Yeah, if I send out a résumé over email, no one ever calls me, which is why I bring a printout to the office in person, so they can meet me." When I looked back at him blankly, he said, "Chanel, my name is José Manuel Hernando. Depending on the room I'm in, I'm usually not Latino enough because I don't speak Spanish, or people assume I'm 'too Latino' if the only thing they see is my name, so sometimes I've used Joseph instead."

I feared the medical world might treat José the same way potential employers did. I didn't know if bias and prejudice would play any role in how people treated him, but it was my job to make certain it didn't. It's why I blurted out, "We have insurance!" It's why I wanted to make sure I was talking to the "person in charge," why I asked so many questions, why I called the doctors (and not just the nurses) by their first names. It must be why I dressed up to go to the ICU that morning. I was terrified, and the only thing I could do was try to up José's chances any way I possibly could. I wanted them to like us.

José had been moved to the ICU. He was still on the breathing machine and had more wires and tubes going in and out of, well, everywhere, than I thought a body could hold. At least a half dozen bags of fluid slow-dripped their way into him. A full orchestra of machines surrounded him; their bings and blips provided a constant soundtrack. Even so, the ventilator was louder. I wasn't even on the damn thing and I hated it. In fact, besides keeping the person you love alive, there is not much to like about an ICU unit at all. Both the ER and the ICU are designed for function, and rightly so; that's where you have seconds to save a life or not. I'm certainly not suggesting an ICU be designed like a hotel foyer, but those areas of the hospital, including the lobbies—the one place that is supposed to be comfortable or at least accommodating, where friends who'd heard about the accident had begun to gather—were about as inviting as the driver's seat in a tank. If I had to rank rooms designed to be aggressively against the human form, I'd put the ER and ICU right up there with being stuck in a submarine bathroom while wearing a straightjacket.

I hadn't been in José's room too long when the attending surgeon came in with a half dozen humorless-looking strangers in white jackets. He introduced himself with words he'd clearly spoken thousands of times already: "Hi, I'm Dr. Lewis Rubinson, the attending surgeon. You're the wife?" he asked and then went back to the chart. He'd picked up and flipped through the papers in the clipboard with the ease of a dealer in Vegas shuffling a deck of cards. *Flip, flip, flip* went the pages as he nodded at the surgery notes and repeated phrases out loud to, it appeared to me, no one in particular.

"Uh-huh . . . forty-three-year-old healthy male . . . note the respiratory . . . consciousness . . . wait and see."

They were very intelligent-sounding but irritatingly clinical nonsense words.

I squinted a bit, my head cocked sideways.

What does any of that mean?

All the residents, standing in a half circle around the foot of the bed, nodded along in deferential agreement and soft-talked among themselves. The doctor flipped more pages.

"Do you have any questions for me?" he said with a conversation-ending tone after a few minutes.

"So, who are you again?" I asked half joking, but not really even that much.

He smiled and, thank god, put the clipboard down.

"It's a lot all at once, isn't it?"

Now he was talking to me, not the clipboard. Or the residents.

"Yeah, none of this medical stuff is familiar to me. This is all, um, new territory." I tried to smile. "If you were talking about building a website I'd be right with you, but I don't know any of this language. I need you to break this down for me. Pretend I don't know anything about medicine and tell me what is happening."

I was grateful he started over and explained: the ICU does this; a team of us work together in shifts; we are looking for movement from José. The first twenty-four hours are the most critical, so we want to keep a close eye on him. Each morning we'll visit the room during rounds to talk with you. Maybe we'll know more tomorrow. And again, all we can really do is take care of José and see how he responds; we wait and see.

"What time are rounds?" I asked.

"We'll come between eight and noon," Lewis answered.

"What are you, the cable guy?"

"Does that not work for you?" He laughed and seemed delighted that I'd flipped him some shit.

"Well, I want to be here as much as I can and still be able to put my son to bed and be there when he wakes up."

"How old is he?"

"Five."

"My daughter is two. How about we come at ten a.m.?"

"She must be adorable. Ten will be perfect. Thank you."

Our main nurse, Laura, had been in the room when I first arrived and listened to the doctors as they talked over the clipboard, but I noticed her main focus was always José. When I asked something probably about as clinically experienced as, "So what is all this stuff?" while still looking over all the machines, she showed me which lines and fluids were what, what the machines did and what to look for (or ignore) on the screens and monitors lined up behind his head.

She asked if José wore contact lenses. I hadn't even thought about them and I guess no one else had, either. But last night, José's contact lenses were probably the last thing anyone cared about. When I said yes, she put some fluid under his lids to moisten them and lightly slid the lenses out. Afterward, she faced me with a more serious tone to warn me before she cleared his airway that his body's gag reflex would respond, and "it can be a little hard to watch." She was not wrong.

When she noticed I was distracted by all the scrapes and road rash on his elbows and legs, she handed me some antibiotic ointment and suggested I help out by keeping his wounds clean, probably just to give me something to do or keep me out of her way. It was a big thing for José and a lot of the cyclists on his racing team to keep the frequent elbow and knee scrapes "wet" with Neosporin or Aquaphor first-aid ointment (there were long, heated debates as intense as "what is the correct way to cook BBQ ribs?" among dozens of spandex-wearing bicycle geeks wearing a giant tomato logo on the front of their Cucina Fresca team jerseys about which method healed faster), so I joked with her that as soon as José talked, his first words would probably be to thank her for keeping him from getting all scarred up.

But the much-needed lightheartedness didn't last long. When I asked how good the chances were that he would wake up, her reply was thoughtful, but she was very slow to answer. "Right now, we're looking for signs for us to be able to be optimistic."

"So we're looking for signs, and being optimistic," I said.

The extra pause as she gathered her response was no less thoughtful, but firm. "No. We are looking for signs that are optimistic so we can be able to begin to be optimistic."

I nodded. Her precise selection of words and careful enunciation threw up double-caution red flashing warning lights. But she said optimistic, right? Maybe this was right around the time my adrenaline surge wore off and my body just caught up with how freaked out and overwhelmed I was. Laura was trying to give as clear a picture of the actual situation as she possibly could, but the language sounded, to me, very vague.

If I focused on her word "optimistic," was I still hopeful, because the word is one that is supposed to invite at least a small amount of room for something positive? Or was it because none of the doctors was saying, "Sweetie, humans can't go without oxygen that long without being brain dead" or "Chanel, I'd like to explain that, unfortunately, your husband's head is disconnected from his spine and we can't really put it back on."

So while I rubbed antibiotic cream on my "don't be too optimistic about" spinal-cord-crushed, went-a-long-time-without-oxygen husband, my critical-thinking capacity felt about as finely tuned as a puppy chasing its own tail.

Who was I going to ask again?

I had a sweaty piece of paper in my pocket that said, "Call her back" in my handwriting and no memory of writing it much less who I had been talking to. I didn't want to throw it away in case it was the only way I'd remember that I'd forgotten something.

And oh yeah, who asked me for the insurance card again? And why does a nurse advocate want to talk to me?

Erin arrived with big, pink pastry boxes from the Macrina Bakery for the ICU's main nursing desk and a pile of notebooks, gum, a toothbrush, hair ties, and an extra phone charger for me. I decided to take someone's advice to start recording conversations on my phone, which I then often forgot to do.

Throughout the day, more friends arrived. Jen's plane landed in midafternoon, and she promptly established with the entire ICU staff that she was José's sister, which was mostly true. José had been out of town visiting our friends Anne and Alan just a few weeks before, and they'd driven from out of state as soon as they heard. Dozens of José's racing buddies in their clicking clip-on shoes and *very* tight, lightly colored spandex cycling "kits" had also arrived. The nurses seemed pretty delighted to watch them walk up and down the hallways. The parade of lean men in spandex was much more entertaining than the dozens of people who came and went from José's room to draw blood, poke his toes, and ask me the same questions someone else had just asked five minutes ago.

The nurse advocate came by with forms for me to fill out. She asked if I had our insurance card with me.

So it was her.

Nope, I'd forgotten the card again. But apparently there are stickers for parking somewhere, and the bathrooms for visitors are down the hall as there aren't any in the rooms (ah, I finally got it—patients in the ICU don't get up).

All day and into the evening, a steady stream of neurologists, pulmonologists, cardiologists, and every other kind of head, neck, spine, heart, and brain specialist circulated through José's room, checked the charts and vitals, asked me more of the same questions, and left.

The shifts changed again and I realized we'd hit the twenty-four-hour mark. José had not woken up yet. He also hadn't appeared to move on his own, reached for the ventilator (apparently people hate being on them and try to grab at them or pull them out), or reacted to any of the poking or prodding. Laura needed a half hour or so to transition shifts and relay all the information, so I headed to the lobby to give them some time and privacy. On the way out, I noticed that the new nurse was not wearing silly socks or any colored pins or buttons on her hospital scrubs the way a lot of nurses on the floor did. This one wore clogs like everyone else, but she had the more badass version with black leather and shiny studs.

About an hour later, the night shift staff had settled in and the whole floor was a lot quieter. The new nurse introduced herself as Kat and told me that she would not put up with the extra visitors that she'd heard had been in the room on the day shift, nor with my getting in the way, at all. She was in charge and José was her priority.

This nurse wasn't fucking around.

In another life we might have bumped into each other at Burning Man or done shots at Sturgis.

Part of me wanted to make her my friend, but mostly I wanted information.

"Can you tell me what's actually happening?" I asked.

She looked around the room and signaled for me to follow her out into the hallway. She looked straight into my eyes. She wanted to know if I really knew, or if the doctors were saying, how really, very serious his injuries were.

I got the feeling she was worried for me. Or about me. And not in an entirely good way. Like she was holding herself back from saying something. So I asked her, "If I were you, and this was your husband, what would you want me tell you?"

She stopped and gave a hand motion for me to follow her around the corner and farther away from the nurses' desk. I moved with the same apprehension as a kid being sent to the principal's office.

With a nod she said, "You asked me to tell you what is going on, so yes, they are spoon-feeding you the information. You have to ask, 'What is the prognosis?' They know how to answer that, but 'What is going to happen' or 'How much better will he get?' will get you the same general answers you've been getting so far."

She looked at me, hard. She gave me the exact answer I'd asked for and the advice I'd wanted—and I did not like it one fucking bit. The only time I'd ever felt this level of fear, like I wanted to peel my own skin off, was when I was thirty hours into labor and delivery. My ob-gyn got a worried look on her face and said something about the baby's heartbeat dropping. One of the nurses said they'd prep for a possible backup C-section. I realized I had to push this baby out of me right-fucking-now—and it was too late for drugs. In this hallway with this nurse, I felt that terror again—and something else. A new feeling was building up and gathering strength inside of me: a hundred-mile-an-hour wave of anger and rage. I wanted to point it in her direction and smack her ass down so hard she'd shut the hell up.

I managed to whisper a thank-you and hurried back to José's room. Jen had stepped out to make phone calls to schedule time slots to visit the next day. We didn't want to have too many people waiting in the lobby but mostly we were trying to prevent some family members from having to bump into each other. I sobbed so intensely I worried I'd pass out.

It was that time of night well past bar closing but not yet dawn. Time to go home. Everyone but Jen had left already. My mom had left a message that she'd read stories to Gabe in my bedroom and he was still asleep on my bed. Jen met me in the lobby, and we walked to the parking garage together. After I yelled at the parking lot attendant for some reason, Jen paid and took the wheel.

Part of me knew what Kat had said was true. The other part was looking for signs to be optimistic.

Hearing the soft breathing of my son next to me, I squeezed my eyes tight against the rest of the world for a few more minutes. There hadn't been any calls during the night from the hospital with changes or news. It was Sunday; those first twenty-four hours had long come and gone. The longer he remained unconscious, the less we could blame the anesthesia for the reason he wasn't waking up. Gabe never slept in past seven or seven thirty, so I knew I'd have plenty of time for a morning snuggle and to make him his favorite breakfast of bacon, waffles, and blueberries. He still couldn't say waffles, so it came out "awfuls," so of course José, Lyric, and I called them "awfuls," too. At the breakfast counter, I tried to be reassuring.

"Papa has been in accident. The doctors are trying to help him," I said.

I couldn't say nothing, and I didn't want to lie, exactly. I tried to tell him the truth, but as little of it as I could. He didn't ask any questions.

In the quiet of mixing the waffle batter and prepping the pans, the slow buzz of worry about the future grew louder.

What will become of us?

How long will our money last?

Can we afford Gabe's new private school now?

Will we lose the house?

Short-term, I was hosed for money but could maybe cash out a 401(k). We had bought life insurance when Gabe was born but hadn't updated it in years. Disability insurance? As I freelanced, I knew I didn't have any. Did José check the box on his new employee forms when he started his new job last year? I wasn't sure, I was waiting to hear. I didn't know his social security number; what else didn't I know?

Chanel, calm the fuck down.

One step, one thing, at a time.

I could find the health insurance card that was in my other purse and call the bank tomorrow when they were open. It had occurred to me that José probably didn't have time after work to deposit his paycheck, which meant the check we'd written for Gabe's tuition payment would likely bounce.

The only things you have to do—right now—are: finish making breakfast for Gabe, get dressed, and go to the hospital.

Everything else can wait.

It'll be waiting for you later.

As I drove to the hospital, I tried to remember the gentle reminders from my doula during childbirth to "do nothing extra," to conserve my energy for the rest of labor. That mantra seemed as appropriate here as it did in labor and delivery. *Save your energy, don't do anything that isn't helpful or necessary*, I thought as I said hello to the new group of spandex-clad members of José's bike team camped out in the lobby, thanked people for bringing food (people love to bring food), asked someone if they could find some coolers to put all the food in, and escorted some visitors back to see José for a few minutes. It was tiring to answer everyone's questions and give the same vague update a few dozen times but I also wanted to see our friends and take a break from the room full of machines.

I dropped the insurance card off at the nurse advocate's desk on the way to José's room. As she made a copy of it for the files, she thanked me for the information and then asked if we had our "affairs in order." The phrase had always sounded silly, or too formal, so when I paused, she asked again if we had our wills or living wills completed.

"Yes, we've done our wills," I replied.

She said something like, "That's great" or "It can really help."

She leaned in, "You're legally married, right? You have a marriage certificate? Not the one you sign at the wedding and frame but one from the state?"

Even as I reassured her that we had been, in fact, actually legally married, it dawned on me I'd need to triple-check that our friend James, who'd married us nine years before, had actually signed and mailed the license to the official state office.

"It makes it easier for you to make the decisions about his care if you have the paperwork done. But you're OK anyway because you're the wife." She seemed relieved and turned back toward the nurse's desk.

I stared down the rest of the shiny hallway toward the room.

Shit, another thing to follow up on that I have to find.

Then I remembered something that stopped me dead in my tracks.

I'd told her we'd completed our wills. Which was true. We had written them. But.

Oh shit.

Ohhhh shit.

Oh shit shit shit fucking fuck fuuuuuuuuck!

All the air was sucked out of the hallway.

The final versions of our will, living will, and power-of-attorney documents we'd done with a lawyer were sitting in my inbox, as they had been for months, waiting to be signed and notarized. We'd finally done them when we bought the new house.

Oh my god.

So maybe we're married but we don't have wills? Maybe it's OK because we drafted them so it shows what José wanted? Maybe we aren't actually married because I never checked that that paper we signed on our wedding day got mailed to the state? What if it got lost in the mail? OK, maybe it doesn't matter because my name is on the mortgage. But what if I go broke and lose the house? Do I have to declare bankruptcy? Ohhhh shit, his very Catholic Peruvian family! What if they don't agree about medical decisions and our living wills are worth shit unsigned and we're not actually married . . . ?

You are such a stupid idiot to . . .

Why the actual fuck did you think you could . . .

Jen was in José's room when I walked in. She looked up and with a one-second look at my face saw the full-throttle internal ass-kicking shame-fest I had just unleashed inside my head.

"What? What happened?" she asked.

Whatever dam I'd been stuffing the heaps of multiplying fears and worries and regrets and questions behind burst under the pressure.

"Oh my god, Jen, I can't believe this is happening but I really can't believe how totally fucked we are. I don't have my shit together. At all. I have no idea what's going to happen to us. Look where we are."

The room spun outward. The machines everywhere. The families sleeping in the lobby with their young kids my son's age spread over their laps. The people here with no visitors. The addicts living on the street outside. The homeless encampment between the hospital and the highway. The *whoosh whoosh* of the medevac helicopter coming and going with more broken bodies to Harborview's level-one trauma unit. The neurologists not saying anything, or anything I could understand. The chronically ill dying here. The suffering. The overwhelming suffering was a weight on me like a pair of soaking wet jeans and a thick, constricting wool sweater I couldn't ever get off me.

I kept talking and waving my arms around. "What's even happening? How do you even do this?"

Spin, swirl, spin.

And just like a scene in the movies where the camera zooms in and pans out at the same time, I understood that no matter how bad it got, if José died and I lost everything except the clothes on my back, I would and could find a way to take care of my son, keep him safe and close to his sister. That in the worst possible moment of my life, I was quite clearly very, very fucked. And, I was going to make sure we'd get through this. And most of the people I passed in the halls or in the rooms next to ours might not.

"OK, OK. Whoa. OK, what is one thing? Just one thing you want, right now. What do you need?" Jen always knows what to say.

"I need to not have to work for a year. I am going to be a wreck for a long time and I need to take care of Gabe."

"Well, there it is. You're not working for a year."

"That just seems crazy. I don't even know where that came from." It was ridiculous. The words came out of my mouth fully formed, a total surprise, and sounded as shamefully indulgent as "a private jet" or "a Porsche." But I needed time. Whatever happened next, whether José lived or died, it was going to be hard, unimaginably hard. I had a young son who was six weeks away from starting kindergarten and did not need a broken or absent shell of a woman as his mother to screw him up after whatever was going to happen next.

Jen paused. "Chanel, do you think those words came to you because they might be true? When the universe talks like that, you might want to listen. The rest we'll figure out."

"Honestly Jen, if I have time, maybe I can actually make it through this."

The one thing that made me feel less suffocated and like a hostage in my own life was the thought that I could have some time. Nothing else would fix anything. Just time.

I hadn't been home for dinner in two nights, and when I arrived back at the house, Erin Brower and her husband, Josh (yes, there are two Erins and they are both married to men named Josh), had just walked in the door with a giant box of food from the farmer's market to make dinner and another box, thank god, full of wine. Both of "the Erins" have very special skills in the trauma department. Erin Galvin was a social worker and had been by my side navigating the ER with me for days. Erin Brower was a counselor trained in early childhood development. Actually, Erin Brower had left a career in fashion to become a counselor, so now she looked incredible, always had something gorgeous on, *and* knew exactly the right thing to say. *Thank god for them*, I thought, as my mom played LEGOs with Gabe, Jen opened wine, Anne and Alan provided desperately needed inappropriate jokes, and I sat down for one second on the orange leather

IKEA couch I'd saved up to buy. Surrounded by my friends and family, I felt like everything was going to be OK.

Or at least OK enough. Looking around the house, I realized that while it felt like time would help in the long term, it wouldn't have gotten me through the moments I had to face in those last forty-eight hours. If I hadn't had people to lean on who were there to help right at that moment, I wasn't sure there'd be enough time in the world to get through something like this alone.

By Monday, José had been in the ICU for over two days and hadn't woken up. I was doing my best to keep the house routine feeling "normal" for Gabe, but he did not, under any circumstances, want to go to summer camp that morning so he was home with my mom for the day. I had told him his papa was in the hospital and had a big owie the doctors were trying to heal, which he understood, but he didn't ask many questions and was quieter than usual. As the "weekend rush" passed, the ICU had more of a "regular workday" feeling. The urgency in José's room slowed, too. The charts and dials were checked a little less frequently, making it easier to hear what the doctors were not exactly saying. The impact was so severe that José's spinal cord was crushed. He'd had an "immediate traumatic cardiac arrest," which meant his heart stopped and left him with no oxygen for a number of minutes, so what brain activity he still had was uncertain.

The whole reason an ICU exists is to keep people alive, and the doctors and nurses were doing an amazing job of that. But the signs we had been hoping for, the ones that would let us be optimistic, hadn't appeared. There were a few more tests they wanted to run, like taking him off of the ventilator to see if he could breathe on his own. And another type of scan, a new one that used some kind of electrical currents or sent a "ping" through his body to see if brain signals were connecting to the rest of his body, was also talked about. It sounded like the results were going to be able to tell us how much damage had been done to José's brain, which meant we'd know his chance of recovery. I half wondered why they hadn't done it days ago.

I got better at understanding the differences between day and night staff, who defers to whom (nurses are always called by their first names, doctors never), and how to get answers (keep asking). I knew where to find the closest coffee, the better bathrooms, and the faster elevators, which shortcuts to take, and which hallways to avoid. I figured out who was better at explaining what was going on (nurses) and who wasn't (neurologists) and that anesthesiologists like jokes (and to tell you about the crazy shit they did in college). I realized I had to ask specific questions, synthesize what they were all saying, and sort out what the hell needed to happen. I was just a few miles from my house but felt like a refugee trying to understand a new language in a foreign land. At best I was stuck in a crappy study-abroad program.

The need to organize was born out of survival mode more than anything else; my brain just could not keep track of the million things I had to worry about, follow up on, track down, or find out. Any power I had left needed to be rerouted to my own emergency life-support systems, which were: breakfast with Gabe, go to hospital, be home for dinner and put Gabe to bed, go back to hospital, go home and sleep a few hours. Repeat. But even though I was operating in minute-by-minute emergency mode, I still needed to be sure dozens of day-to-day things were happening, like covering Gabe's childcare, updating Connie so she could decide how (and when) to tell Lyric, coordinating with José's aunt and cousins who were flying in, and figuring out who would feed the dog and two cats. And now I needed to find some critical pieces of information and fill in the blanks on which insurance policies we had and what exactly they covered for health, disability, and long-term care. Also our automotive coverage. I could barely think about money, except that we didn't have any to cover what our insurance wouldn't—unless I cashed out our modest retirement funds.

Just finding the phone number to call the life insurance company felt emotionally impossible and I knew I'd have to search through my unsorted email inbox to find the policy information or dig through the plastic storage tub marked "to be filed" that contained years' worth of policies, certificates, car registrations, and financial records along with used checkbooks and recipes I'd always wanted to try. It would take hours.

What started off as friends organically helping where they could quickly became a system. Having one person in charge of one specific task—like childcare, fielding phone calls, scheduling food drop-offs, coordinating hospital visits, pet wrangling, or searching through our files for information on our insurance policies—meant I had to connect with only one person about one thing.

Just as in a MASH unit or command center, or on a project team, I needed a single point of contact and a very clear decision tree. My mom was in charge of Gabe. Sunshine handled donations. Carrie, the general manager at José's company and an old friend of mine, took the lead on finding out about our health-care plan or any additional insurance coverage through his work. Josh confirmed the terms of the individual life insurance policies we'd purchased shortly after Gabe was born (I'd secretly feared we'd missed a payment or screwed up the autopay account) and regularly updated the private website we'd started through CaringBridge to share updates on José. Erin G. managed visitors because the ICU allowed only two people in a room during visiting hours, and his big family along with friends plus his whole bike team wanted to see him. Jen attended to the two very separate sides of José's family. Our friend Curtis was back in town and helped sort out my money situation. He followed up on the tuition at the new school Gabe was to start in just six short weeks.

People wanted to help, and it was hugely reassuring to know I had a team of high-functioning friends who were great at organizing the shit out of the important stuff. And now that there were point people set up for the handful of big, immediate issues, I spent way less time playing telephone and none hunting through boxes of receipts and envelopes labeled "To File." That meant more time in the room with José. That meant I could be a teensy bit less distracted while I was putting Gabe to bed or making him breakfast in the morning. I felt better knowing that friends were helping to get the answers I needed. Even if it was bad news, really exceptionally bad news, financially, legally, or otherwise, I just wanted to know where I stood.

It's better to know exactly how I'm going to be totally screwed than have no idea.

"So, I've got some good news and some bad news," said Carrie on the other end of the phone.

"OK, some good news would be good," I said.

"Well, now I know why Doreen wasn't calling me back. I just got off the phone with her, and she said, "'Carrie, I just don't know how we are going to tell Chanel that José signed all his documents listing some woman named Laura as the beneficiary!!!'"

The whole wing of the ICU must have thought I had finally lost my mind because the howling, bent-over hysterical laughing was wildly inappropriate for (a) a Critical Care Unit, and (b) someone who was supposed to be way, way sad. For minutes, Carrie and I snorted and howled, and I almost peed myself. Carrie tried to gulp air on the other end and needed a few minutes to wipe her eyes before she was able to speak.

"Doreen said she didn't sleep all weekend and couldn't bring her-self to call me!"

"I can't believe she spent the whole weekend thinking José had named some other woman instead of me. Of course she had no idea my middle name is Chanel and José had probably tried to *avoid* any confusion and just written my legal name down!"

After another round of howls, she got quiet.

"So that's the end of the funny part. You do have a year's worth of José's salary for life insurance, but he doesn't have any disability insurance."

José dying was the very worst thing I could imagine, but over the last few days it had become clearer that it wasn't necessarily the worst possible outcome. It was Tuesday and he hadn't woken up or responded to me or anyone or anything (lights in his eyes, poking his toes, my voice). From the very first hours at the hospital, the saddest and darkest thoughts would cross my mind. As hope was fading, it was hard to hold them off.

Every cell in my body wanted him to wake up, but what would happen if he did? He would be devastatingly hurt. How much better could he get? The spinal cord in his neck was crushed and could not be repaired. What would the long slow spiral down look like, death from his injuries or eventually pneumonia from living on a ventilator? They'd done the breathing test the day before and when they shared the results, it wasn't exactly clear what they meant. He'd been off the ventilator for maybe ten or twenty minutes, which was supposed to be good news, but the doctors were worried about his oxygen dropping, so it sounded to me like he couldn't breathe completely on his own for long.

After telling Jen and Erin G. the latest update, they suggested we take a walk and dragged me outside for a break. Stepping out of the controlled madness of the hospital into the sunshine of an epically perfect day to sit on the manicured lawn was like walking onto a movie set: a little island of grass, on a very hot day, the three of us sitting in the sun with our shoes off and iced coffee drinks. We could have been at the beach or a regular park if a picture of us had been taken at the right angle at the right moment. But we didn't have trashy magazines, and we weren't commenting on celebrity fashion fails. I was getting some air before my meeting with Dr. Darrell Owens, the Palliative Care director.

On that little patch of grass I finally cracked, in some combination of total surrender and complete implosion. Every wild scenario that had been spinning through my head, every manic hope and crushing fear that had been at a growing simmer finally boiled over.

"Oh my god, you guys, I can't take it anymore. We've been here for days and he's not waking up and people are looking at me differently now. I can hear how their tone has changed. The nurses are not checking things and moving stuff around as much anymore, and I know what's coming, like I almost really knew when I was driving here. The 'signs to hope to be optimistic' aren't happening and there's no body activity and his brain tests are coming back I don't know when, but we've gone from 'Wow, we're so lucky he's alive' to 'Maybe we can totally deal with paralysis from the waist down' to I don't know what we're even talking about. Neck down? Or him lying there blinking out messages to me like the guy in *The Diving Bell and the Butterfly?*

"I don't know, you guys, I really don't know. If his brain works, we can work with the body piece, and if his body works and his brain is damaged but functional, then he could just, like, ride his bike all day and play video games, and we can work with that. But locked in? He wouldn't want that. And I sure as fuck know if I let him waste away in a hospital bed, maybe conscious or blinking or not even conscious at all, and I had to drag the kids to see him every Saturday at some creepy building that smells funny and the kids cry every time and complain, 'Mama, don't make me go to the scary place. Papa looks funny and I want to go to the birthday party instead,' I would lose my mind. And José would kill me for letting that happen. And that is no life for him and I feel like such a selfish asshole for admitting it, but that is no life for *me*. José wouldn't want that for me, and he certainly wouldn't want that for Gabe and Lyric.

"I just can't do it, and I don't know if his mom or dad are going to try to stop me, but this can't go on. I dunno if that means I'm the one killing him or if he's already dead and I have to stop all the tubes and machines and beeping getting in his way. What if he can feel something and is suffering? But his mom? Or his dad's family? I will not end up like one of those Terri Schiavo horror shows that go on and on. This is not a fucking Sally Field movie where everything sucks and is a struggle and we're supposed to suck it up to the bitter end. I am not doing it. None of this is OK. We can't do this . . ."

It was hard to say out loud, but I had to. I had shifted from hoping and praying he wasn't dead or wouldn't die, to realizing I was more afraid he'd be stuck living out a long, slow death full of this misery. As much as I didn't want it to be true, it was.

Erin started to say, "Sweetie, no one would want . . ."

But then—*sprinklers.*

All the sprinklers in the grass exploded and we squealed like thirteen-year-old girls at the beach, getting sprayed from all sides, grabbing shoes and purses and drinks, toe-jumping across the grass trying to dodge the streams as we ran to the sidewalk. Soaked all the way through, we wiped the dripping water off and deplastered our hair from our faces, still giggling and laughing like teenagers.

Looking back up at the hospital, my laughter faded. It was time to go meet the Palliative Care guy. He had come by José's room to request a meeting. Some friends and family were with me at the time, including José's mom. Swaying on her feet a bit unsteadily, she said she thought it was "too soon"—but no one else said anything.

Guide:
When the Shit Hits the Fan

If someone comes along and shoots an arrow into your heart, it's fruitless to stand there and yell at the person. It would be much better to turn your attention to the fact that there's an arrow in your heart.

—PEMA CHÖDRÖN

At any given moment during the first few days following José's accident, you would have seen a long list of questions swirling around inside my head. The ones that I didn't have answers to or wasn't sure about picked up speed and got louder with each circling lap. *What happens now that something bad has already happened?* Once you get your bearings (a bit) and get those you love located, safe, informed, or looked after, you move from *What the actual fuck is happening?* to *What the hell do I do now?*

First, I should come clean: I am absolutely *not* trying to sell you on a fantasy that having your power-of-attorney document handy, or even having the fat packet of insurance coverage and exclusions your employer's Human Resources department gave you on your first day of work right there in your purse, will make a life-and-death situation less shitty, scary, or unfair. However, when I was trying to figure out what 50-50 meant, it made me feel crazy that I didn't know where to find those pieces of information or remember what some of them said.

Having a few more things taken care of in advance would have turned the noise level down, at least lessened the quantity of stuff I was worrying or wondering about.

For example, having our wills, power of attorney, and living wills signed, notarized, and shared with those named in the document would have meant hours less of my brain making up stress-induced worst-nightmare what-if scenarios. Had José and I discussed his benefits package when he took the new job, I'd have said, "Oh hell yes, you should pay for that company-subsidized disability insurance since you're the main breadwinner in the family and we just bought a new house with a big, fat, two-income-family mortgage." Had we been more organized around paying our bills, I wouldn't have had any doubt that our life insurance policies were solid. If we had been more on top of our finances, one of us could have easily called our insurance agent (in less than a minute) and asked to increase our policies. None of these things were hard to do, and we did not lack the time, ability, or resources to do them. They just *seemed* so impossible to do.

Having options, even if just a few, made a difference. Having friends and family to lean on kept me standing. However, it was painfully clear that the things we didn't have ready, completed, figured out, or easily findable were like numerous, continuous sucker punches from two giant monsters named What I Should Have Done and What I Wish I'd Had.

Top Three Things I Needed, Wanted, or the Hospital Asked Me For

1. Paperwork

Think of it this way: we do much harder, scarier things in our daily lives all the time. Running a marathon hurts, but millions of people do it every year for *fun*. Applying for a job sucks. Saving someone from drowning is scary. Labor and delivery was HARD. Making a hollandaise sauce that doesn't break or a really light, buttery, flaky pie crust seems impossible to me. The truth is that signing up for life insurance isn't much more complicated than ordering a pizza delivery. And take it from me, getting an annual mammogram is way less pleasant than reviewing your retirement plans once a year. Yet many of us get our boobs squished like clockwork but can't recall the last time we checked our credit card interest rate or how much we need to save for retirement.

Doing your will takes less time—much less, including the final ten minutes to get it signed in front of witnesses and a notary—than buying a car. Setting up a 401(k) or opening a savings account and autopaying 5 percent of each paycheck to start an emergency fund? Not harder than yanking your son's $200 retainer from the garbage disposal and getting the damn thing to start spinning again. Paperwork is a pain to do and not any fun, sure. But none of these are, in fact, all that *hard* to do.

When I was in the hospital, I felt dumb, ashamed, and embarrassed whenever I had to answer, "I'll have to check" or "I'm not sure" to half the questions, and on-my-knees grateful for the *other* half, the things we *had* figured out or already completed. Here is a short list of low-effort and high-reward things.

Don't worry if you don't have all these items or don't know what some of them are. We'll cover everything in more detail in "The Tangled Web We Leave" (page 161) but for now, this list will help you get them organized.

VERIFICATION: IDENTIFICATION AND DOCUMENTATION CERTIFICATES

- ❑ Name and ID (state-issued driver's license or identification card).
- ❑ Birth certificates (original or certified/stamped).
- ❑ Marriage and/or divorce certificates (official ones).
- ❑ Other (veteran status, social security card, green card, student/diplomatic visa).

INSURANCE: WHAT KIND OF MEDICAL INSURANCE COVERAGE DO YOU HAVE?

- ❑ Health insurance.
- ❑ Medicare/Medicaid coverage.
- ❑ VA benefits.
- ❑ Secondary coverage through spouse or parent.
- ❑ Long-term care insurance.
- ❑ Disability insurance.
  - • Short-term disability.
  - • Long-term disability.
- ❑ Life insurance (some kinds pay for your medical expenses/ care).
- ❑ Annuities or annuity-based insurance.

NOTE: Confirm if coverage includes any "pre-death benefits."

- ❑ Auto, home, umbrella insurance.

2. Money: Do You Have Easy Access to Funds?

❑ Access to your bank accounts (account numbers, passwords, and/or PINs to withdraw funds or transfer money).

❑ An emergency fund (quick access to cash for unexpected expenses). **NOTE:** Many financial advisors recommend that this money be kept in an easy-to-access savings account (not a CD or investment account).

❑ Savings account (in case you have to dip into the vacation funds).

❑ Credit card (with room for emergency purchases like last-minute travel). **NOTE:** This is another good reason to keep credit card balances low, in addition to improving your credit score.

❑ In a pinch: Do you have friends or family you can ask? Collect donations from work, your community, or set up an online donation request (GoFundMe, etc.).

3. Legal (aka Estate Planning):
Do You Have Your "Affairs in Order"?

❑ Your will (Last Will and Testament).

❑ Your living will (also referred to as an advance care directive).

❑ A power-of-attorney document (POA).

❑ Other health-care forms or instructions, such as a do-not-resuscitate or -intubate order (DNR/DNI), a letter to your doctor, a physician's order for life-sustaining treatment (POLST), a consent form for organ donation, a Five Wishes document, or other additional requests.

REMEMBER! Include full legal names and reference any nicknames or abbreviations that could cause any potential confusion. Confirm that each document is complete, signed, the most recent/current version, and legally binding and/or notarized per your state's laws.

Help: How Can I Help You? What Can I Do?

Information Gathering

While some of the information or details you (or the family) are look-ing for won't be given out due to privacy, legal reasons, or Health Insurance Portability and Accountability Act (HIPAA) rules, there is a lot of legwork that can be done on your (or someone else's) behalf to locate policies, start gathering information, or send a crucial docu-ment to a verified email or overnight it to someone's home address if they need to print it out or sign it themselves.

- Contact the employer's Human Resources department to ask about benefits, family and medical leave, vacation time, or if coworkers can donate sick/vacation time to increase some-one else's paid time off.
- Coworkers or a business partner may need to be alerted in cases where people are self-employed or are small business owners.
- Some companies offer free or discounted legal or financial advice through their benefits package.

Information Sharing

It is wonderful to have friends and family who care and are eager to get updates on a hospital visit (even the planned ones), progress reports, or test results, and often any news they can get their hands on (even a quick call that there is no new news) is appreciated and incredibly helpful. At the same time, updating even a few people a day is time consuming and can be exhausting. To alleviate some of that stress:

- Create an email list, free at the CaringBridge website (or others) for health-related community updates, or a private/ closed Facebook group. With these tools you can provide one-to-many people updates.
- Find your high-functioning friends, then ask them to use their type-A, get-shit-done skills to help you. If someone close to you is a good organizer, project manager, or communicator, it will be easy for them (and a huge gift to you) if they can set up spreadsheets or calendars and manage them for you.

REMEMBER! Ask for help. Accept offers of help. Let people help. Just because your world came crashing down on you doesn't mean the day-to-day realities of life stop. Kids need to be fed, pets looked after, laundry done, bills paid, and appointments scheduled and driven to on time. The dishes do not do themselves.

People will want to help you. It actually makes people feel better if they can do something. If you don't know what they could do to help (and my mind was blank a lot of the time), put one person in charge of organizing help, and they can get food delivery, carpooling, housecleaning, donation drop-offs, or a crowdfunding website set up for you.

Family Meeting

The family meeting had been arranged after Darrell and I had finished talking on Tuesday, just the day before. The head neurosurgeon at the hospital would attend along with Lewis and Darrell to talk to us at two o'clock about the findings from all the tests, including what I referred to as the "ping" test, to determine José's brain function. These results would provide a comprehensive look at everything they knew and, as I understood it, tell us something conclusive about his prognosis. It didn't even cross my mind to issue specific invitations to the family meeting. I just told everyone about it.

Around noon a resident came to José's room and introduced himself; his name was José. Just as I was starting to like him, he announced that he was asked to sit in for Lewis as he had a conflict and couldn't attend. But, he went on, we weren't going to have the meeting at two that afternoon after all. It needed to be rescheduled or canceled. He said something about Long-Term Care or someone not being able to attend. I was holding my breath so hard I could have cracked my own ribs. This dude, new to our little team and unfortunately named José, needed to stop talking and stop fucking up my plans so I could figure out what the fuck my actual plans could even be.

I had been counting down the hours until this meeting. I was wound so tight one of the bike team members had arranged for his wife, a physical therapist and masseuse, to come to the hospital and help me relax before it. Now I was about to pop a vein.

"This meeting was scheduled yesterday. People are flying in specifically for this meeting."

I made that up, but the pressure was real.

"There are test results we are waiting to hear. Darrell is on board and you are covering for Lewis. I'm not changing the plans we already made. So, tell me who wants to cancel this and why?" I was barely holding it together.

Jen and the new day-shift nurse were just a few feet away and stared at me as if the room were wired with explosives and the timer had ticked down into single digits.

Fuck, think, fuck. I need reinforcements.

"Jen, can you come over here and help me think through this?" I asked before turning back to the resident.

"José, here's the deal. We need to know what the hell is going on. I need to know what the test results from yesterday tell us. The neurosurgeon, Darrell, and Lewis planned this meeting yesterday. No one even mentioned Long-Term Care or whoever was going to be there. This meeting needs to happen with or without them. *Today.*"

Pause. Breathe. Pause.

"There is a big group of people who will be here, at two o'clock, driving and flying in, to make the meeting you guys set up, again, yesterday. And when you say there is going to be a meeting at two o'clock to tell the wife and family if her husband has any brain function," now I was stabbing my finger toward his face, "then there had better Be. A. Fucking. Meeting. At. Two. O'clock. So, this is when I'll now thank-you-very-much in advance for making sure everyone knows it is *still* happening. At two o'clock. Now, I'm late for my massage."

He backed away, slowly, not just a little wide-eyed, out of the room. Jen started laughing her ass off, the nurse seemed beside-herself delighted, and I was pretty sure that the resident hadn't been ripped two new assholes like that by "the wife" before. The whole nurses' station was on fire like Godzilla was approaching the city as I walked past, and after a minute of feeling smug and not just a little pleased with myself, I spent the next hour trying to stop shaking while sobbing in the massage chair. With my face leaning into the tissue paper–lined head cradle, I had a perfect view of the spit, tears, and snot that pooled on my lower lip and poured over in a long string toward the floor.

The meeting began promptly at 2:00 p.m. in a small conference room. Lewis was present; he had apparently canceled his conflict. Poor José the Resident was nowhere in sight. About twenty-five people came. I registered José's mom, his sister and her wife, and his brother. From the Hernando side of the family, I saw his dad and his wife, Tía Martha, Tía Marcia, and José's cousin Rose, who was a nurse in Chicago and had been helping to explain the medical information. José's cycling-team friend, who had been relaying news back to the team, was there, as well as Erin, Jen, and my mom. Another dozen people huddled just inside the door. It occurred to me that the group here had pretty much "self-selected" and that seemed perfectly reasonable to me.

As people were still filing into the room, Darrell whisper-asked me if I really wanted this many people at the meeting. "Are they all family?"

"Well, yeah, mostly. I didn't invite anyone specifically and what am I supposed to do? Uninvite them now that they are already here?"

Private, very personal information would be discussed, Darrell reminded me.

"Darrell, whatever gets said will be communicated out anyway, and honestly, the more people who know what's happening means the less people I'll have to talk to."

He paused. I felt that he was still uncomfortable, but I just needed this meeting to get started already. At this point I didn't care if a busload of tourists wanted to join and take pictures.

"I guess it's kinda like in *Jaws*," I said. "Looks like you're gonna need a bigger boat."

"OK. We'll get a bigger conference room." I swear he smiled as he shook his head from side to side at me.

These were the facts: The damage to José's brain was significant and devastating. His body wasn't functioning. His nervous system wasn't firing. He would not be able to come back in any meaningful way. Unrecoverable. Brain dead. They explained softly and were as caring and professional as I can imagine anyone could possibly be. Then, maybe twenty minutes in, I realized they were just saying the same thing over. And over.

I asked if there was anything else, any new information to add that hadn't already been said.

There wasn't.

"OK. Thank you for all you have said. I need to pause this, if we are done."

The three doctors had been sitting in a row to my left. All three were now quiet; all three nodded. I fled.

If it were possible to run out of my own body I would have. After a full-throttle ten seconds, I made it to the corridor by the elevators and froze.

Wait a minute. Where am I going? Where the fuck am I supposed to go?

I paced like a caged lion who knows there is no escape but tries rubbing up against the bars anyway.

What am I supposed to do?

I smashed the down button on the elevator over and over.

Where do I want to be?

In the elevator? No.

Out on the street? No.

Home? Without José? No.

Back in that meeting room? No no no.

There was nowhere.

The only person who could console me about José being almost or already dead was José.

Then Erin was right in front of me, with one hand on each of my shoulders steadying me, her eyes locked on mine. She'd followed me out of the room, and just as I could see a serious social-worker mental-health moment coming, I heard, "Excuse me, Chanel? You're Chanel, right?"

"Hi there," said a very enthusiastic woman with bouncy hair and very friendly eyes. "I'm a friend of José's. Well, we used to work together. We haven't met, but I remembered he liked music, so I made this CD of a bunch of very soothing, relaxing, tribal music I thought you could play in his room for him."

There was a very long pause while I tried to blink myself back into reality. Autopilot kicked in. "Thanks so much for coming by, it was very thoughtful of you to—"

Erin cut in. "Okayyyy. Let's wrap this up. Thank you, but the timing is bad. We're done here," she said in her no-patience, zero-fucks-given voice.

The well-intentioned woman walked away. I have never been more grateful for Erin's suffering-no-fools skills. Otherwise, I might have just stood there talking to her for another five minutes hoping the ground would open up and swallow me.

With her hands still on me, Erin said, "Where are you trying to go? Outside?"

I'm pretty sure I said nothing, or maybe mumbled, "The room," before I pulled away and race-walked down one more corridor back toward the ICU. A path to José's room cleared for me, the look on my face sending everyone cringing away to melt into the walls. I fell apart in José's room, collapsing over him in another round of keening, hyper-ventilating, convulsive, bent-over, spit-and-stomach-acid-dripping-out-of-your-nose vomit-crying just like I had that very first time in the ER. It felt like years ago even though only five days had passed.

No more talking. No more wondering. No more waiting. The normally bustling unit was so quiet I could hear the swing of the metal-on-metal rings sliding slowly across the rod as someone closed the curtain behind me in what I imagine was a futile, but still sweet, attempt for privacy.

The choice wasn't mine; he was dead. But I had to make the decision to let him die.

Empty

"I need to lie down with him," I told the nursing staff.

They said it was against hospital procedure. I told them I really had to do it, and I would do it anyway, so they could either help me or worry I'd mess up their lines. I had to *know*. They said they understood. During the day was too hard; it would be easier at night. They told me to come at midnight, and they'd arrange it with the night crew.

I had to be *sure*.

When I arrived that night, I took off my shoes and crawled up onto the bed. All the nurses left, closing the curtain behind them, and we were alone for the first and only time that whole week. I lay down, put my arm over his chest, slid my foot into that one exact place it had been every night for years now, above his ankle, trying to mimic the same position, wanting to get it right. José smelled different. His neck was swollen, and he had started getting a fever.

I closed my eyes and just tried to lie there, feel him. I had no idea what I was expecting or hoping for, but I was compelled to be there out of instinct or desperation. I had all of the facts a team of trauma and neurology experts could give me, and I felt very solid about what he would want. I was even more certain about what he wouldn't want at all. The decision was so black-and-white, it was almost made for me: medically, José was dead. But I wanted to *know*; I needed to be *certain*. I wanted to get as close to him as I could, to see if he was still with us. With my nose in his neck and my eyes tight next to him, only one word came to me: *empty*.

My eyes flashed open. This was not comforting. I didn't feel better. His body wasn't lifeless, or cold, but there was no connection. This didn't feel good at all, no matter how close I tried to get to him. I couldn't reach him. Or find him. Or feel him. I felt almost as if I were embracing a wall. He wasn't there.

I climbed out of the bed, slid my shoes back on, straightened my shirt, tucked my hair back, and walked out, closing the curtain behind me.

I went to the nurses' station. "Thank you for tonight. It means, well . . . I needed to. So, please give him everything you can to make him as comfortable as possible. I don't want even the slightest chance he feels any pain—nothing, not even on a cellular level."

It was after two in the morning when I walked out the after-hours exit past the two security guards and a metal detector. When I walked into the kitchen from the garage, Gabe was sitting on the couch, totally awake and all alone. His eyes were the size of terrified soup bowls.

"Sweetie, you're awake."

He gave a big nod as he stood on the couch. I rushed over to pick him up.

"Did you come look me for in my room but couldn't find me?"

Littler nods on my collarbone came through the big hug.

"Were you worried you were by yourself?"

"You weren't in your bed or down here," he said.

"I bet that was scary. I was at the hospital so I wasn't here, but do you remember that Grandma is here staying with us and is sleeping in Lyric's room?"

He stayed silent. I couldn't tell if he remembered or not.

"Let's go upstairs and have a cuddle in my bed after we go take a peek and see Grandma."

I carried him upstairs. "I just want you to see that Grandma was here the whole time and that I wouldn't leave you at home by yourself."

I turned the handle on the door and we both leaned in a few inches into the dark room where my mom was sleeping.

Gabe looked up at me and smiled. "That's Grandma."

"Yup. She's been right there sleeping the whole time. I probably should have reminded you that Grandma is here in case you woke up and I was at the hospital during nighttime." He nodded a sweet little five-year-old nod.

He crawled into my bed and, as usual, arranged his little body in the perfect configuration to take up 75 percent of the space.

"I want you to know that even if I'm not here, I'll make sure you are OK and aren't alone, sweetie. I'll always make sure that someone is here to take care of you. You don't have to worry or be scared about that."

He scooched in closer and flipped over for a back scratchy. As I made little concentric circles over and around his back I counted the few hours of sleep I'd get and wondered how long he'd been sitting downstairs on that couch by himself feeling alone and abandoned.

"I'd never leave you alone. You don't have to worry because I'll make sure someone is always here and you'll never have to be scared you're all alone. I promise, kiddo, I'll always make sure that you'll be OK."

At the hospital the next morning, the head nurse at the desk caught my eyes when I arrived and asked if I would like her to let the doctors know I was here and ready to talk. Everyone had pretty much left me alone after I ran out of the meeting room the day before, but now it seemed that they were waiting on me. I said yes, and a meeting was quickly called.

I sat down in the maroon and gray conference room and picked at the sandwich someone had shoved in my hand. It was a much smaller group now: I'd asked just my mom to come with me to meet with Lewis, a nurse, and Darrell. As soon as we settled into seats, Darrell asked if I knew what I wanted to do.

"Yes, I have made the choice to approve removing medical intervention."

Darrell, Lewis, and the nurse continued to look at me, as if I were supposed to say more.

"Do you need to hear me say it back to you, explain it to you so you know I fully understand?"

They all nodded, relieved.

I got it. It was important to be certain. I had to say it. Out loud.

"Geez guys, I get it, but . . . OK." I took a breath, and prayed that my very, very highest self would show up as I replayed the long conversation I'd had with Darrell two days earlier. It had been just us in the meeting room, and as soon as I'd sat down, I'd felt relieved. I'd asked him to tell me everything about the dying process and how long it takes, what it looks like, what happens. Darrell had explained the difference between palliative care and hospice. He had asked me what quality of life meant to José, what he absolutely would not have wanted, and how much he would have to get better to get close to a quality of life that would be meaningful for him. He'd explained what "comfort care" means and what would happen if José stayed on the machines. And he'd explained what it would look like and what José's body would do if I turned them off. I remembered the compassion and reassurance Darrell had shown me when I'd told him that I'd been living in fear all week that José would die at any moment but now I was more terrified that he would—we would—be stuck like this, in a long slow death that only meant more suffering. I didn't want it to be real, or say it out loud, but I had to say what I knew, what they all knew, to be true.

"I am removing medical support, which I am now calling medical intervention because what we are doing to José now is only prolonging his death, which is certain. José is in a place where he cannot get better. The damage to his brain means he cannot function to sustain his life on his own; his spine is injured so badly that it cannot be repaired; his brain and his body can no longer talk to each other; he has no chance of recovery. You used the word *unrecoverable* yesterday. He also said he had never in his thirty years seen anyone with injuries as severe as this even make it to the hospital alive. And if you had met José before, you would understand why it does not surprise me one bit. But that does not mean he is really alive. I know this is not a life—to use your words, the 'quality of life'—he would want to have. To honor him and his life in the very best way I can and as his wife and the legal decision maker, I am asking you to remove all medical support. I understand completely that I am instructing you to remove everything that is breathing for him and has been keeping him alive.

"You will remove the breathing tube and everything else, like nutrition and hydration. He will then be free to show us what happens next. I understand that he could die very quickly, in minutes or hours, but it is also not unusual for it to take more time, like a few days. In some circumstances it could go longer, maybe a week, but very rarely two. His body will likely be calm and peaceful but in some cases might jerk or have muscle movements, and while it looks distressing, it is part of the process and does not mean he is suffering. We will make him as comfortable as possible and be there to love and support him. We will look to José and hold space for him however he leads us, to allow him to stop suffering unnecessarily. His sacrifice to stay with us this long has already been far too great."

Long silence.

Darrell shifted in his chair. "I have never heard anyone describe it so well before."

Lewis said, "I wish we could have videotaped that."

I sat back somewhat dazed and felt some satisfaction I had at least advocated and pushed for José as best as I could. But no matter how capably and competently I could have navigated the ICU process or understood medical terms, this was an unwinnable situation that left me completely hollow. I noticed the nice nurse who'd been around all week and said, "Oh, you dyed your hair. The color looks great on you."

My higher self had clearly left the room.

We got down to logistics. I'd need to decide on a hospice; one of the nurses would call about openings. Did I have a preference for a certain part of town? In the meantime, they would move him out of the ICU to another room in this hospital.

Oddly, this was the moment it all got really, really real, and I got really scared. Nervous scared. Like when your water breaks and you don't want to go to the hospital. You can't go through with it but you must. You can't not. But you just. Can't. Just because I'd said the words didn't mean it was over. Now they were, we were, going to have to do it. Whatever calm I'd felt was entirely gone, and I was entirely and completely petrified.

"I need you to understand that if you think José is strong just by still being alive, just wait. If the record is two weeks in hospice with no food or water, he is so stubborn, he will beat that fucking record and make it three. His resting heart rate was just one or two beats per minute higher than Lance Armstrong's a few weeks ago. I don't think I've got another week in me, certainly not two or three. And oh shit, I don't want to do this all over again at some new place. So I don't know how long it will actually take or what I can ask, but I am very specifically asking each of you, out loud, to please do everything you can and in your power to help him and make this go as peacefully and painlessly as you can.

"Now that the decision is made, what needs to happen to do it here, tomorrow, at noon?"

They turned to each other, and the conversation no longer included me.

I understood that his time in the ICU was coming to an end. It was unsettling to realize that I had gotten used to the routine of being there: breakfast with Gabe before arriving at ten, the nurses' names, the good lot to park in. Since the moment our lives changed, everything had unfolded in this building. These small walls had held the chaos and confusion in check. Now a bigger unknown loomed ahead of me outside of these rooms. When I leave here, what do I do? I couldn't stay in the ICU, but I had come to feel comfortable there, and leaving meant José would be gone. Not just dead, but really actually never ever going to be with us again. Anymore. Ever. Gone.

I was calm, but tired, weary, and stripped bare. We stood up. Lewis gave me a little shoulder squeeze and, with a "how're you really doing, kiddo?" kind of look, said, "Do you want to get some fresh air?"

I nodded. I thought I had gotten the hospital down by now, but there was a whole new maze of hallways and staff elevators that took us straight out into the big afternoon sun, past the loading dock, and toward the lawn with the sprinklers.

We sat outside on the cement seats. Like regular people. Like someone who had compassionately just requested no longer prolonging a death, which no matter how true and right and correct it was, still might have felt a little like someone who'd just approved killing her husband.

"So, I heard you gave our resident José quite a time yesterday," Lewis said with a bit of a smirk.

"Um, yeah. I'm kinda sorry about that, but I really didn't get what he was doing."

"He was just trying to do his job."

"I know, but he wasn't. And frankly, he didn't know what was going on, or he was really messing with me at the very worst time. Why was he trying to cancel the meeting?"

When he didn't answer, I continued. "Besides, you really shouldn't send a lightweight into a heavyweight ring anyway."

He laughed, agreed, and suggested I should seriously think about going into medicine. The idea sat with me for maybe a full second, until I realized there are likely very few thirty-nine-year-old soon-to-be widowed single mothers in med school.

I heard myself say "was" later that day. I'd like to say it was practice, but it just came out. As it hung in the air, it didn't sound false, but I also realized that very soon it would be true. Soon I'd start sentences about him with, "Remember when . . ." I'd overheard two friends in the lobby reminiscing, and one said, "He used to . . ." And I'd caught myself earlier and stopped mid-sentence, "José was . . ."

The only thing that terrified me more than actually making the decision to stop medical intervention was forcing him to continue to suffer. I'll admit I was afraid José's dad's side of the family might want to stop me from removing medical support. If I am being honest, I was trying to avoid them. I froze when "the *tías*" and José's cousin Rose walked toward me in the hallway outside his room.

These were the grand matriarchs of the family, who had shown me nothing but acceptance and kindness, but I still felt a relative to dread as they approached. The only thing that might come close to their deep, do-anything love and loyalty to their family was their faith in the Catholic Church. The same church that has historically been very anti-anything involving removing medical support or hastening what is a certain death to, in my mind, avoid unnecessary pain and suffering.

Tía Marcia was in the middle. It had been only about a year since she had lost her husband to Alzheimer's, and the final years had been a long, slow, incredibly painful decline. Her eyes were full of love and strength, but there was a rawness to her that was new. She appeared smaller, and even though her smile was as grand as it always had been, there was something broken, or breaking, and frail about her now.

Do I look like she does? Like a widow?

She approached me, unsteadily, with her hands outstretched.

"You are doing the right thing," she said.

The fog lifted. I know she said other things about love, and God, and the duty of a wife, and how it's the women who keep the family together. Also about José, when he was just a sweet little boy whom she called by his middle name, Manuel. She still called him Manuelito or Lolo.

Tía Marcia didn't look like a widow to me anymore. Any vulnerability or fragility I saw before now looked like grace, mercy, and true love. I needed to hear I was doing the right thing from someone who knew how impossible losing a husband feels.

Later that night, I sat on a swirly barstool at the kitchen counter at home trying to find the words to prepare my son for his father's death. He knew José was in an accident and that he needed to be in the hospital because he had a big owie, but I had been vague, because, well, I didn't know what to tell him. What should I share or try to explain? What do I say? *Sorry, your dad is dead but technically not till tomorrow? I am so sorry, babe, that I am going to unplug your papa tomorrow, and then it might take a few minutes or a few days for him to be all the way dead?*

I'd been practicing what to say, what I should say, to Gabe for days inside my head, but knew tonight, finally, I had to say it out loud. "I want to talk to you a little more about Papa still being in the hospital. He is doing everything he can and working so hard to heal up so he can stay with us, and the doctors are doing everything they can too, but Papa's owie is still pretty big."

"Is the owie in his neck? Was there blood?" he asked.

"Yes, his neck is the biggest owie, and when I got to the hospital I didn't see any blood."

"Is Papa's owie going to get better?"

"Papa is so strong and loves you so much, he is trying so hard to get better. But some owies are just sometimes too big."

His whole body slumped.

As we went to read books together before bed, Josh posted an update to José's CaringBridge page:

> *We want to express our profound gratitude for your ongoing outpouring of love for José and his family.*
>
> *We are not receiving visitors at the hospital at this time.*
>
> *Immediate family only is with him.*
>
> *Thank you for honoring this request and not coming to visit.*
>
> *We deeply appreciate you continuing to hold him and his family in your thoughts and prayers.*

The Last Day

I didn't see any reason to arrive early on the day we stopped intervention.

I had no idea what would actually happen, how long it would
take, or how I'd react once I was there. If actually dying once he
was off the machines *could* take somewhere between minutes and
days, even weeks, *would* it drag out or be swift and merciful? Could
I be calm, or would I feel like I was being drawn and quartered and
dragged through the streets behind a horse? Would I change my
mind, run out of the room? Passing by the nurses' station, I felt their
always friendly faces and concerned eyes follow me. I wondered what
a walk toward the gallows in the middle of the town square would be
like. So many eyes.

I whispered, "only prolonging death, medical intervention, unrecoverable injuries" to myself over and over, each phrase a little bead
to rub my fingers over, to keep myself walking.

Chanel, you're not killing him, because he already died.

He's already dead.

The machines are in the way.

Let him go.

The paper gowns and hats we had to don were a small price to pay
for the private room we'd gotten the day before. The doctors had
found some bacteria that required José to be isolated, but I secretly

wondered if there wasn't any infection. They were doing what little they could to make things easier.

The room was small, the blinds drawn and spun half down. There weren't as many machines; the familiar beeps were gone. There were a few screens with low numbers. I didn't ask what they meant. It didn't matter anymore. The critical details and questions desperately documented in notebooks during the week, the timing of things, the chronology of events, no longer meant anything. Time bowed deeply and excused itself from the room.

I was shattered beyond weariness.

Walking toward the same spot at the right side of his bed as I did a week ago when in the ER, it hit me as clearly as knowing you are in love: *He is so much closer to death now.* The words landed immediately as I entered the room. *Close, lower somehow.* They were as true as the words that came back to me when I crawled into the hospital bed with him after midnight, just two nights before. That empty feeling I'd had, remembering tucking my foot under his two calves with my right arm on his chest like hundreds (thousands) of nights, was still there, but he felt so much further away from me. He was really going away.

José was all I could focus on. The family members in the room all blurred together in a line of hospital-issue light-blue-colored paper gowns and caps.

Lewis controlled the room; his movements carried intention and calm as he began removing lines, lifting the white tape to remove long needles, giving reassuring instructions to the nurse, who had a big-eyed, in-over-her-head look. The walls holding up the room panned out. José was beyond pain. The only thing that was true or mattered was surrounding him with pure love. To release him from just the smallest of his suffering was a gift to give, not a burden to bear.

Blood spurted from José's left forearm when one of the last IVs was removed. The nurse apologized ashamedly for the mess.

"Shhhhh. No talking," I held up my hand and started to shake, sucking deep scoops of air to anchor the vertigo.

Only The Tube remained. That long, ugly plastic tube that had been shoved down José's throat and taped to his face, rubbing his bottom lip and breathing for him. After the first day or two, I had to turn my head when they cleared his airway; his body choking against it was just too much to watch. I closed my eyes one last time, knowing that whatever they pulled out of him was not an image I wanted to have seared to memory or replayed over and over in my head for years to come.

Nothing left to do, Lewis made a half bow to me, and moved back a foot or two away from the bed toward the side of the room next to the now-dark machines.

I covered José with as much of my bent body as I could, getting as close to him as skin allowed. When breath came out of his mouth, I pulled it into my lungs, infusing him into my body.

I cradled his face, my nose inches away from his. And for a while the bridge between us held. I couldn't vibrate any higher, feel any lighter, or breathe any deeper.

And then, José went beyond where I could go.

He was there. And then he wasn't.

Just like that.

I saw it.

The moment.

If dying can take a long time, the exact moment it happens does not; it was a flash, an instant.

Staring into his face, I watched and saw the instant he was no longer there.

The rest of him was. The dark hairline around his face, the crinkles around those almond eyes, the little mole near the tip of his nose. Those lips. The thick stubble of his beard that rubbed my cheeks raw. I was still locked into every slice and molecule of him, but he was different, gone; what remained was his body.

Thank you.

Falling onto him, those two words exploded out of me. There wasn't room for anything else to exist. Only light.

Thank you, thank you, thank you, thank you.

There was no room for anything other than pure gratitude for his life, our son, the life we had together. All of it.

It wasn't from me, and in that split second I knew that whatever I felt wasn't just from José. It was that something *other*, enveloping everything, originating from nowhere specifically but also everywhere.

Thank you.

That voice, my voice, the true voice. Life and death comes in and goes out and for that second there was no difference and the two felt exactly the same.

Everything is all so very simple.

For that second of everything and nothing, I held them all together.

"This. It's this," I heard so very softly.

Thank you.

Reentry Protocols

I am covering his body. I went with him as far I could, but the thread goes only so far.

For the first time this whole week, my husband is dead. Not half-dead, could be dead, might have died, or technically died at the scene. There was no more marveling that he was still alive, fear that he could die at any minute, or worry about how long he could or would stay "mostly dead." Now he was really in past tense. He died.

I was no longer waiting for him to wake up, come back, or come home. Or guessing how dead he was going to stay or how alive he might ever be again.

I don't know how long I remained crumpled over him, but the weight of the room eventually pulled me back into my body. Gravity. Time was working again. Mostly. I heard the low shuffles of feet and the swing of the door as the room began to empty. I understood at some point that I'd need to do something, so I began to uncurl my arms from around his head. In slow motion my face pulled back far enough to cup his cheeks and stroke the hairline above his brow down to the temple on what everyone would immediately begin referring to as "the body." It was a cloudy slow dance in between heavy air, my hands, and his face. I almost asked how long I'd been gone.

I heard someone shift in a chair and my eyes opened. George. As if on cue, he moved near the foot of the bed and Jen came up to the right side of the bed. Only then did it register that Jen and George were the only two remaining in the room. I noticed George's blue denim shirt and matching Levi's jeans under the paper gown and the faint smell of his rolled tobacco. He'd been a close friend to us and like a brother or almost father figure to José. He had raced San Francisco traffic, conjured a last-minute plane ticket the night before, and sped from the Seattle airport to the hospital. He'd been running late and I'd worried his flight had been delayed, but waiting felt wrong. I'd just said, "José is ready, we need to let him go, now," when George walked into the room.

George leaned in. "Let's get those things off of him. Let's make him comfortable."

Of course, I thought. Make him comfortable. He'd had so many tubes and needles in him, and I wanted everything off.

I picked at the corners and started peeling off the medical tape. Some came off like the wrapping paper tape you use to put kid art or postcards on the walls, but the hardcore hospital grade stuff stuck to him like very mad duct tape. I placed a blanket over him and pulled the thin gown down, one shoulder at a time, and used a washcloth Jen had found on one of the shelves to wash and clean "the hospital" off of him.

I really had no idea, kissing a hand, what his body was doing or how fast. Kissing the other hand a few minutes later, *Does this one feel cooler than the other? Already?*

Rounding his knee with a warm washcloth, I felt the strong, lean thighs he'd beg me to rub out after a long race, his hipbone I couldn't help but grab onto where he was ticklish and he'd squirm away. After being married nine years, I knew every curve and line. Everything was so familiar. As I washed him, I noticed his skin turned a muted tone. Not yellow but more like an absence of color.

Even though I had no idea how to do it or what I was supposed to do, I was washing and caressing his body. I felt a deep, cellular calm with the familiarity of the movements, though each motion held the purpose and care of performing a tea ceremony or carrying a sacred scroll. I loved him the same as I had hours or weeks before. I did not want to leave the room, and now I could take care of him and love him a little longer.

I'm sure I never said, "I am preparing his body" out loud, but I thought it over and over again.

This must be what people over thousands of years have done.

The phrase *being with your dead* vibrated low and chantlike in my head.

To prepare?

Prepare for what, I am not exactly sure. But I look back at those moments as fondly as I do memories of his being alive.

Whom it served most, I also can't say, but whether or not part of his presence remained or slowly trailed away, preparing his body must have prepared me to begin to live without him. Right there in front of me I could see and feel and touch with 100 percent certainty that it was only his dead body that remained.

And even though I was as comfortable as on any of the thousands of intimate nights we'd shared in our bed, I got self-conscious about how to place his arms. I didn't want to do it wrong or make it weird somehow. To make them look less posed, I kept adjusting his hand, or arm, the bend of the elbow on his chest, then lower, then on his stomach and then higher again. Nothing looked right, but I didn't know how long I could just keep moving him around. I started to feel how different he was, the body was.

Do his muscles feel tense because he is already starting to stiffen?

Are the color and tone of his skin dissipating?

The changes happened so quickly. In just a handful of minutes.

Even if I wasn't sure I was preparing him correctly, touching him felt far more natural than doing nothing. It occurred to me I was relieved that strangers weren't touching him anymore.

The red-and-black Pendleton blanket I'd brought from home a few days before now covered him, the corners folded down around his neck like a robe, and we'd placed on his chest the bundle of sage and cedar tied with red string that George had brought with him. Jen, George, and I stood at the foot of the bed admiring him.

"He looks like himself again," Jen said.

"It's weird, all that swelling around his neck is gone now," I noted.

"Wow, for a dead guy, José is still one good-looking man." George's eyes twinkled with love as he smiled and shook his head in appreciation.

I smiled. Then chuckled. And laughed a real laugh. The deep, loud kind ladies aren't supposed to make in public, but everyone still turns to look with a smile. The simple fact that I *could* laugh meant maybe I could still walk out of here, on my own feet, with enough of me intact that I could, well, feel human again.

Jen walked small groups into the room. A sharp intake of breath from José's *tías*, and from behind me it sounded like his dad, Marco, was saying prayers in Spanish. There were murmurs and good-byes from José's mother, Pat; his brother, Robert; his sister, Shelley; and her wife, Angela. I couldn't hear well, because I remained at the window with my eyes locked on whatever life continued on across downtown Seattle as the final visitors came for their last good-bye. Staring out the window felt forced and awkward, as if it were rude to be so obviously removed from everyone else, but it seemed like the least crazy and most normal-ish thing I could do. Also, I couldn't figure out how else to arrange myself, and I could not turn my head to meet anyone's eyes or unclench my arms from my chest.

It was too much for me to take in anyone else's suffering. During the last few days, some empathic swell inside of me made others' grief and pain ring in my ears. Their fear smelled like an electric fire or the air when the sky turns Jolly Rancher–candy green color before a tornado hits. The worry in their eyes was so suffocating, it was hard to breathe. All their words piled up around me. The hugs that were supposed to make me feel better made me want to crawl out of my own skin. So I stayed at the window pretending to watch the people of downtown Seattle move around like pieces on a board game. The tint shading on the glass reflected my own opaque image back to me, showing that my jeans now slipped past my hipbone and my jaw left a hollow space under my cheekbones when clenched. Catching my own eyes taking myself in didn't feel like anything, as if I'd come across a photo someone had taken of me long ago.

And then the door stopped opening and closing.

I turned from the window to find only George and asked, "So now what? Do you just go home?"

"Yes, you go home," George replied.

After a week in the ICU, it was done. I thought the ordeal was "over," so my plan was to crawl under my bed for a few years. I was so incredibly wrong. The rest of the hard part was just beginning.

Darrell was waiting for me at the main nurses' desk. I could see the stacks of empty pink pastry and pizza boxes my friends had brought every day to the nurses. They looked at me with downcast eyes. I would have slipped out the back door if there'd been one. Darrell held a piece of paper in my direction.

"Wait, I have to pick a funeral home, right now?" I asked.

I didn't even know what palliative care was a week ago and Darrell had been so helpful, but now I was over it.

Aren't we done yet?

"Yes, before you go. The body is usually moved from the hospital within twenty-four hours," he replied.

I glanced at the photocopied paper he'd just handed to me: funeral and burial, burial and cremation, cremation only, out-of-state residents, and so on. It was hard to read or know what to choose. I knew he'd wanted to be cremated, but not at one of those funeral places with the shiny brass banisters and dusty carpets.

"You know, I am trying to look at this list and all I can see is a shitty off-center photocopy I can barely read. And by the way, why do all the crappy handouts I've gotten this week have names like 'parting rainbows,' or 'bridges crossing' or 'journey passageways'? It's so, just . . . can't you get some better handouts for all this death stuff?" I was out of steam.

"You're totally right, but you still need to pick," he said with enough older-brother bossiness that I knew I had to.

"OK, what about this one, in Kirkland. I never go to Kirkland." A few funeral homes were closer, but I didn't want to have to drive past it all the time on the way to the grocery store or a friend's house. I'd have a hard enough time going anywhere in this city without a memory of José linked to it. I didn't want any more triggers, thank you.

"They've been around a long time. But you're going to pick one that is farther away?" he asked.

"Yes, them," I said decisively. "Now, I have to go call this trauma-expert guy so he can talk me through how I am supposed to tell my son his dad is dead. Anything else? More paperwork?"

That shut him up long enough so I could walk past.

And that was pretty much. That.

Then . . . I went home.

Guide:
Quality of Life,
Death, and Dying

You only live once, but if you do it right, once is enough.

—OFTEN ATTRIBUTED TO MAE WEST

Quality of life. You know it when you see it, right? Or more likely you know it when you feel it. You'll really know it when you don't feel it, or don't have it, anymore. Determining quality of life often comes down to a gut check, an instinctual knowing that's hard to explain. When I had to answer the question "What does quality of life mean for José?" my immediate, unwavering, and unequivocal response was, "Not that. It's absolutely not being mostly dead and only kept alive by machines."

His prognosis was unrecoverable. I knew he wouldn't want to live like that because we had talked about what quality of life meant to him—and this wasn't it. My choice was almost decided for me. I did not have to guess, wonder, and doubt. Many others do not get that same mercy. And that is exactly why we need to define what our quality of life is, talk about it, and write it down.

While the term *quality of life* is applied to everything from where we live and how long of a commute we'll sign up for, all the way up the scale of importance to very challenging health decisions, it's generally understood but also hard to nail down. What *exactly* does it mean? How is it measured? Because quality of life can mean different things to different people and be applied to a variety of circumstances, it's critical to be thoughtful and specific about what it means to you. So let's do that.

Define Quality of Life

Having conversations with your close friends and family about your definition of quality of life is an important step, but those discussions are not legally binding. In order to make them so, you complete a document, called a living will, outlining your wishes and specific instructions for what types of medical care you want (and don't want) when you are at, or nearing, the end of your life. (Specifics on how to create a living will are covered on page 220.)

Years after José's death, I asked Darrell, based on his thirty years of experience working in palliative care, what makes a living will "good" and what are the most common mistakes people make when creating one.

Darrell emphasized that it's important to have a living will, period. Without one, things can get complicated very quickly. But he'd also seen documents that specified *who* should decide but provided no instructions on what they should do or any details about what the person wanted. Medicine is often not black and white. Darrell has watched loved ones without clear guidance struggle to make decisions for dying patients; everyone suffered. All on their own, they have to come up with goals of care and guess what they would have wanted. For example, how much mobility would maintain their loved ones' quality of life? A living will reduces the stress and strain on your family and prevents you, according to Darrell, "from possibly being stuck with a health condition that is inconsistent with the life you want."

Darrell suggests that your living will include answers to these five questions:

1. What and how do you define a meaningful quality of life?
2. What is unacceptable to you?
3. If you were very sick or injured, how much better would you need to get to meet or maintain your quality of life?
4. How little mobility or how much disability are you OK with?
5. What is *most important* to you?

In *Being Mortal*, Atul Gawande asks, "What does a good day look like?" If it's being able to visit with friends, walk your dog around the block once a day, or still enjoy a scotch at night, your living will should include it.

As you define what quality of life means to you, use specific situations or examples. For instance:

I want to be able to go to my daughter's wedding.
I want to be able to verbally communicate for as long as I can.
I want to know who is in the room with me and be able to engage with him or her.
I do not want to be in pain or suffer unnecessarily.
I wish to be able to eat food and drink water independently.

The same approach is useful as you define what does *not* meet your definition of quality of life and identify what you don't want. For example:

I hate the ventilator and never want to do that again.
If there is no chance I will get better and be able to return to my home, I do not want to go to an institution or nursing home.
If aggressive treatments and surgeries have little chance of

improving my health and will likely diminish my quality of life, I
do not want those treatments.

Thinking in terms of real-life situations and being specific is important, because your family and friends may think they know what you want or have a general idea, but they could be way off base when it comes to the details. Have you read the book *The Diving Bell and the Butterfly*? The author, Jean-Dominique Bauby, was paralyzed in an accident and suffered from locked-in syndrome. He was only able to blink one eyelid, and this became his sole means of communication. Would Bauby's prognosis meet my definition of an acceptable quality of life? Nope. Would it for my friend Mira? Not so fast.

"If I am not in pain, and that is important, I do not want to be in pain, and I can be awake and present and see out of one eye . . . I can see out of one eye, right?" she asked.

"Sure," I replied.

"Well, if I'm not in pain and I'm coherent, I could spend that time finally reading all the classics I've never been able to." She thought about it for another few seconds. "Yup, I could do that. If I could read books and not be in pain, that would be enough for me."

"When you say 'no pain,' do you mean absolutely no pain or a little pain?" I asked.

"Maybe a little, but not a lot," she replied.

"How would you rate that amount of pain on a scale from one to ten with zero being absolutely no pain at all and ten meaning constant terrible pain?" I asked.

"Hmm. A two, maybe a three, but not higher," she replied.

I know Mira well, and I love books, too—but there's no way I would have ever guessed that is what she would want. However, a casual talk with a friend about quality of life and drafting your living will is one thing. How do you talk about end-of-life wishes if you are nervous about bringing up the subject with your spouse or a parent? Or don't want to talk about death at all?

Dying Well: A Conversation with BJ Miller

On the way to the hospital, when I told the social worker to do everything possible to keep José alive until I arrived, I hadn't really thought through what I was saying and what it could mean. In that moment, I just wanted José to be alive. But soon afterward, that changed. I didn't want him to be in pain or suffer. I didn't want him to be afraid. Keeping him comfortable while we waited to see if he would wake up was always on my mind, even before I knew what "comfort care" meant.

BJ Miller is a hospice and palliative care physician, a national speaker on death and dying, and the coauthor with Shoshana Berger of the upcoming book *A Beginner's Guide to the End*. When we first spoke and shared our "how we got here" stories, BJ immediately understood how my panicked words to "do everything possible" matched the common reaction that doing everything is the same as doing the right thing or the best thing on someone else's behalf. As much as I wouldn't have realized, or wanted to admit it, I shared an outdated assumption that I had to choose between, as BJ described it, "quality of life *or* quantity of life." He went on to say, "Palliative care and hospice are just about helping you live well, as comfortably as possible, and that often ends up being longer."

When a patient asks about palliative care and hospice, that is, when one may need them or meet the criteria for benefiting from them, many people are surprised to learn they may have more care options and a wider range of services (including home care) available to them than they had thought. In fact, hospice is a subtype of palliative care when someone has six months or less to live, but palliative care is often available anywhere along the trajectory of serious illness. As BJ said, "There's so much that we know, there's so much that we can do to bring peace and comfort." And, if you change your mind or feel better, you can even *check yourself out* of hospice. Who knew? I didn't. Which could be why many people don't find their way to hospice care until just a few days before they die.

When I asked what can make a real difference for the patient and family facing end-of-life decisions (whether in hospice or not), he replied: "One thing that is strategically very important is [for the patient] to name their proxy." And then, "Have the conversation about quality of life. It's really about the conversation 'being known.'"

BJ clarified that, while the way to approach the conversation about end-of-life wishes depends on the person's age and beliefs, many patients are relieved to talk about their wishes or fears. But not everyone is. For those who are resistant to talking about their own death, he's seen the apprehension shift "the second you say, 'Oh, advance planning is one of the kindest things you could do for your family, so that they don't have to worry about what you would have wanted, and they don't have to fight with each other.' That often gets people." Or gets through to them.

Avoiding family stress, disagreements, and fighting is no small thing, but a low-drama, no-lawsuit death is not the main goal. Writing a living will and discussing end-of-life decisions and quality of life is really about kindness, to yourself and those close to you. Of course we want to be cared for, comforted, and made comfortable with as much love, dignity, and respect as possible as we near the end of our lives and die. Communicating your wishes for what you want (and don't want) is important, BJ says, "because you want to be known. . . . You want your doctors and whoever's caring for you to understand who you are as a person." Not only does your family know what to do, you get what you want and are able to receive what makes you most comfortable.

That's what we did for, or on behalf of, José, as well as we could. When I was uncertain, it was often about stuff like whether I should play more music or bring some pictures to place around him. Or slippers? Would he have liked to have been shaved? I knew what he "wanted" in the big picture, but not necessarily the little incremental things he'd have wanted. To be honest, I worried I was maybe doing it wrong. So I asked BJ, what have you experienced that can make this whole thing easier on everyone? In addition to kindness and compassion in general, it was helpful to be reminded to trust ourselves and listen to what feels right.

"Dying is a part of the living process, and you know a lot about living," he reminds us. "This is something our species has been doing forever. We all have a relationship with loss. You know more than you think you do. You're not going to screw it up."

Tell the Truth;
Not Too Much

Have you ever wished you could light yourself on fire, fling yourself out of an airplane, or turn immediately to ash instead of telling someone the truth about something? If so, you'll know how I felt, sitting in my oppressively hot garage, staring at the door to the kitchen, sweat pooling in my bra and slipping off my elbows, wishing I could do anything else instead of going inside to tell my five-year-old son that his father was dead.

The last time I'd checked out of a hospital, I'd also felt terror-stricken, but it was the entirely opposite *joy-terror* of going home with our newborn son. I had cherished the morning sickness and swollen ankles—even the maternity overalls. I had been focused for so long on being pregnant and having a baby, I hadn't thought about what came after. When it was time to put Gabe in the borrowed infant car seat and go home, it hit me that they were just going to let us leave. With a baby. And we had no clue what the hell we were doing. I was wheeled out cradling a baby in one hand and a vanilla milkshake in the other.

My time in the ICU with José was so intensely about tests, breathing capacity, brain function, consciousness, dying, and death that I hadn't thought about what happened next. It hadn't occurred to me that I'd just go home. To my son. All alone. What the hell should I do next? Where was my milkshake now?

As I'd pulled into the driveway and opened the garage doors, I called the trauma expert whom the social worker had recommended. On this hot summer day, it was double sweltering inside the garage. I noticed all of the bikes lining the wall: training bike, mountain bike, commuter bike, time-trial bike, backup race bike. The Cervélo hook was bare. And then of course there was the trainer, the bike stand, the shop table full of shiny Italian metal and who-knows-what carbon-fiber pieces everywhere, the team jerseys, and the old helmets. I was surrounded by everything José loved.

José, you fucking-fucker you. If you were here right now, I would kill you all over again, a million times, for leaving me here to go in-side that door and tell our son his papa is dead. Alone. Fuck.

I was off the phone but was repeating the words the trauma guy had said. "Chanel, your son just lost his dad. He needs his mom right now."

They weren't much, but those words were some sort of rope to hold on to as the nauseous knee-buckling waves pushed the panic up into my throat.

Oh god. No. No. No.

It turns out the hardest thing I'd ever have to do wasn't removing medical support; it was figuring out how tell Gabe his dad was dead.

I realized I'd be walking through the same door that José had walked out of a week before, almost to the hour.

"You have just been through a profound trauma," the trauma expert had continued. "The difference is, your son is about to experience a great loss, and at such a young age, understanding what this means is going to be a long process for him."

When I asked what I should say he got very quiet. "Tell the truth; not too much."

OK, Chanel.

Me, trauma. Gabe, loss.

Parent now. Cave later.

Before I even entered the kitchen, I'd almost convinced myself that telling him tomorrow was a totally fine plan. I'd have rather pushed a boulder up a mountain and faced daily eviscerations for the rest of my life—anything, anything else, but having to tell him.

But I knew that if I didn't do it immediately I might never do it.

I sat down on a kitchen counter barstool next to him, overcome with the urge to squeeze him tight and sob till passing out.

"Baby, can I talk to you about Papa for a minute?"

Big eyes looked back at me.

"I'll talk while you finish your snack."

My mom exited the room.

"Remember last night when I said Papa has been working so hard all week to heal his owie so he can stay with us because he loves us so much and would never ever want to leave us?"

"Yeah." More big eyes. He dropped the blueberries he was holding.

"And that sometimes owies can be too big to heal?"

His eyes looked down as he slumped. He knew.

"Well, baby, I am so sorry that your papa's owie was just too big for the doctors to heal. It was too big for your papa. He tried so hard and was so strong and brave, but he couldn't. Your papa died today."

The words were globs of heavy concrete thrown down a damp well with no bottom. They hurtled. And spun.

"He died?"

"Yes. I'm so sorry. Your papa's body died."

He fast-walked into the living room, running away from me, to flop on the couch. My reaction was no different than when he'd fallen out of the raft on the river, was about to touch a hot stove, or fell off a swing. I was halfway across the room, arms out to scoop him up or catch him, before I knew I'd moved. He flung himself face-first into the back cushions. I sat down next to him and put my hand on the back his leg. I worried that I'd scared him. He half squirmed on his side, face scrunched, as if he was working hard to make any of what I was saying make sense.

After a few minutes of pushing me away, he ran up to his room and shoved the door tightly closed. Then big noises. He barricaded the door with his tubs of LEGOs, the giant Playmobil castle that took a whole weekend to build. Books. Trucks. Stuffed animals.

I sat on the carpet with my back up against the door, talking to him in soothing tones. The way I would when he'd have a tantrum.

"I'm right here, Gabe. I'll be just right here on the other side of the door so you know where I am. I am so sorry, baby."

After an impossible few hours, he allowed me into his room. But I could only sit on the very tippy-top corner of his bed next to his pillow. No lying down. I couldn't touch him.

"OK, kiddo, I'm just going to sit next to you on the bed, so you know I am here. So you can ask me any questions or talk more if you want to. I'll just stay right here."

I tried to give him the room he asked for, but every few minutes my hand would wander over to scratch his back and he would shake me off. My need to console him was overwhelming, but he didn't want to be touched and could not be consoled. He didn't cry. The often easy tears of sadness, hurt, anger, or frustration could not be found. His face searched, so confused. My baby boy. It was a new language he was forced to understand. The language of acute sadness. So foreign and visceral, it didn't fit right in his body, in his every atom. I thought he might have fallen asleep, but then he spoke.

"Mama?"

"Yes, baby?"

"Where is Papa?"

"Well, I think he is in the sky and trees and sunshine and everywhere, and in the wind so we can feel him hugging us with every breeze."

"In the wind?"

"Uh-huh. I think his spirit is everywhere, and he will always be with us in our hearts, and maybe we can close our eyes and imagine him."

"But *where* is he?"

"Where?"

"Where did he go? Is he in the ground?"

I realized he wanted the details. The physical. The tangible. His body.

"That's a really good question, babe. Some people get buried in the ground in a cemetery after they die. But we aren't going to do that."

"We're not?"

"No baby, your papa wanted to be cremated instead."

"What is that?"

Oh fuck fuck fuck.

I am in a white panic.

I can't say, *"Well, kiddo, right now your dad probably is in a refrigerator in the hospital basement, or maybe in a moving van or being driven to a place where they are going to put him in a big furnace and burn him up."*

My lower back and whole body were squeezed so tight I could almost levitate.

Tell the truth. Not too much.

"OK, remember in Star Wars? The real movies, not the Clone Wars ones, when Darth Vader remembered the good side of the force before he died? Well, he was such a great and brave and very special Jedi that Luke Skywalker made a giant fire to honor him?"

I can hear him nodding.

"You can't use your body anymore after you die, so we are going to give Papa the same kind of Jedi ceremony and let his body go back out to the stars."

"Like Darth Vader?"

"Yeah, we're going to give your papa the biggest ceremony just like the good Darth Vader."

The two of us drifted in and out of our own thoughts in a little single bed on top of his Clone Troopers sheet set. He eventually stopped pushing my hand away.

"Was there any blood?"

"When I got to the hospital, I didn't see any blood."

"When Papa died, does that mean he'll be dead all year?"

"Yes, baby, but not just all year, OK? When your body dies, it has to stay dead. When Papa's body died, it means he can't ever come back." I repeated it to make sure he understood.

Finally, Gabe slept. I didn't move one inch in case I'd wake him even though my arm had fallen asleep and was on fire. At some point, I dozed off too.

Found and Lost

am in a field. Or on a farm.

The bite in the air feels like fall, but the rustling of bare branches is too loud for my skin.

Everything is grayscale.

Tall fingers of wheat wave with a crinkle like dry straw.

I am certain I am alone but being watched, like prey.

Hurried and scared, I can't find José.

Find him before dark. You have to find him now, I keep repeating while I search empty barns, look behind fences, and scratch past overgrown bushes.

No. I am searching in the bushes.

Branches catch my face. Grass tangles in my hair. Blood streams down my knuckles. My heart beats like a howling wind in my ears.

I hunch lower in a thick patch—and find him.

I pull tangled branches off his chest and see his ashen skin under the torn places in his shirt.

I have to bend down to reach the last branch near his collarbone, and through the empty spaces see his face is caked with dirt.

I can't make my eyes look at him again and my hand won't lift, but we can't be here, and just before I remember to breathe, everything goes dark.

PART II After

We think that the point is to pass the test or
to overcome the problem, but the truth is that things don't
really get solved. They come together and they fall apart.

—PEMA CHÖDRÖN

Aftershocks

No matter how many times I ask, I cannot remember what happened that entire weekend after José died. Something about going to the beach and jumping on blown-up air mattresses in the water. Gabe got a scratch from the nozzle on his shin.

I lost Saturday and Sunday, but I remember Monday morning vividly. I'd fallen asleep in Gabe's room while putting him to bed the night before. I registered the faraway ring of my cell phone but didn't dare, or care, to move. Gabe was still asleep, my arm tucked under his head, but I'd been awake for hours.

The adrenaline surge I had experienced on the way to the hospital that first night and the shockwaves I rode dozens of times during the past week had worn off completely, and I felt shelled, depleted. Hollow. I was swimming in a sea of worry, panic rocking me in wave after endless wave.

So now I'm a thirty-nine-year-old single mom with a five-year-old son and twelve-year-old stepdaughter. I'm a widow. I still can't guess the password to get into his phone or his laptop. We "completed" our wills, but we never signed them, so, probate court. I have no paid time off, no steady income, and a mortgage I can't afford on my own, so the money situation needs to get figured out.

Remaining perfectly still so I wouldn't wake Gabe, I spun my wedding rings clockwise with my thumb to try to keep blood flowing through my arm. I felt grateful to be home and tucked into bed with my son, but the comfort of the moment was temporary, as every second carried the feeling that we were pretty much fucked. Basic things I wish I had done and the other things I had to figure out deluged me.

Life insurance will help a lot, but it won't last forever. The cats keep peeing on the couch. I have to plan a funeral. The kids have no dad.

The phone rang again. Then footsteps up the stairs. Then the soft *tap tap tap* of a knuckle lightly on the door.

The next tap at the door was louder and clearly a *knock, knock, knock*. The door opened just a second afterward. My mom leaned in to say there was someone on the phone for me. She stayed in the doorway.

"I'll call them back, Mom," I whispered.

"Well, he says he needs to speak to you."

"I'll call back."

"Well, he called twice and says it's urgent he speaks with you."

I remained silent.

"He's waiting, on your phone, and said he has to speak with you, directly."

I didn't respond.

"It's the coroner."

I slid my arm out from under Gabe's.

Why the hell is the coroner calling? Is this normal?

"Mrs. Hernando?" he stammered.

"Ms. Reynolds. And yes, this is Chanel."

"I apologize to have to bother you, but the . . . I'm calling about the . . . body of Mr. Hernando, your husband?"

I could feel my eyes rolling into the back of my head. *What now? What could you possibly want. From me. Right now? It's nine a.m. on Monday morning.*

"It was . . . again, I am so sorry to call. It appears he was moved before anyone called me, sometime over the weekend. They were supposed to call me, to schedule, first. I'm so sorry." He finally stopped talking.

"So you're calling me, um, because you need to know where he is—or went?"

"Yes, they usually call me. I need to schedule the autopsy, before . . . immediately. I hope it's not too late. So, can you . . . ?" His voice trailed off.

"Before they cremate him you need to examine the body?"

"Yes."

He was embarrassed. I didn't care.

"Why?"

"In a case like this, an accident, or homicide. The autopsy confirms the cause of death," he said.

I looked around to make sure Gabe wouldn't overhear me. All clear, but I still lowered my voice. "Doesn't it seem like the part when the van ran him over would be the cause of death?"

"It's the law. I'm sorry. We have to."

I was too tired to think of what to say next. The sheer impossible dumbness of the conversation was too much to take in.

I filled in the blanks for the coroner, found the telephone number for the funeral home on the crappy handout, hung up, and major league baseball–style whipped my arm back to throw my phone across the room as hard as I could to shatter into a million stupid asshole pieces.

Then froze in midair. I dropped it back into my lap. I hadn't backed it up in a while and couldn't afford to lose all the contact information, and I still couldn't get into José's phone. And screw it, my arm felt tired and heavy anyway.

So I stared at the wall. There was no comfortable way to arrange or put my body. I couldn't turn off my thoughts, and with so many people coming, going, or gathering at the house to offer their condolences or help plan the memorial service, I had no privacy. Nowhere to go. Autopilot mode told me to go hide in our—nope, now *my*—bedroom.

Walking back up the stairs, my brain got stuck on the nervousness in the coroner's voice. It quickly dawned on me that someone, some-where, had seriously fucked up.

What the hell? They lost "the body"?

Maybe "the cremation" of "the body" had already taken place. What happens if the autopsy guy doesn't get there in time? Was someone going to get their ass handed to them or get fired on the spot for screwing up "the burning up" or the "returning to the earth," as the funeral people like to call it, of my husband? Don't tons of people die at Harborview's world-class trauma unit all the time? Shouldn't they, you know, know who to call? Have a list maybe?

How many people piled up over the weekend?

My god, who's even running this monkey show?

Shutting my bedroom door, I took a few more robotic steps to the closet and pulled down José's perfectly folded sweaters off the shelves, the ones I'd been mad at him for buying because they were more than we had budgeted.

"But it's the half-yearly sale!" he'd insisted.

I dropped them one by one into a pile on the floor and curled up on top of them.

I cannot un-know that the autopsy is where they peel skin off and weigh your organs. At least that's how it works on TV. A picture of incisions and cold metal tables formed as I shoved his favorite black V-neck sweater into my face, the softness of the cashmere smooth on my cheek and cradling my neck. I smiled as I remembered how his $200 sweaters looked great on him, but as I smashed my face harder into the sweaters, hoping they'd muffle the howling, I thought they tasted just as dry as any old flannel shirt would have.

The coroner needs to find him, so he can carve him up before some other guys burn him down to a container of gravel-size nuggets and cement-looking dust.

Breathe in. Breathe out. Again.

Lying on the closet floor, I practiced saying it. Even to me it sounded a little too much like advice from a yoga-goddess-heart-hugger type who'd also encourage you to look at your vagina in a mirror or drink your own pee, but I had more than occasionally noticed I'd only been taking these teeny sips of air at the tippy-top of my chest. When I breathed more deeply, my stomach didn't lock up and I felt a little less panicked.

Breathe.

It won't always feel like this.

Breathe.

It won't always be like this.

I didn't feel better, but on top of that puddle of sweaters, it did help to think that if I took things second by second, breath by breath, eventually I *could* get up.

"Mama? Mama?" Gabe knocked on the door.

The palms of my hands were already wiping my eyes and nose dry before my head had finished popping up.

"Yep. I'm here, kiddo," I said, trying to sound normal and cheery. I didn't want him to see me like that. I had to get up. Go parent.

"Can we watch *Scooby-Doo*?"

"Yup. I'll be right there. Just give me five minutes, OK?"

"OK."

"You can tell Grandma to start it and I'll be right down."

In the bathroom, I redid my ponytail and washed my face, but my eyes still looked puffy yet also somehow sunken with dark circles smudged underneath. Reflected in the mirror, I saw a framed photo from a retreat in California taken three years ago. Even backward, the hand-swept, cursive letters painted onto the square, wooden sign hanging from the willow tree clearly read, "breathe, you are alive." My friend Laura and I traveled with our toddlers together to the meditation retreat at Deer Park Monastery with Thích Nhất Hạnh; Laura had taken the picture and framed it for me. We'd been much closer back then, but she and her husband, Josh, had come to the hospital in the middle of the week when it was clearer how serious the injuries were. She was a social worker who specialized in trauma, so when she said, "If anyone can do this, you can," I believed her.

Looking back at myself in the mirror, I forced myself to take one long, very deep breath and watch the exhale. It stuck in my chest a few times at the end but I managed to expel all the air. I'd never have guessed that one day the sign in that photo would mean "breathe, your husband is dead. Now go watch cartoons with your son."

OK, Chanel, if anyone can do this, you can.

Meridians

While José and I almost always agreed on our parenting style, our childhoods were dramatically different. As were our families. José's parents split up when he was young, and he spent far less time with his father's Peruvian side of the family than with his mother and two siblings. Who we come from and family-of-origin stories run deep.

José's dad, Marco, stowed away on a boat to the US from Lima, Peru, in his early twenties and landed in the States with no money and very little English. José's mom, Pat, was a graduate student with two kids whose family settled generations ago in Montana after first exploring the "New World" as French fur trappers. The few pictures that survived a garage fire, which no one really talks about, show Marco as a handsome, big-grinned soccer player who had that swagger that gives him away as a Latin American man. Or maybe it was the moustache. Or the Erik Estrada haircut. But you get where I'm going with this. José's mom has the kind smile of a social worker but the core of a woman who is built 100 percent of strength and get-through-it-ness.

José was in that group of kids who find themselves squarely in the middle of not fitting in exactly. The Peruvian and French made him look more Italian, but everyone said he looked like Antonio Banderas—which he didn't, but that was the only lighter-skinned handsome Spanish guy people seemed able to think of, so the comparison happened frequently. He wasn't Latino enough in many groups, but when he wore a beautiful leather jacket he'd bought to celebrate a promotion and his (white) coworkers and friends "joked" that he looked like a Colombian drug lord, he stopped wearing it.

José created things by coding them into life with 1s and 0s on a keyboard or by moving his fingers over the strings of a guitar. His favorite was a 1980s Steinberger. He aced the SATs without studying because he was incredibly smart, had an incredible memory, and just "saw how the test worked." He was intimidatingly good looking, intelligent, and filled with old-soul grace. And he was a terrible dancer. Really, a hard-to-even-look-at, awfully bad, really bad, bad dancer. He was even worse with money. When we got married, my credit score tanked.

He had a sweet tooth for the type of candy I can only describe as the "hard stuff." He destroyed whole family-size packages of Starbursts, Skittles, and Hi-Chews in one sitting. The smell coming from the small pile of wrappers alone made my teeth hurt.

We met when I was a young twenty-four and he was an even younger twenty-nine. On our first date, I got into his car by sliding through the driver's-side door and over the stick shift because the whole passenger side was smashed in. We shared a giant piece of chocolate cake from the Bauhaus coffee shop on Capitol Hill and sat upstairs. Where you could smoke. Inside! It was 1994.

While he was playing guitar in a rock band with women's phone numbers falling out of his pockets like confetti, I was backpacking through Central America working on independent films. We needed a few extra years of practice to be any good at being grown-ups, but by the time I was thirty we had chosen to make a life together helping raise his daughter and hopefully having our own children. Because we had done the work, the vows we said to each other meant even more to me. They were earned.

When we were planning our wedding, we'd already had dozens of dinners and celebrated numerous holidays with his mom's side of the family, but he'd been estranged from his dad and all of the Hernandos for a solid ten years or so. His mom and dad hadn't seen each other for over twenty years. As it often goes, there were many, multilayered reasons how and why it got to there, and no one would likely agree on who said what or whose fault that other thing was, so we might as well skip that part. There were a lot of feelings that go way, way back, mostly of the disappointed and angry kind, and it's all very, very complicated.

So when I heard from my mom that the Hernandos were waiting for a callback so they could come visit, as lovely as they all may have been to me, I felt stuck in one of those dreams where you are late for a test that you forgot to study for or the plane is going down and you have to fly it. I did not feel prepared or qualified to meet with them on my own. I didn't know how to handle being responsible for managing, tending to, or repairing José's decades-long family narrative. I didn't want to do it, but I equally didn't want Gabe to grow up not knowing his Latino side of the family, as José had.

So in case someone you love died and you wished you could see them again so you could punch them in their stupid, dead face for dying on you and leaving you to take care of their family's unfinished business, know you're not alone.

Tía Marcia and Tía Martha walked through the door on each side of Marco carrying a lot of things that looked like casseroles and presents for Gabe. When José and I were planning to get married and he wanted to reconnect with his father's family, it was the *tías* he reached out to first. They were matriarchs, and I admired the way the family seemed to orbit them at the family gatherings and holiday dinners. Marcia was always smiling and exuberant. Martha had this unwavering get-shit-done air about her.

In addition to gifts and food, they brought a manila folder with a check and cash donations and one impossible question. We sat on the orange L-shaped leather couch. The standing fans blew hot air at us in oscillating swipes that made our hair look perfectly windswept in six-second intervals that would play just right in a Wes Anderson movie. That's when Marco turned to me and asked me what his son was like, if he was more like his mother's family or a Hernando.

I was so deep into my own grief, I was a fish breathing its water yet totally oblivious to the depth and vastness of the ocean. Here was a man who was asking me who his son was. He hadn't spent a lot of time with him, and now it was too late.

After the good-byes and "Please let us know if you need help for the service," I slid down the back of the couch with a migraine that started with an arc of prism light and spread across my vision like a terrible high school laser light show. I was sticking to the couch but didn't want to move or have to talk to anyone so *why not lie here a minute to stare out the window as the thoughts go by* must have seemed like the best idea available.

I couldn't move, out of sheer exhaustion, and when that swirly rainbow of light started to flicker in my vision, I knew a full-on migraine was just about twenty minutes away. But I was relieved. My conscience was clean. It may not seem like much, but at that moment it was everything.

I'd had a successful—not perfect, but loving—marriage for nine years. I couldn't think of anything that I regretted, had been left unsaid, or I wished I could undo.

Of course, if I'd been able to pick the last words I'd say to him, they would not have been "OK, I'll kiss you but I'm still mad at you." But I loved how they showed the honesty and partnership we'd built and nurtured over the course of our marriage. We were, in fact, current.

A few days later, I woke up quickly from a hard, dreamless sleep to a house full of voices and clanging. My dad, my brother Scott, and my brother's wife, Julie, had arrived from Minneapolis the afternoon before. With the familiar sound of LEGOs in the plastic storage bins, it sounded like a regular day in a normal house. Coming downstairs, I saw that my dad and Scott had ripped the whole kitchen sink apart. The faucet was in 147 little grubby gray pieces, and bits of pipe were scattered on newspaper covering every available surface.

When I shuffled in, Mom was reading Gabe a Dr. Seuss book on the couch, and Julie was gathering more books to read to him. I just wanted a glass of water. The glass(es) of wine and Valium I'd downed last night to help me get to sleep were likely not helping the headache

I'd had for days go away, but sleep seemed more important, and I felt like shit anyway. A hangover was the least of my worries.

"We're fixing your faucet!" They smiled proudly.

"Wow!" I said. "You sure are."

My eyes widened with all the surprise or relief I could muster.

I grabbed a glass from the cabinet and tipped it half sideways in the bathroom sink next to the kitchen, calling out to them, "So, it looks like you've got a little project going on there?" Somehow the Minnesota accent is back so I am using my *Fargo* voice.

"Oh yeah," they called back in unison, pleased with their progress.

"Your faucet was leaking, so we thought we should fix it for you," said Scott.

"Two trips to the hardware store later," my mom called out.

"I think we nearly got it." My dad wiped his hands off on the bright green kitchen towel they'd sent us as a Christmas present the year before.

I wandered back into the kitchen in my bathrobe and watched Gabe over the top of the glass during a long sip of water. He was happy looking at all the sink parts scattered everywhere while his grandma read a story. He said, "Hi, Mama" when I kissed him on the top of his head. Julie had brought coloring and sticker books, and they were working on putting each puppy and kitten sticker next to a drawing of an adult dog or cat that was most likely its mother.

"OK, this is great, thanks so much."

I made myself walk back upstairs and take a shower. I didn't care about the faucet. I didn't care if the whole house burned down.

But clearly my family felt this was exactly the right time to spend hours repairing a not actually very leaky faucet. It was a regular ol' Midwestern-style home that day after all. Less talking. More fixing.

Being raised in Minnesota with parents who both had heartland values formed by either farm life or military hardiness, I've nailed many helpful life skills. We fix stuff. However, asking for help and being good with feelings are absolutely not among them. No one actually comes out and really *says* what it is, but somehow you're supposed to just know; you are never ever, ever to talk about your feelings. Asking for help is OK if you really need to, sure, especially if it's physical labor or advice about where the fish are biting, but emotional support triggers your inside voice that suggests you're probably just being a big fucking pussy. Suck it up. Walk it off. Don't be a baby.

Of course, your neighbors will jump into a frozen lake to grab you or drive through a blizzard to yank you out of a ditch, and then deliver a twenty-pound casserole from their great-aunt's recipe with crumbled potato chips on top.

Compassion, duty, responsibility, and doing the right thing, however, should not be confused with sadness or sensitivity—being emotional, god forbid. I'm not sure if the recent wave of popularity of the idea that emotional vulnerability is what one *should* strive for resonates in the Midwest; I hope it does, but growing up we read *Having It All* and *Getting Things Done*. Brené Brown and "opening your heart" were *not* a thing. Struggle and suffering were always things to cover up or get over as quickly as possible. Dramatic responses are unwelcome in public. Losing your shit is meant to be a private, indoor weakness. No one wants to acknowledge it or have you feel embarrassed about it afterward, so your inappropriate display will go unmentioned. If we can get away with it, we'll pretend it just *never happened*.

You will be praised for how well you're holding up, how much you can suck it up, how well you're getting through it, and how strong you are. Growing up, I remember one news story about that teenage kid who walked a mile or two home after the combine ripped his arms off, dialed 911 holding a pencil in his teeth, and then waited in the bathtub for the paramedics so he wouldn't get blood all over the carpets.

Talking about your feelings seems to naturally pair with an ability to ask for help. In Minnesota, when someone asked if you need help, you should clearly answer no.

So, Chanel, looks like ya might need a hand there?

Naw, I think I'll be OK.

Well, I'm sure you're right, but, well, I can see your clothes have caught a little bit on fire there, and I have this extinguisher handy right here, so . . .

Ohhhh no no no. Don't you bother. I'm sure I can take care of it.

After two decades in Seattle, the accent is gone, but I know that the minutiae Garrison Keillor dishes on *A Prairie Home Companion* get laughs because he is 100 percent spot-on. I lived *all* the jokes. I couldn't wait to move to a place where half the phone book wasn't filled with Andersons and Gundersons. But for better or worse, I can also change my own flat tire, drive a tractor, clean my own fish, and still kick some ass at the air hockey table. If there were some sort of zombie apocalypse, I've always assumed I would be one of the few to make it through the night.

Because I took all of this to mean I was a strong, independent, resilient woman who was lucky to be called a tough girl or even a badass, I've love-hated the whole "being vulnerable" movement. My usual gut response to "try to not be too much of a pussy" didn't help at all when I asked the coroner how many official, stamped death certificates I'd need. There is no "sucking it up" when the nice mom with the kid Gabe's age asks at the bakery what his favorite cupcake is and you start grief-spilling your entire story like the *Exxon Valdez*. I'd have to remind myself I shouldn't be so judgy and cut myself some slack. Admitting I was scared or worried or needed help was already hard, so I had to try, really try, to not squirm out of, or run from, those moments. Because as much as I wished it wasn't, it was so overwhelmingly true that I was so overwhelmingly vulnerable. The crosstalk in my head wasn't pretty at all.

Get off your ass and don't be such a baby. You're in a lot better shape and much luckier than most people.

I mean, you can do this. Just be gentle and kind to yourself.

But get your ass to a kickboxing class.

But cut yourself some slack. Just be in your body.

And so went the Bootstraps versus Buddhist verbal fistfight in my head.

While the Buddhist voice was always the consistent and trusted one, the Bootstrapper was louder, fought dirty, and had decades more experience pushing my buttons. Kickboxing class was one of the few places where both voices shut up for a little bit, so I was really glad when my trainer, Shari, called and invited me to come see her outside of class for a private session whenever I was ready.

I replied, "How about tomorrow?"

Not only was Shari a great personal trainer, but she also had the *look*. Even if you were bigger and taller, she would absolutely clean the floor with you without smudging her lipstick. She could probably even do it in four-inch heels. Plus, she'd given up her law practice to start her own business. If she wasn't the most thoughtful and generous person I'd ever met, I would have absolutely hated her.

In her studio, we went through a few warmups. Then, she picked up two practice pads used for punching and suggested some speed drills. I put on my red boxing gloves, pulling the Velcro around the wrist on the second glove tight with my teeth, walked to the middle of the mat, and got into fighting stance. The small group classes had a mixture of very athletic women and those just getting back into shape. I was somewhere in the middle but took the bag and pad work seriously. She knew I liked to hit—hard.

A starting drill is something like left jab, left jab, right cross, left jab.

Then you work up to more combinations and add the kicks: left jab, left jab, right cross, left jab, right under hook, left body, left body, right cross, right kick, right kick, switch kick left. Then you do that nineteen more times—for your first round.

On a good day, when I've had enough sleep, am well hydrated, and have eaten some carbs or protein an hour or two before, five or ten minutes of these speed drills is enough to leave me panting with sweat dripping into my eyes. I hadn't done any of those things that day, but I still wanted to keep going. I didn't care that the light-headed feeling was coming, or that I knew I was blowing past the point where if you rest now (when you're only deep-coughing while salivating), you can likely cut short the full puke close on the horizon. I kept going.

One wall was mirrored like a dance or yoga studio, so it was easy to see that the white ring around my mouth from dehydration was even more noticeable next to my beet-red cheeks. My skin had stopped sweating a while ago and I felt woozy, but I wanted to punch as long

as I could. It might have been just a few indulgent minutes of a widowed mom grief-punching, but I felt like Muhammad Ali; hearing the
smack-smack-thump of my glove, the *whack* of my lower shin on the
dense, vinyl-covered Everlast pads, I could have dropkicked the Rock
or a Range Rover if I'd had to. I should say I felt like Muhammad Ali
right up to the moment I fumbled to open the sliding glass door as fast
as I could with my boxing gloves still on and then bent over Shari's
rhododendron bushes to throw up what little was left in my stomach.

Shari came out after a minute and put her hand on my back and
asked if I wanted to talk about the legal questions I had now. I said
we should do another few rounds and then talk about when and why
people hire a lawyer when accidents like this happen.

I can't blame her for looking unsure, since I was still bent over her
rhodies with my hands on my thighs to prop up my upper body, but
she just nodded when I said, "This isn't the hardest thing I've had
to do. Let's do two minutes more, and then we can talk about what
lawyering up looks like."

The Celebration-of-Life Memorial-Funeral-Ceremony-Service

couldn't tell if I was ambivalent, afraid, overwhelmed, or going numb, but I really couldn't get myself to care at all about the Memorial. It felt like it was "what you do," but I really didn't even want to go.

If it's not a funeral service or a wake with a casket, is a memorial better or too formal? "Celebration of life" sounds closer but still too Hallmarky or euphemistic. So what do you call it? Whatever it is, it's only two days away.

We settled, or someone else probably decided and I don't even remember, on a memorial celebration. I couldn't possibly have cared any less whether we even had one at all. People asked about the flowers (don't know), what to say on the announcement (don't care), what kind of food to serve on such a hot day (whatever), whether there should be music (doesn't matter), and if there should be signs to point out where to park (seriously?). I didn't care about most of the details at all—except I wanted it to be outside, and I didn't want him to be in a shitty plastic urn with the fake flourish and funeral-industry fonts. Other than that, it seemed easier to let other people organize it, and they seemed happy to be doing (or able to do) something. Just like the week in the hospital, people showed up and I leaned on them, probably harder than I realized.

While José was in the ICU, Connie and I had talked a few times on the phone about how and what to tell Gabe and Lyric, and when. Lyric had come home early from camp and been to the hospital. On the day José died, Connie and her husband, Michael, talked with Lyric at home in their backyard. Now, our conversations were focused on the memorial and how we could organize it so both kids would feel included. We'd had a very supportive and friendly blended family and often went to Lyric's track meets or dance recitals together and had dinner afterward. Connie and Michael had Gabe overnight the previous New Year's Eve to watch fireworks with Lyric so José and I could stay out late. Connie and I were 100 percent aligned that keeping the kids together was critical; the years-long regular coparenting schedule, which had Lyric at our house every other week, wasn't going to make sense anymore, but without even having to say it, I knew we would keep the kids together, whatever it took. They were siblings; they'd both lost their dad.

Michael called around for locations and rented a beautiful spot at the Arboretum and Botanical Gardens. Curtis took me there to look at it ahead of time. Wendy, whom we'd known through Gabe's preschool, was a doctor, and in addition to vitamins for stress and something better (and nonaddictive) to help me sleep, she brought me a dress because I couldn't stand the thought of putting on clothes from our shared closet to wear to his funeral. Erin Galvin was on logistics. Erin Brower took care of dinners at the house. Jen dealt with the funeral home. Connie and Jake, whom we used to swap childcare with, made programs for the memorial. Deborah, an old friend, brought me to the shop of a local artist, Greg, who had a gorgeous collection of urns and glass gravestones he made by hand. José's sister, Shelley, was a chef and wanted to organize all the food. Dawn and her partner, Mike, were new friends of ours and brought over a case of wine.

Each person used her or his superpower to help prepare for the day. The organizing we'd done during the hospital days remained life-saving, both logistically and emotionally. The rest of our grieving friends or distraught coworkers, who seemed a bit lost about what to do or say, posted a comment or story on the CaringBridge website, which also posted the memorial details and sent an email. On Facebook, people posted pictures or sent notes to José about how much they missed him, or they sent condolences with a message or note. It was sweet, and really we were all just figuring it out as we went, but I didn't have the energy to spare or explain to anyone if something else would be helpful.

So that's what you do. You organize stuff. You gather. Pay your respects. Show up to the thing. And I was the wife. So you go.

People flew in, drove up, and came together for the memorial. Writing this now, it just occurred to me that I have no idea where people stayed or who got picked up at the airport.

My mom's side of the family knew exactly what to do. They were military. In fact, they were multigeneration West Point, two-star-general military and moved to a new base in a different country every year. While I'm certain it was rarely spoken about very directly, death must have always been a lurking presence at the dinner table. Especially when fathers and sons were away during the wars. In my generation, the daughters were captains and pilots too. There were unwritten rules, such as never "stop by" someone's home unexpectedly, as the sound of a doorbell out of the blue would stop a heart. My mom's oldest brother, Curt, had been retired for years, but even without the uniform, the American flag tie clip, haircut, and his precise posture gave him away.

On the morning of the service, my mom's family gathered at the big counter in the middle of the kitchen. The breakfast table and most of the hardwood floor space had been taken over by the half dozen or so clear plastic toy bins full of thousands of teeny plastic pieces. Either Gabe had been to the LEGO store or someone had brought him a new box containing another Star Wars set every day since José died. A piece from the new set was missing. Everyone assured me they looked everywhere. *Everywhere.* As if this were closing time at a bar on Saturday night and a fight had been brewing all night, everyone was on edge. It was like the room was holding its breath.

I sat down with the instructions. "I bet we can find one that's the same shape from the other bins."

We do. It's the wrong color but the right size. I hand it to Gabe. "It looks like it goes on the inside so you'll never see it's a different color."

Gabe seemed happy with the replacement, disaster avoided. I almost felt like saying, "Resume regular peacetime activities."

I got up from the floor to grab my coffee from the table.

"Yes, I can see you both are going to be OK," said Uncle Curt.

And whether or not he believed it was true didn't matter at all. For the first time (even though I was nearly forty), I felt like an adult around him, and I realized this must not have been the first time he'd visited a home that had just lost a husband and father. He seemed to know what he was talking about, and I was damn glad to hear it.

I didn't know where to sit. Or look. I couldn't hide or flee, but I felt both totally exposed and invisible the whole time. It was hot. James, who had married us along with his wife, Linda, was going to direct the service and asked if I wanted to talk, or say something, and I really couldn't answer. There was no way to know whether any semblance of words would be the right thing to say or if I opened my mouth, I'd only make shrieks that no longer sounded human.

The kids had wanted to have big bowls of all of José's favorite candy out for everyone, and there they were—giant glass and crystal punch bowls filled with candy on the long table next to the dozens of photographs and framed pictures everyone brought to share.

Gabe, on a crazy sugar high, was overwhelmed and not understanding much of what was happening around him. He ran laps around the lines of chairs facing the podium and then on every other spin would sprint down the middle and bob off to the left or weave to the right like an Olympic bank robber on his way to the getaway car. Having one of those "good mother moments," I hurried after him to try to get him to calm down, or slow down, or sit with me. Or just do something other than what he felt like doing, which when I caught up to him seemed like the most reasonable thing to be doing, actually.

At the few funerals I'd attended in the Midwest, the children did *not* go whirling dervishing around in half-feral laps as the emotionally reasonable adults talked about the weather, food, or whispered about how who was holding up. But the calm tones and reserved emotions gave me this overall feeling that they were all holding their breath, as though something else bad would happen if anyone there acknowledged that something bad was already happening. The monster lurking in the closet can hurt you only if you look at it.

When I looked at Gabe, I saw his raw and emotional child version of Paul Revere yelling, "The Monsters are coming, the Monsters are coming," as he raced past all of our emotionally regulated faces. Even though I was just trying to get through the minutes and keep my shit together and had no real reason to stop him, I had to fight a strong urge that wanted to contain him. No one else seemed to care, and even if they did, fuck it. A kid should be able to do pretty much whatever he wants at his father's funeral. I spent most of the rest of the service focused on breathing in and out of my mouth to help feel less nauseated, counting the seconds until it would be over. And wondering what, if anything, I should even say to everyone.

I had no idea if I would do it, but when James started to come to the end and everyone else who had planned to speak had already given their talk or shared their story, he looked over to see if I wanted to say anything. I waited until the last possible second to decide, but I nodded and stood up.

I stood at the podium, opened my mouth, and something very close to this is what came out:

I wasn't sure if I wanted to say anything, and I didn't plan anything specific to say. But I do want to say thank you. Thank you for being here and for all the help and support we've gotten the last two weeks. I am very grateful for everything. And all of you. It made a huge difference. And you all have taught me a lot about what showing up looks like. What showing up really means. And I just want to say thank you so much for that.

In the car on the way home, Gabe was quiet, and I kept trying to "normalize" José's death and make sure to talk about it so he would know we could talk about it. But not be crazy or obsessive about talking about it so I wouldn't force or push the dead-dad issue if he didn't want to talk about it. I was given advice by the ICU social worker about talking to the kids—not to make any assumptions about what they do and don't hear, see, or think or believe to be true. Kids know more than we think they might and can also misunderstand what's happening around them, so I reminded myself to keep checking in with Gabe.

We were starting to weave through the curving road south through the arboretum toward the lake and toward home. I made it a point to drive on Lake Washington Boulevard, because it was the nice way home even if I couldn't make myself go all the way down to Seward Park, where he was hit.

"Hey, kiddo, what did you think about Papa's memorial, um, party today?"

Stared out the window. No answer.

"That was so much candy at the candy table, huh? Did you try every single kind?"

"Yeah, there was Starbursts and Skittles and Hi-Chews."

"All the favorites, huh?"

"Uh-huh."

"What did you think about the party, sweetie? Did anything surprise you?"

Looked out the window again.

"I wanted to get a present, too," he said.

"A present? I don't think I saw presents. Do you mean the gifts or flowers people left for us on the table?"

"No, the ones the guy at the front gave out. He didn't give me one."

Was it the programs? Or did someone hand something out?

I was racking my brain when it hit me. All the ashes didn't fit into the urn I'd picked out, so we put the small mound remaining into two nice little wood boxes for José's mom and dad. James had handed them the ashes and they looked like gifts. Like little presents.

How am I ever going to be able to think of everything and get this right?!

"Do you mean the little boxes that were passed out during the ceremony?"

He nodded.

"Oh honey, I see. That wasn't really a present, exactly. It was something special for José's mom and dad. We have a bigger one. It's in the back of the car with us right now."

What if he asks what it is? Do I say it is the remains? Do I say what it looks like? What if he wants to see? I told him about the Darth Vader fire, so I guess I can say it's like the charcoal left over.

We crossed Madison Avenue, and the road started turning us toward the lake. I peeked in the rearview mirror. He seemed OK with my answer. He was just looking out the window. Not saying anything. I'm supposed to pay attention and tell the truth—but let him help guide how long the conversation goes.

Shit, this is tricky.

"Well, kiddo. If you want to see the big wood box or ask me about it we'll have one at home and you can ask me about it or see it anytime."

"OK, Mama. We're going to the LEGO store later or tomorrow?"

"Yup. Tomorrow you have a playdate to go to the LEGO store with Josh Lipsky because he really wants to build a Star Wars set with you. OK?"

"Can I get a big one?"

"You can get any one you want except the Millennium Falcon." I had to be precise. José and Gabe had salivated over (what was then) the biggest set ever produced. They used to look at pictures of it online. It also cost hundreds of dollars and would take dozens of hours

to build. Just thinking about the sustained energy required to build it
with him paralyzed me.

Remind him that whatever he is feeling is OK.

And none of this is his fault in any way.

Ask him what he thinks. But don't make it his job to figure any-
thing out.

You are the parent. Don't assume anything.

Guide:
After Death

The bitterest tears shed over graves are for
words left unsaid and deeds left undone.

—HARRIET BEECHER STOWE

spent a week with José in the hospital and bathed his body once he
had died. I felt his family and community had cared for and tended
to him, sat vigil, tried to provide comfort, and taken care of him the
best way we knew how. However, because I had no context or experience of being with our dead as other cultures so comfortably do, I
didn't know I could bring his body home. Had someone not suggested
it, I never would have known I could, or would have wanted to, stay
with José after he died, clean his body, dress him. I didn't know we
had the option of a funeral at home or a green burial in a forested
cemetery. Or that cremating him released about six hundred pounds
of carbon dioxide into the atmosphere.

I knew that embalming became an industry practice in order to
transport dead bodies over long distances or store them for long periods of time, because I'd watched some Ken Burns documentary about
the Civil War, but there were tons of other things I hadn't picked up
randomly that I wish I had known or learned beforehand. I knew

he preferred cremation to burial, but I couldn't remember one single conversation about whether he wanted his remains on the mantel sitting next to the smaller urn with his cat Alex's ashes, tossed onstage during a Bill Frisell show, or perhaps shot into outer space—probably space. In fact, now you *can* release your cremains into space—well, across the Kármán line, the boundary of Earth's atmosphere, so technically outer space. Good thing I kept his ashes.

Death Professionals

Caitlin Doughty is the founder of the death-acceptance collective The Order of the Good Death (of which I'm a member). She's also YouTube's celebrated *Ask a Mortician* host and creator, and *both* of her books, *Smoke Gets in Your Eyes* and *From Here to Eternity*, are *New York Times* bestsellers. When I first sat down with Caitlin face-to-face and talked, really talked, we were in Austin, Texas, eating an overpriced and not very delicious salad at a packed hotel restaurant during the massive South by Southwest Conference. It had been four years since José's death, and my website had gotten a ton of press. Besides our bangs, our lives didn't have much in common except that both of us thought, talked, and wrote about death all the time. As Caitlin and I walked through the slide deck for the session we were copresenting the next day, I realized that while I knew something about what happens before and after someone dies, I still had a lot to learn about the actual death and dying part.

First of all, the only real knowledge I had about the death and funeral industry came from watching *Six Feet Under*. I wanted the real, inside scoop on what actually happens and who the players really are.

What is a mortician exactly?

What about a coroner? Is it weird that he called me like that? Does that mean that he lost the body?

What does the medical examiner do?

The funeral director?

Essentially, how many people, and who, touched my husband after I left the hospital room that day?

There are a lot of names you've likely heard from crime scenes on TV shows, but here is a short list of death jobs and what they actually are. Many of these people or roles you will never see or meet, because they work behind the scenes.

Coroner: An elected official who confirms, certifies, and sometimes investigates the cause of someone's death.

Medical examiner: A medical doctor trained in forensic pathology who examines bodies, performs autopsies, and investigates suspicious deaths.

Funeral director: A professional, also called an undertaker, who often works with the family to organize and arrange the care of the body and funeral plans and rites. He or she may work independently or at a funeral home.

Mortician: A death professional who prepares the body for cremation or burial and, much like a funeral director, oversees funeral arrangements, arranges necessary documentation, and supports the family.

Funeral home: A professional business that provides full-service funerals, wakes, and cremations.

Burial and cremation services: Businesses other than traditional funeral homes that provide alternative options for the care of the body, memorial services, cremation, and burial.

Caitlin and many others are kicking down the gates of an otherwise very staid and old-fashioned death industry of $20 billion in annual revenue, reminding us that we don't need that industry. The average funeral costs $8,000 to $10,000, but we have the option to care for our dead ourselves; only a handful of states *require* you to use commercial funeral home services. An independent funeral director or cooperative funeral organization is often a smaller, locally run business and can be far more affordable. As Caitlin points out:

> For thousands of years of human history, your family was your burden from cradle to grave. There was no option to shift responsibility to a funeral director or mortician. You washed the body, shrouded or dressed the body, sat with the body, and finally accompanied the body to the grave or crematory. It's a beautiful experience for the family to have.

You probably didn't even know you could care for your dead. Let her dispel two other common misconceptions:

1. A dead body won't harm you. A lot of people think dead bodies are somehow dangerous. They're not. Only if your loved one died of a highly contagious disease would certain precautions need to be taken.
2. Taking care of a dead body is legal. Your county or state *may* require you to be assisted by a local mortician or funeral director, but it may not. Find out the law in your state through the Home Funeral Alliance nonprofit organization or your state's licensing department.

PLANNING FOR DEATH

- ❑ Collect or create estate-planning documents (see page 208, "Guide: The Tangled Web We Leave," section 4, Legal).
- ❑ Document medical wishes and desires (there's more in the living will section on page 220).
- ❑ Sign medical release-of-information forms to share documents with your family, doctor, hospital, hospice (HIPAA release form, POLST medical order), etc.
- ❑ Express and define your end-of-life care wishes, what you do (or don't) want when you are near death—for example: music,

visitors, candles, pictures, comfort items, poems, prayers or silence, and so on.

❑ Discuss preferences or make plans for your body after death.

❑ Confirm health coverage or financial assistance with costs of care (disabllity payments, Social Security, other insurance or benefits, etc.).

❑ Call the medical insurance company and/or Medicare about what services, procedures, and treatments are covered and if pre-authorization is needed, for example, for home assistance or hospice care.

❑ Are there other assets to confirm or collect, such as the contents of a safe deposit box or gold bars buried under a tree? Are there details to document (accounts and passwords, online assets) and add to your essentials list? Complete any missing documents or outline additional wishes.

❑ Are there letters you'd like to write, trips to take, videos to film, phone calls to place, or conversations you'd like to have?

NOTIFICATION OF THE DEATH

If death does not occur in a hospital or other medical location or a doctor was not present, notify a doctor, the police, and/or a coroner.

❑ Arrange for organ donation (if it had been requested or if it's possible).

❑ Complete other upon-death instructions (DNA sampling, science, cryonics).

❑ Obtain several death certificates (certified copies).

Death Certificates FAQ

Why do you need one? A death certificate is a government-issued document that declares the time, date, and cause of death. Copies are needed to show proof of death in order to collect on any life insurance policies, and are usually required to close bank accounts and administer an estate.

Where do you get it? Usually, the funeral home or funeral director will file the official death certificate document with the state or county health department and request copies for the family directly.

How many certified copies do you need? The fee for a certified copy varies by state (or county), but it's usually about twenty-five dollars. Jeff Jorgenson, founder of Elemental Cremation & Burial in Seattle (my funeral instructions say, "Call Jeff and he will come get me.") suggests that, while the default has been to order five or ten copies, you can start with two or three. According to Jeff:

Bank accounts and investment firms will take a photocopy. If you walk in with an original certified copy, they will make a photocopy and hand you your original back. Pension and life insurance companies will often take the original and not return it. Additionally, if an estate needs to go to probate, you will probably have to leave an original with your attorney.

He notes that if cost is a concern, you can always order more, should you need additional copies.

How do you order more copies? Certified copies can be ordered on your behalf by the funeral director, third-party companies offer this service for a fee, or you can order them directly through the state (or county) health or records office where the person died.

CARE OF THE BODY

- ❏ Is there a living will, a letter, or funeral directions expressing wishes?
- ❏ Execute wishes or, if no instructions, make informed decisions.
- ❏ Hire professionals, if needed.
- ❏ Move the body to your home, another location, a funeral home or crematorium, or to a different state.
- ❏ Invite or reply to requests to view, wash, or dress the body and/or to witness the cremation.

Wakes, Funerals, Memorials, and Life Celebrations

Immediately following a death is a hard time for the family to think about these types of events for the first time. There can be an overwhelming number of issues to consider, including logistics for out-of-town travel, costs, and the emotional needs of the family. If you or your loved one can express your wishes beforehand, it will help a lot. If that's not possible, know that you have a lot of options—there's no "right" way to go here—and try to focus on what's most important; as so many choices are presented, it's common to feel pressured to decide quickly. There are options for you to plan in advance for your own death and questions for you to ask yourself when planning or assisting with someone else's:

What would be most meaningful to the person who has died?
What would be most meaningful to those grieving?
The type of service?
Location?
Attendees?

Maybe a large traditional religious ceremony would be most meaningful, or a modest home viewing of Uncle Hank in his favorite Elvis jumpsuit with ABBA playing nonstop. If you have a religious or cultural tradition to follow, some of the decisions may be easier; if not, and you just can't handle making one more decision, you can wait. You also don't have to have one big event. Sure, there are timing considerations with a traditional or natural burial, but you can gather to mourn or celebrate someone's life any damn time you want to. You can have a small gathering, even several, or wait a year before you plan anything if that is easier. Someone's ashes can sit around for years (and have), if that's what you prefer or need to do.

WAKES, FUNERALS, MEMORIALS, AND LIFE CELEBRATIONS CHECKLIST

- ❑ Review any directions or instructions that have been left or requested in a will or premade funeral plans.
- ❑ List friends and family members who can or would like to help with the service(s) and tasks below.
  - Write an obituary or announcement. Ask others to contribute or share stories, if desired.
  - Send invitations via mail, email, and/or other social channels.
  - Coordinate logistics with out-of-town guests.
  - Arrange for photos, music, food, and other items.
  - Confirm who will speak.
- ❑ Some recommend a family member or friend to stay at the bereaved person's home (or your home) to care for the house and pets, or to be there during the funeral to help with logistics or assist out-of-town guests.

Strangers in a Strange Land

The day after the memorial, it had been two weeks since the accident and one week since I removed life support. The heat wave still hadn't broken, and there were moments I felt like I was on fire alongside José in the crematorium. I lay awake that night, staring at the ceiling, telling myself not to get into the car and drive to the spot where he died so I could lie down on the pavement. I knew that even if I could find the exact spot, I would still not be able to talk to him. Or find him. Or know where he went. I also knew it would be a strange situation to explain if a passerby called the police to check out what the crazy lady was doing in the middle of the street at three in the morning.

Funny story, Officer, I am merely trying to locate the spot where my husband died to see if I can feel him or know where he went. Nothing to see here.

My body hurt and burned, and José's not being in our bed, downstairs, or on his way home throbbed like a phantom limb. My cells ached and the blood in my own veins felt alien, synthetic. The quiet at night felt loud, the house so empty. The sum of my collective parts didn't add up anymore. I had grief-vertigo so intense I'd have to ride it out like labor pains, force myself to stay calm, holding my breath the way you're taught to do if you're pinned underwater and waiting out the next set of waves. *One, two, three.*

I must have looked dead in the eyes half the time and couldn't force myself to eat much, but I'd get swells of energy as if I'd just drunk twenty shots of espresso and felt more alive than I ever had. Even if it was as temporary as a five-year-old on a sugar rush or the turbo charge of a truck stop energy drink (before the headache and stomach cramps), I loved those fleeting moments when I could've grabbed grief by the balls and kicked its stupid, unfair, sorry ass.

What strange land had I just washed up onto?

Curtis and Brad are the very best kind of friends. They offered me the beach house they shared on Vashon Island as a place to get away with my family after the memorial. They sent me off with a couple of bottles of wine and made me promise to stay as long as I wanted. Scott and Julie had a few days before flying back home, and my parents would stay another week. José and I had spent weekends out there, and Gabe loved the ferry ride over and the Vashon house for its long private beach and "secret" pirate cove (we made that up). We'd light fireworks and barbecue, making a visit to Vashon feel a little like camping out—while sleeping in a very lovely home.

Despite being a quick ferry ride from Seattle, Vashon Island felt a lot like "the country." Deer wandered across the roads at dusk; orca whales were visible from the beach house porch; a sea otter family would sometimes play on the raft of two-by-fours the neighbor had hammered together and tied an anchor to so it wouldn't float away with the tides; and the raccoons threw all-night parties in the garbage cans year-round. The locals have bumper stickers that say KEEP VASHON WEIRD, so it seemed like the perfect place to start figuring out whatever I had to figure out.

As soon we drove off the ferry, my shoulders relaxed down a full inch. The food people had dropped off the previous week was packed in coolers in the back, crowding most of the space our dog Hannah was used to. She'd spent over a week with friends and fellow golden retriever lovers Dierdre and Patrick, so she was still acting anxious, but when I made the final turn down the curving, densely green and mossy, forested road to the parking area, like clockwork Hannah started wagging and whining and pushed her head farther out the window. Here she could run up and down the beach, ecstatically rolling in sand-caked, days-old washed-up dead things and smoosh them into her (easily infected) ears and into fur-mats on her stomach and neck. We'd have to wash her down on the deck dozens of times with the garden hose and extra-strength dish soap to get the smell off her before we could bring her in for the night.

The first day there, we played on the beach and looked for starfish at low tide, ate food, and mostly sat and stared at the water from the deck.

In my chicken-scratch handwriting, I'd started a list of things to do or find out.

> *Mortgage, ask about payment options.*
> *Insurance: How does the life insurance pay out? When?*
> *Legal stuff: probate process, call attorney.*
> *Death certificates must be certified = order more $20 each.*
> *Hospital bills: How much? Who pays? What do I have to pay?*
> *Call Apple about hacking into José's phone?*
> *MONEY!!! How much money do I have? How long will it last?*
> *Notify people to change my status to widowed, José's to deceased.*

My first call was to the bank that held our mortgage.

"Hi, my name is Chanel Reynolds, and my husband and I have our mortgage with you. I am calling to notify you he was recently killed in an accident and I need to talk to someone about . . ."

"Ma'am, let me first say I am sorry for your loss."

"Well, um, thank you. I appreciate that. And I . . ."

"Ma'am, again, I am sorry for your loss and will transfer you to the appropriate department who can help you."

After a surprisingly short time on hold, I learned I could claim a "hardship" and defer mortgage payments for six months, given that my household income was now exactly zero dollars. It didn't feel like much of a win to have to explain that I was now a widow and broke, but even if it wasn't much of a victory, it bought me some time, and the mortgage was one less thing I'd have to worry about for a while. The bank would send me forms through the mail, and all I needed to do was fill them out and return them with a certified death certificate.

Next I called the insurance company that held our car-insurance policy. Someone on the bike team had mentioned that even though José was on his bike during the accident, our auto policy should include some personal injury protection or property coverage. I wanted to find out about that and remove José from the policy as, well, he wouldn't need it anymore.

The little neighborhood insurance office was owned by a husband-and-wife team, and it seemed their entire family worked there. The wife was clearly in charge of operations, and I had always appreciated her friendly reminder phone calls every six months that the next payment was due so I could give her the billing information over the phone. When she answered the phone and I explained why I was calling, I could hear her put her hand over the phone so I wouldn't hear her tears. But through the muffled jostling of the phone, I could also hear her calling out to everyone to stop what they were doing and help me. She would mail me all of the information and documentation I needed and call me in a few days to follow up.

Then I called the health-insurance company. Depending on how quickly the hospital billing system worked, I figured they may already have seen a ton of charges coming though and red-flagged our plan into a "something is seriously up" group.

I called the main number and started in, again, with why I was calling. "Hi, my name is Chanel Reynolds, and my husband and I are covered on his plan through his work. I am calling to notify you he was recently killed in an accident and I need to talk to someone about . . ."

"Ma'am, let me first say I am sorry for your loss."

"Well, um, thank you. I appreciate that. And I . . ."

"Ma'am, thank you for calling to notify us. I will transfer you to the appropriate department who can help you, and again, I am sorry for your loss."

Apparently, there is some group that specifically handles the when-someone-dies phone calls, and I was always transferred to them right away. I came to call these the "I'm sorry for your loss" departments, as they all seemed to read from a pretty specific script, and generally the first phone call kicked off a flurry of forms and paperwork for months to come. We covered the essentials in the first few minutes with a dozen questions: policy numbers, additional health insurance or other coverage (nope), something about the company office being based in California so the Employee Retirement Income Security Act (ERISA) laws applied (huh?), and what our maximum out-of-pocket payment was ($10,000). After that, I stopped taking notes and tried to follow the gist of what the associate was saying to me, which was impossible. More paperwork was coming my way, though.

Just a few weeks before, I'd complained that filling out forms for summer camp or the beginning of the school year was unbearable. Oh man, I thought that was bad? Just hope no one you know ever, ever dies. Ever. Not knowing what to say or how to help aside, after just three phone calls, it was overwhelmingly clear that we do not do death very well in this country. The cordial yet uncaring voices on the other end of the phone, the codification of José's death, and the energy it took to take notes and answer questions about the cause of death, date of death—my surviving-spouse status made me feel stuck in the death section of customer service hell. I couldn't breathe. I needed to go for a run.

Putting on my jogging clothes as fast as a teenager caught in the act, I wondered how long you'd have to train for an ultramarathon. Anything to not have to feel so bad, so stuck like a hostage in the current state of my life. Or to maybe be able to feel anything. I laced up my shoes and headed out.

A gravel trail runs along the water hugging Paradise Cove, bends to asphalt at the parking area, and runs steeply uphill for nearly a mile before hitting the main road. Getting a little speed before the hill was ideal, but the trail was littered with garbage from the raccoons' latest bacchanal.

I tried to avoid the bigger piles and more solid pieces but my foot overturned a coffee filter, spilling damp clumps of grounds onto my ankle and into my sock.

Excellent. Really fucking excellent. Thank you, universe, for reminding me that no matter if your husband has just died or not, things will still go wrong and you will have to deal with them.

I squatted down and started scooping used yogurt containers and diapers back into the bin and rage-mumbling very dark curses at my brother (why hadn't he put the lid on tight like I'd said!). I was almost finished wishing my brother an endless spiral of near-death torture that might have made even Prometheus wince, when the most lovely, incredibly ancient couple appeared from behind a giant, well-manicured hedge.

They appeared to have been together for about a thousand years. They even had that merged look normally reserved for Florida retirement communities, but instead of matching tennis visors or golf windbreakers, it was more like they'd become one person. Clearly on their morning cardio walk, they swished their arms enthusiastically and in perfect unison. If there'd been a prize for the most energetic old couple on the whole planet, they'd have won.

With soft but very real pity, the lady soothed, "Oh, well now dear, that looks like the worst thing I can ever imagine!"

I stared back, unblinking, for probably too long.

I had the ferocious urge to fling garbage at them while screaming and then run into the woods and punch some trees.

It is occasionally convenient to be "out of your body." From above, I could see that doing that would be, as my mental health–worker friends would say, an "inappropriate emotional response."

So I allowed the squinty-eyed snarl parked on my face to thaw into something resembling a smile. "Yes, thank you, it really is *awful*, isn't it?"

As they swished-walked off, I kicked the rest of the garbage into the overturned can, stood it up, tightened the lid down with the bungee cord, turned up toward the very steep, windy, forested road, and ran up it like a motherfucker. I pushed past nausea the whole way up, but by the top I couldn't take it anymore. I puked and sobbed next to the fencepost at the main road, horses hoofing at the grass nearby while cars whizzed past to catch the ferry or get to the farmers market. It was berry season.

I wiped my face with the least garbage-smelling wrist with up-through-elbow hand motions and cried all the way down the hill—to do it all over again.

Up.

Puke.

Down.

Sob.

And again. Till there was nothing left in me.

And then, eventually, you get cold or tired or thirsty or hungry, or even bored, and go back inside to make lunch and play with your kids so they know you're there and haven't lost your mind.

When we left, just a few days later, I was equally dreading and looking forward to going home. My friends were mostly back at work, Gabe was excited to spend the day with Lyric at her mom's house, and my family would soon be flying back to Minneapolis. The few phone calls I'd made felt like a small victory, but heading back to Seattle, I felt I'd only confirmed we could tread water financially for a while and perfected the art of casually puking on the side of the road and cleaning up garbage spills.

Having kids to care for kept me more grounded, more aware, and certainly more informed about the grieving process and how it may look different for kids. Seeing them do well made me feel better, too. Parenting Gabe alone, taking care of him, of his grief and mine, while remaining a solid stepparent to Lyric, felt like learning how to juggle in zero gravity. There was no way to really know what the right thing to do was, so I went about tethering us as much as possible and getting support. We were signed up for a family grief-support group in the fall, and I had a weekly session with a counselor named Delia starting soon.

I was single-parenting now. I was all on my own—all of the time.

There would be no more running-to-the-store-real-quick, no I-drop-off-you-pick-up coverage, no one else to read the bedtime story, walk the dog, take out the trash, go to parent-teacher conferences, shop, clean up, or cook three meals a day plus snacks. *Single* single-parenting, I would say. And, yes, it was hard to not be unsympathetic when I'd hear divorced friends complain that daddy weekends were off schedule, child support was late, or an ex was drinking (again) or back in rehab (again). For a long time, even watching some of our friends go through divorces, even the heinous ones that napalm an entire family for years . . . pretty much *any* scenario other than mine sounded pretty fucking awesome. If he hadn't died and I was *only* betrayed and abandoned, at least the kids would still have their dad around. From where I was sitting, I would have happily taken that trade.

I just wanted my life back.

However, there weren't any time machines, so my mission was to get smart and be brave enough to figure out this grief shit without fucking up the kids or myself in the process. That was my job for the next year: get us out the other side alive and healthy and as happy as anyone in a situation like ours could possibly be.

I told myself that all I had to do was get through the remaining weeks of summer vacation. That seemed workable. And though I often got blindsided, I also got a few things right.

Toward the end of August, with a new school year starting in a few weeks, Connie and I had arranged for me to have both kids for the weekend. Taking them to the park down the street was an easy way to make things seem normal. We spread out a few beach towels on the grass close to the swings and play structures to be out of the way of the Frisbees and footballs being tossed around. It seemed everywhere I looked there were smiling dads throwing balls, walking dogs, or riding bikes with their kids. Both kids were halfway through destroying a pack of Hi-Chews, and each had another roll in a pocket. It had been José's favorite candy, so we had a lot of them around the house.

The classic Radio Flyer–style red wagon we used to haul coolers, towels, toys, snacks, and/or kids was parked next to us. I pulled out the giant flat of strawberries we'd gotten at the farmers market along with the water bottles, juice boxes, candy, and donuts we'd just picked up from the café and pizza place on the corner. Lyric took charge of the donuts and showed us how to hide them under the blanket so the crows wouldn't find them while she told one of Gabe's favorite stories. He loved hearing about the time Lyric was his age and a crow stole her cheeseburger, just swooped down and flew away with it while she was playing Frisbee with her mom only ten feet away. Lyric chased that crow yelling, "Give me back my cheeseburger!" over and over again for the length of a soccer field. At that point in her retelling, Lyric ran around pretending to jump up trying to grab the imaginary crow. Gabe laughed extra hard. Just as she got to the ending, where the crow didn't give her cheeseburger back and she cried and cried, we heard a familiar *ding-ding-ding-ding-ding*.

The kids froze like prairie dogs and in unison yelled, *"The ice cream man!"*

"Can we have ice cream?"

"Do you have money?"

"Where's the money?"

"Can I have a Fudgsicle or a Bomb Pop?"

"No, I want a Push-Up if they don't have ice cream sandwiches."

"Do you have dollars?"

"How much money do you have?"

They were dancing in front of me like they hadn't seen sunshine or tasted food in *decades*. "Guys, guys, guys." I tried to calm them down. "I don't have any money with me, and we have all of this food, and donuts, already with us."

"Ice cream, ice cream ice cream ice cream," they chanted.

"So, here's the thing. I don't have money with me and you were really excited about these donuts five minutes ago and we just bought all this candy."

They were not impressed with my logic.

"In fact, you guys were just eating candy, you have more in your pockets and, wait a minute, you both have candy in your mouths.

You were so excited about the idea of the ice cream man, you forgot you have candy. In your mouths. *Right now*."

And then they just shrugged, got up, and ran over to the play structure and hopped from monkey bars to climbing wall to rope ladder to the two swings without touching the ground playing "Don't step on the hot lava." Just like that.

I was able to feel pleased with my awesome-mom-Buddhist-parenting moment for a solid few minutes before a Frisbee hit me in the head. When the man jogged over, apologetic and smiling, I caught myself checking out his ass and looking to see if he was wearing a wedding ring.

What the fuck was that, Chanel?!

And then I remembered I was still wearing mine. I still felt married.

The man tossed the Frisbee to his kid as he jogged back over to his spot. I looked around the park almost wanting to count how many stupid dads were there playing with their dumb kids. But as I watched my kids chase each other, busy having a blast while taunting the peril of the burning lava waiting to engulf them with any accidental slip or misstep, I knew that even now, at this one moment, I had candy in my mouth, too.

Border Crossing

From a long hallway I am shown to an opening door that leads into a room. It is long and skinny with a wall of windows at the end. Airplanes are visible across grayed-out concrete. It is a private room in an airport lounge for VIPs or frequent fliers. Clean and comfortable but not quite fancy.

José is half asleep on a well-worn black leather couch. A carpet with a pattern designed for bulk purchases is the only other object in the room. José has the half-open half-shut satisfied squint he'd get after a big bike ride. Exhausted, spent.

This is an in-between place. A border station. The quick sprint to connecting flights. I am getting a special visit. I am aware of the time.

"Do I get to touch you?" I rush over and lie on top of him, left arm tucked around his neck and right hand on his chest.

"It's really you!" I say, my eyes scanning him.

I put my hand under his shirt.

I feel his chin slide down toward the top of my forehead so his lips can press at my hairline.

"You feel exactly the way I remember." I am starting to hurry.

His hand on my back presses lightly between my shoulder blades. Fingertips and palm.

"Can we be together again?" I sound desperate and don't want the real answer.

My face nuzzles his neck. I can't see his face.

"Well—you have to swim out really far. And then it gets . . . complicated."

The air grows thinner.

Time.

I should go faster.

Rushing to get my clothes off, remove his shirt, feel him, rush to make love to him one last time . . .

I could feel it coming.

Sliding out of sleep.

I was pulled away.

Out.

Death by a Thousand Paper Cuts

As for what had actually happened on the afternoon of José's accident, it took weeks before the pieces really came together. The police report was ninety-seven pages. Some pages had blank squares where diagrams of the intersection were drawn in. Others were filled with quotes from eyewitnesses. Reading a single page was a feat of endurance.

At 6:35 p.m. on July 17, José was riding south on Lake Washington Boulevard, a pretty, tree-lined residential street busy with bikes, joggers, dogs being walked, and families going swimming in the lake. Headed toward a soft left curve, José had passed another cyclist moving quickly. A car swung out wide when there was a break in the traffic in the oncoming lane and passed José, as cars frequently do on that road, given that drivers get impatient with the speed limit of thirty-five and the frequent bike riders slowing their pace. The main boulevard ahead split off in a Y, left toward the park, with its sweet little swimming beach, or to the right and up a little hill.

A van carrying four people had just come in the other direction from the park and was waiting to turn left, to follow the fork up the hill. José had ridden this road hundreds of times.

The driver says he didn't see him when he pulled across the oncoming lane. Into José's path. The police report notes that his girlfriend, in the passenger seat, screamed, "Look out!" to avoid the cyclist. The report notes that the driver said the sun was in his eyes.

Then the accident report also notes that the driver commented later that he could see José "was braking hard." That was the part where everything went upside down and my perspective of the accident flipped from being in the van to seeing it from José's eyes.

I couldn't un-know that José could see what was coming, saw the van pull into his path. Unable to avoid the van, José's body and bike collided into and tore the passenger-side mirror off; a bystander said it was so loud, it sounded like two cars crashing. Someone nearby was a wilderness medic, one of the folks who volunteer to hike out into the middle of nowhere to find plane crash survivors or lost hikers; she had her kit with her, the report said.

The report said when the driver gave his statement on the side of the road, he wasn't wearing any shoes or a shirt. The report said the breath and toxicity tests all came back negative. The handwriting was hard to read; I squinted harder, but the words stopped working and I had to get up or lie down or maybe go throw up.

The autopsy report was in a double-sealed envelope and not as thick. It did, however, pack a much bigger punch. It was a tidier and more compact document. Very formal. Textbook-tight grammar. The spaces on the first page or two, which was as far as I got, had room for specifics to be documented in numbers and to detail accurate information. The matter-of-factness of it made the police report appear casual by comparison.

I wanted to see how they described the injury and what the coroner put down as the cause of death. I also wanted to see if the reports identified the placement of the "jagged laceration" in the same spot on his body. The memory I had from the hospital was a line of long, puffy stiches on his neck going down, but it was fuzzy. I'm not sure why reading any of it mattered to me. To see if I was right? To reassemble what hit where, so I could create a Polaroid in my head of the actual collision?

Halfway down the page, I chuckled to myself: José *had* been saying he was an inch taller than he really was. "Ah-hah! I knew it!" I yelled out loud as I thrust my hand up in the air in some kind of Super Bowl touchdown gesture.

On the very next line, the examiner noted his measurements by section, in pieces, and specified whether he was circumcised or not. I yelped and tossed the report off my lap. Too much. I wanted to know what happened to my husband, not read a well-documented measuring of his centimeters.

If I were you? Never read the autopsy report!

Another piece of advice? If not knowing feels like a red-hot coal sitting in the middle of your lower intestines slowly liquefying your guts and you have to scratch at that burn, go slowly. Dip very slowly into the reports. Enter these medical files and police, autopsy, legal, or court reports (or any of the documents they throw at you) the way you would enter a very hot hot tub with a broken thermostat.

Don't go alone. You can always have a friend be there, or even read it to you, so it isn't right there in your hands. There may be answers in there—and maybe they will help and be exactly what you need, but they may not make you feel better or change anything.

At the time, reading those reports felt necessary. I didn't want to *not* know anything; I wanted to understand. But guess what? Reading those documents so I could get a timeline together in my head was *not urgent*—even if it felt like it.

It had absolutely not seemed urgent to call the police detective back even though I had been given the detective's business card at the hospital and was supposed to call "when things calmed down." They had not. However, she started calling.

The first couple of phone conversations were brief and business-like—I had to sign something, they had to mail something—but when the police detective tried to reassure me for the *third* time that the driver of the van felt so distraught and sorry, saying yet again, "in case it was a comfort, I just wanted you to know, in case it is comfort to you," I tasted metal.

I remembered that detectives see unremorseful people do terrible things to defenseless people, including children, every day. This police detective was probably just trying to make me, a nice widow who didn't drown her own children or blow up an entire family in a meth lab explosion, feel better about the shitty, shitty unfortunate accident. This guy felt bad and I wasn't a felon, so this must have felt like a vacation day at the office for her.

There was no physical threat, no bear to be seen, but my heart raced, all of my organs somehow squeezed oddly upward, and each additional word that came out of her mouth made me more furious.

I'd met the detective for the first time a few weeks ago. I had to pick up José's bike—the one that weighed as much as a kitten, the one he'd been riding during the accident—from the police station. She wasn't very big but was wearing combat boots and uniform pants. She reminded me of a cross between Holly Hunter in *Raising Arizona* and Linda Hamilton in *Terminator 2*. As I opened the back hatch on the Toyota RAV4 and started awkwardly trying to get the bike into the back, she said, "Well, I know this is more for me than it is for you, but I'm going to hug you anyway."

I stood there getting force-hugged by a law enforcement officer. I just let her hug me, closed my eyes, and waited for it to end.

But alone in my car, speaking with her on the phone miles away, my reaction changed. I put the phone on speaker, placed it faceup on the dashboard, clenched my jaw, and charged.

Shaking the whole car like a rabid middle-aged woman trying to choke out the steering wheel, I yelled and yelled at that well-intentioned but boundary-blind woman, who was (in her own mind) really just trying to help.

"I am sadder! Do you hear me? You need to stop saying how sad he is, because I am *sadder*. It may be a comfort to you, but it is not a comfort to me. You have said how sad and sorry and destroyed or whatever he is a dozen times, and *I believe you but I don't care. I am sadder!*" I shouted.

She must have apologized.

I think I remember hyperventilating in the front seat for another five or ten minutes.

I do remember going inside Costco, getting an incredibly delicious, sweet berry smoothie and sucking it down in big mouthfuls while shopping for toys to take with us for Christmas vacation. I tried to breathe out the parts of me that wanted to go find some more bears to scream at. I had another hour before pickup time at Gabe's school, so I bought another smoothie and sat near those giant relish and mustard dispensers and watched people shop for electronics.

Urgent, Important, and Fuck It

Even when life is good, or even just *good enough*, it is a challenge to get things done. We all struggle and procrastinate doing taxes, refinancing the mortgage, setting up a college fund, and, you know, updating your insurance policies or finishing your wills (not to mention also making time to exercise regularly, sleep enough, and eat well), but now I *had* to do exactly all of those things. Calling the mortgage company and getting those big monthly payments on hold for a while? Urgent. Calling about José's student loans felt important, but taking care of the bills in my name that affected my credit score should have happened first.

Good thing you're a project manager, I said to myself, but it turned out that the little Post-it notes I left all over the house (but then lost track of) weren't working.

Order marriage certificates
Gabe immunization record
Rest of school forms
Life insurance
Insurance adjuster taxable? (What even is that?)
Call lawyer who did wills—probate?
Toyota is leased in José's name
    payoff amount?
    give it back?

Start a diary
    record events, dates, and times and who was there, process,
        what happens
Ask if associates or paralegals work on cases
Cost estimates and financial analytics (like $$ forensics)
Call physicians?
Accident reconstruction
Bike expert
Unsafe conditions or history of accidents at street/intersection
Financial planner
Life insurance timing?
Schedule haircuts
Wood chips for playground

Writing stuff down isn't the same as doing what needs to get done—and none of these things were happening. The *Getting Things Done*–style prioritization grid that helped with work projects didn't seem appropriate for my life's current emotional and financial Armageddon, and the urgent and important things were all mixed up with the totally optional stuff. All the while, I berated myself—making a single phone call each day or signing one individual piece of paper shouldn't be so damn hard—but I started to measure the mail, bills, and summary of medical services letters in inches instead of pages, and the fat three-ring binder was quickly overflowing. I felt like giving up.

Hoping to find some answers, I picked up Atul Gawande's *Checklist Manifesto*. I was still reading the *introduction* to the book and was already you-had-me-at-hello lovestruck. He offered a simple strategy that allows for the way we humans will fail, make mistakes, and generally get stuff wrong: "It is a checklist."

The *Checklist Manifesto* suggests that checklists be specific and precise. Gawande explains how even highly trained pilots can get so caught up in checking dials, looking at the altimeter and the maps, and trying to restart the engines that they need to be reminded to actually fly the plane. It is, in fact, in bold on the pilot's specific emergency procedure checklist. The emotional part of me just wanted to sleep for the next ten years, but the single parent who needed to get shit done and figure out what to do needed a constant reminder to keep my house, my son, and my life upright. My life was on fire and the engines had quit; nevertheless, I was the captain and I needed to *fly the plane.*

I tried to make a more specific checklist to better sort and triage the pile of to-dos so I could tackle the urgent things first, and most important, avoid accidentally steering our plane into the side of a mountain.

Guide: The Tangled Web We Leave

We live in a rainbow of chaos.

—PAUL CÉZANNE

B elieve me, getting your shit together (before or after shit goes down and your life goes sideways) is easier than you think. Start exactly where you are. I'll walk you through it. Worrying about it is often more sucky than just doing it. The things that hit me hardest, in roughly the order they hit me, are grouped into four basic categories that are easiest if approached and tackled together: essentials like phone numbers and passwords; insurance coverage, what you have and maybe also need; money, from emergency funds to retirement planning; and legal items you need to have or should know about if someone gets sick or dies.

Keep in mind, all this figuring out, finding out, and financial forensics took many months, and sometimes years, to get resolved. Be patient. Your mantra is: *This is a marathon, not a sprint.*

More important: Take care of yourself while you take care of business. Your heart and body could probably use some extra love before and after you crack open your to-do list.

Perhaps most important: the actual things you have to do aren't individually hard to actually do. You likely do, have done, and will again do much harder things than tackling one phone call or form a day, or even one a week. Trust me. If anyone can do this—you can. You already know: *hoping for the best is not a plan.*

OK, my friends, it's time to put your big-girl panties on. We're doing this. Stick with me. Here's an overview of the four main areas we'll cover:

1. **Essentials.** A great place to start. When things go wrong, the essentials are often the first thing you need. Really, really need. When it comes to your life details, you'll likely have more to track down than the ten essential items recommended for backpacking or a hike, but I'll bet you can make great progress in just ten minutes. Plus, you do *not* need to document how many punches you have left to get that free coffee or sandwich, memorize your entire family's Social Security numbers, or even the passwords to every single online account. However, knowing where that information is and being able to access it quickly is very helpful. Really, really damn helpful.

2. **Insurance.** Insurance was one of the things that helped the most after José's accident. Life insurance is usually discussed as a good way to manage risk and is meant to serve as a bridge from your old life to the new one after someone dies. Policies are often advertised toward married couples and/or parents as a way to replace income for things like childcare, monthly expenses, paying off a mortgage, or to cover college. A few types of insurance are required (auto and health) and are intended to protect yourself and others when big things happen—expensive medical bills (think heart surgery, a long hospital stay) or property damage (a tree falls on your house, your kid smashes into the neighbor's new Mercedes)—and you don't have the funds to write a check, nor could you pay it off if you worked a second job for the rest of your life. You may really need some or more

(perhaps even less) insurance to cover your most vulnerable spots—for example, a short- or long-term disability policy—so the goal here is to cut through the crap to help you figure out what types are best for you and what you may need.

3. **Money.** Overnight, *we* went from a two-income family to *me* being a widowed, single mom of a no-income family. We're focusing on the basic planning most of us need and few of us have. That means having a backup plan (aka emergency fund) in place so you're not living one accident or illness away from financial ruin, as well as saving for short-term goals (vacation, braces) and long-term goals (a down payment, sabbatical, or retirement). There are shelves full of books about beating the stock market, getting/being/staying/marrying rich, optimizing returns, hedge funds, or the futures markets, but still, as a country *we suck at saving.*

A 2018 Bankrate survey showed that 65 percent of Americans save little or nothing for retirement and only 39 percent have enough to cover a $1,000 emergency. But there is good news: managing money is a *learned* skill, so instead of believing you just suck at money, try saying instead, "I *used* to be bad at money, but now . . ." and fill in the blank with your top financial priority. For example ". . . but now I have a one-year plan to lower my credit card debt and start an emergency fund."

4. **Legal.** When it comes to the legal stuff, what professionals call estate planning, I have to tell you, many of the lawyers and financial planners I spoke with admitted (usually when I was sitting across from them at their desks and they were charging me money) that they didn't have their wills done, either. To be honest, hearing that made me feel a little better and certainly less ashamed that we never finished ours. So on the one hand, "*Phew*, it's just not me." Or you. But on the other? This is really, really not good. However, this is a problem we can solve, and for most people it's pretty straightforward to fix. A long, messy,

expensive battle over money or custody is very avoidable. We'll review the main, or foundational, documents (I call them the Big Three) in a standard estate plan: your will (Last Will and Testament), power of attorney (POA), and living will (advance care directive).

1. Essentials

For every minute spent organizing, an hour is earned.

—ANONYMOUS

According to a 2016 Intel Security survey, the average person has twenty-seven (27!) separate online logins, and 37 percent of people forget a password at least once a week. Keeping track of your email, banking, and online subscription accounts is already hard enough to manage. Now imagine that your partner needs to gain access to them—or even just *one* of them. Without any help, password-guessing can be a needle in a haystack. A very irritating haystack on fire that makes you want to scream and throw things.

Like the time I called the hospital a few months after José's death to get an estimate of his medical bills. The woman in the billing department told me she could not give out the information to me, even though I claimed to be his wife, because the paperwork noted his status as single and not married. I suggested that I send her the marriage certificate and the death certificate to clear things up.

She laughed and asked, "Who on earth would you need to send a death certificate for?"

"The death certificate for my dead husband who died in your hospital? That death certificate?" I replied.

She squeaked out a few horrified apologies with "Oh, my heavens" and "Oh, dear" and suggested she get her manager to help me immediately.

"Yes, thank you," I said. "Why don't you go do that."

It's not her fault. She just answered the phone. Don't yell. Don't yell. Don't yell. Breathe in, breathe out, breathe in, breathe out. It's not her fault.

You'll save yourself (or your family) hours of misery and stress by compiling essential information, such as important contacts and all of your banking, credit card, social media, and other online account details and log-in information. Thanks to our computers auto-filling many log-ins, you likely take these bits of information for granted every day, but without them your daily life would come grinding to a halt. Take it from me. It is a punishing task to call credit companies and government offices saying over and over again, "My husband died and I'm trying to get access to the folder where our baby pictures are stored." Also, the company you have an account with may not be legally required, or even permitted, to grant access to your family, depending on your state's laws and/or company policy. The digital world has made life easier (or at least more convenient and entertaining), but if you have a PayPal/Venmo/Bitcoin account that nobody else knows about, it could just drift away (with your money in it) if you don't keep track of it.

Getting organized around happy things seems easier, so try telling yourself that this is not a chore but part of the anticipation of something fun, like shopping for a present or planning a vacation. When I was pregnant, we had a phone tree, a food-delivery schedule, a (lengthy and overwritten) birth plan in place, and all of our medical and insurance info in a tidy little binder. Now *that* is what I am talking about.

The Big List of Essentials to Round Up

This roundup of essentials should provide an overview of some things you might have forgotten about, along with some items you can skip over. It may also jog your memory for additional items you should add.

Contact Information

My full legal name:_____

Nicknames:_____

Address:_____

Address 2 or PO box:_____

Phone number(s):_____

Email(s) and password(s):_____

Birthdate:_____

Social Security number:_____

Emergency Contact

Full name:_____

Relationship:_____

Phone number(s):_____

Email(s):_____

Address(es):_____

Family Members

Full name:_____

Relationship:_____

Phone number(s):_____

Email(s):_____

Address(s):_____

Full name:_____

Relationship:_____

Phone number(s):_____

Email(s):_____

Address(es):_____

Full name:_____

Relationship:_____

Phone number(s):_____

Email(s):_____

Address(es):_____

IMPORTANT DOCUMENTS, LICENSES, AND CERTIFICATES

- ❏ Birth certificate(s)
- ❏ Marriage certificate(s)
- ❏ Death certificate(s)
- ❏ Social Security card(s)
- ❏ Passport or other resident/visa documentation
- ❏ Driver's license or other IDs
- ❏ Deeds, trusts, mortgage, stocks/bonds, etc.

Legal and Insurance

(Make sure to note full legal name and/or nicknames)

Lawyer: _____

Phone number(s):_____

Email:_____

Power of attorney (page 218):_____

Phone number(s):_____

Email:_____

Medical power of attorney/health-care advocate (page 219):_____

Phone number(s):_____

Email:_____

Financial power of attorney (page 220):_____

Phone number(s):_____

Email:_____

Digital power of attorney (page 220):_____

Phone number(s):_____

Email:_____

Guardian of child(ren) and/or pets (page 215):_____

Phone number(s):_____

Email:_____

Executor of will (page 214):_____

Phone number(s):_____

Email:_____

Health-care insurance company:_____

Agent name:_____

Phone number:_____

Email:_____

Policy number:_____

Account username and password:_____

Auto insurance company:_____

Agent name:_____

Phone number:_____

Email:_____

Policy number:_____

Account username and password:_____

Home/renter's/umbrella/business insurance company:_____

Agent name:_____

Phone number:_____

Email:_____

Policy number:_____

Account username and password:_____

Life insurance company:_____

Agent name:_____

Phone number:_____

Email:_____

Policy number:_____

Account username and password:_____

Disability (long and/or short term) insurance company:_____

Agent name:_____

Phone number:_____

Email:_____

Policy number:_____

Account username and password:_____

Long-term care:_____

Agent name:_____

Phone number:_____

Email:_____

Policy number:_____

Account username and password:_____

Other:_____

Banking and Money

Checking account(s):_____

Account(s) username and password:_____

Savings account(s):_____

Account(s) username and password:_____

Other bank account(s):_____

Account(s) username and password:_____

401(k) (list all):_____

Account(s) username and password:_____

Mutual funds:_____

Account(s) username and password:_____

Retirement funds:_____

Account(s) username and password:_____

Stocks:_____

Account(s) username and password:_____

Account(s) on autopay (utilities, cell phone, cable, charities):_____

Account(s) username and password:_____

College savings (529 plan):_____   _____

Account(s) username and password:_____

Debt (credit cards, school loans, car loans):_____

Account(s) username and password:_____

Mortgage:_____

Account(s) username and password:_____

Other:_____

Medical and Health

Medical insurance company:_____

Policy number:_____

Account username and password:_____

Existing conditions:_____

Medications:_____

Allergies to medications:_____

Allergies:_____

Preferred pharmacy:_____

Primary care physician:_____

Phone number:_____

Email:_____

Preferred hospital:_____

Specialist(s):_____

Phone number:_____

Email:_____

Therapist:_____

Phone number:_____

Email:_____

Pediatrician:_____

Phone number:_____

Email:_____

Dentist:_____

Phone number:_____

Email:_____

Other:_____

My medical records are located:_____

Digital Assets and Your Online Life

Home computer username and password:_____

Laptop username and password:_____

Tablet username and password:_____

Cell phone code to unlock:_____

Email accounts and passwords:_____

Social media usernames and passwords (Facebook, Twitter, LinkedIn, Pinterest, Instagram):_____

_____

Movies and TV usernames and passwords (iTunes, Netflix, Hulu, HBO):_____

_____

Books and audiobooks usernames and passwords (Amazon, Audible, Barnes & Noble, Kobo):_____

_____

Music usernames and passwords (iTunes, Pandora, Spotify):_____

_____

Gaming usernames and passwords:_____

_____

Coupon, membership, or discount sites usernames and passwords (Groupon, LivingSocial):_____

_____

Airline miles programs usernames and passwords:_____

_____

Travel points or credit usernames and passwords (Orbitz, Priceline):_____

_____

Digital dollars usernames and passwords (PayPal/Venmo/Bitcoin):_____

_____

Storage services usernames and passwords (Dropbox, iCloud, DocuSafe):_____

_____

Password-management usernames and passwords (LastPass):_____

_____

Art, intellectual property, and creative assets usernames and passwords (YouTube, Vimeo, Flickr, Creative Commons, Etsy, Craigslist, eBay):_____

_____

Keeping Your Information Safe

How and where to safely store and share this critical and sensitive information is a big concern for most of us and comes up as a question (sometimes even a heated discussion) all the time.

When it comes to how to record and store the information, pick a method or tool that will work for you, your life, and your preferences. If you've already got an organizing system in place, then I'd suggest sticking with what works for you.

The rest of us often go with one of these: writing it down on a piece of paper or in a notebook, creating a Word document or spreadsheet on your computer, or using a free or paid service that can store documents and save online account information.

Save, Store, and Share

Once you have all of this information, you don't want it to just lie around or be too hard to locate. Store a copy of your list of essentials (or information on how to access it or who has access) with the other important paperwork we listed on page 168.

- Keep a hard copy and/or a flash drive with your digital files somewhere secure, such as a lockbox, safe, or other secure container in your home, and let only a few trusted people (like the ones listed in your will) know where it is.

Digital Assets: It's Complicated

The laws around digital assets have not moved as quickly as technology. The good news is that most states have laws that include digital assets, but yours may not. Look up the Revised Uniform Fiduciary Access to Digital Assets Act (RUFADAA). Having a digital power of attorney named in your POA allows you to leave legally enforceable access and directions for your digital assets. Otherwise, access to digital assets is determined by each company's terms-of-service agreement, often meaning locked-down accounts and denied access. I hate to think of how many baby pictures are lost, just floating out there somewhere in the cloud.

Finding Lost Information and Locating Accounts

Even the best and most organized among us might overlook an account or two. In my case, there were dozens of times over the next several months (and years!) when I had to do some very intense sleuthing to find certain "oh yeah" accounts and items, such as a receipt for store credit, a backup email account, a gift certificate, or vacation photos from years before. Here are a few things to try:

- Look through a computer's Internet browsing history to find banking, doctor, pharmacy, or other important websites previously visited. It's worth a shot.
- Check email folders, archives, and the trash bin for monthly statements or electronic billing receipts or invoices. Many people rarely clear out their trash and downloads folders or delete old or archived emails.
- Search for key words such as *insurance, account, statement, prescription, policy, confirmation, payment, receipt,* and *taxes*.

Keeping Private Things (Ahem) Private

Many of us have a few secrets, right? I've heard stories from folks about things unearthed very publicly that *shouldn't have been found*, at least not by parents or children. Ugh. Unless you live in an incredibly sex-positive milieu, specifics on what kind of kink, costumes, or toys you preferred are likely not part of the image you want to be remembered by, so keep your private, mutual-consent adult stuff hidden securely or locked up.

TIP: Ask a trusted friend (aka The Cleaner) to be responsible for managing the R- and X-rated items, and make sure they know where to find your stash and have the ability or access (house key or passwords) to take care of it. A serious conversation and handshake agreement should suffice. You don't have to write the deal into your official documents.

THE ESSENTIALS CHECKLIST

- ❑ I have created my Big List of Essentials in case of emergency or illness, or in case someone else needs to retrieve it on my behalf.
- ❑ I have detailed any products or services (such as a safe, a

safe-deposit box, or online services) I am using to hold, save, or store any documents or assets for me:

_____

_____

_____

- ❏ I have listed a digital power of attorney in my POA document (page 168) and on this form:_____.
- ❏ I have updated my account information and passwords to my online accounts on (date) _____.
- ❏ A copy of my details list is here (location):_____ _____, and/or (name/s) _____ has access.

2. Insurance

People who live in glass houses should take out insurance.

—UNKNOWN

As soon as I was a widowed, single parent, getting coverage became critical because I was the *only* parent. I increased my life insurance so there would be enough money to support Gabe through school and college, reviewed my health plan, and updated my auto coverage. On the one hand, these changes made me feel much better, but on the other, I was using my late husband's life insurance payout to buy more, and more expensive, insurance. Smart? Probably. Creepy? Yeah, a little bit.

Let's be honest, insurance is weird. We pay a lot of money for a service that we don't ever want to use or need. But here's the deal, and it can be a major player in having your shit together. In a final conversation about you, no one should have to say, "I had to go into deep credit card debt because he/she died. I had to take off three weeks from work, pull my kid out of school, and travel across the country to take care of everything, so I lost my job and had to put the whole funeral on my credit cards because that bitch didn't even leave any money or have any insurance to take care of *anything*." (OK, so now you know what my inside catastrophic-thinking voice sounds like. It's not pretty, but hey, it's not wrong, either.)

Why do people buy or need to have insurance? Well, getting your shit together can cover a lot of territory and types of policies:

Medical/vision
Dental
Auto
Homeowners and renters
Umbrella (or liability)
Life

Disability
Long-term care

That's a short list and it already feels overwhelming, so you may have put off buying (or even thinking about buying) insurance. It's confusing, it can be expensive, and you might just *hate* the idea of paying money every month for a service you hope never to have to use. If you're worried that insurance is a scam, or you're just throwing money down the toilet, well, you're not alone, but you *still* might need to get your ass covered right. First, the basics.

Getting Insured

If you're employed, the company you work for may offer insurance benefits to you. If you opt in, a portion of each paycheck is set aside to cover the premium (payment). Or you can choose to buy a policy on your own directly through a specific company or through a service that compares rates among dozens of plans and providers.

REQUIRED INSURANCE You are legally obligated to carry some kinds of insurance. Auto insurance is a perfect example. Since the 1970s, drivers have been required to have minimum liability coverage; the amount varies from state to state (note that New Hampshire does not mandate it and some states have exceptions). If you buy a house with less than 20 percent down, most lenders require you to get private mortgage insurance (PMI). If you are a doctor, you're required to have medical malpractice coverage in most states. Under the Affordable Care Act, Americans had to have medical insurance or face a fine. There are plenty more types of insurance policies (plus add-ons and riders), but you get where I am going with this, so let's get into the details.

OPTIONAL INSURANCE There are even more types of optional insurance. An umbrella insurance policy and renter's insurance are fairly common, and many of us have (or have been offered) pet, travel, and crazy-expensive-new-phone insurance. Life insurance, disability insurance, and long-term-care insurance are frequently discussed for estate, retirement, and end-of-life planning, so we'll focus on those.

LIFE INSURANCE If I can't be at Gabe's high school or college graduation, I'd like to make sure he can throw himself a party or take some time to backpack through Europe or wherever the kids go to get drunk and laid these days. If I couldn't see Lyric's first gallery opening or attend the cast-and-crew screening of her feature film directorial debut, I'd like her to have some cash to get the good appetizers and a really fabulous outfit for her moment at the microphone.

What the insurance money provided us after the accident was pretty much *exactly* what life insurance was created for—a financial cushion. Even though I didn't know what our long-term plan would be, just knowing that some life insurance was coming, even a modest amount, bought me the time I desperately needed. Honestly, I came to think of it as our life raft—maybe not the biggest or most fully stocked, but one that would keep us afloat for a while, and for that I was immensely relieved.

However, it wasn't nearly as much as it should have been. We had each purchased a small life insurance policy when Gabe was born. We had a safety net for a few years, but nowhere near enough to replace José's income or pay off the mortgage.

Because we hadn't increased the insurance policies after buying a new, more expensive house, I had far fewer options than I would have wanted. Believe me, I felt lucky that we had *any* options, but I also had a permanent red spot on my forehead from the hundreds of times I slapped myself with the palm of my hand because we hadn't followed the standard advice of how much life insurance to carry. I never took the two minutes to call the insurance agent and ask for new quotes.

So, friends, let's get back to making sure your family has plenty of options and is, at the very least, not totally screwed without you. As Suze Orman said, "If a child, a spouse, a life partner, or a parent depends on you and your income, you need life insurance." For the most part, there are two basic kinds: term and whole.

TERM LIFE Term policies are considered a cost-effective way to manage your family's financial risk if "something happens" (you die) during the policy length. The payout is called a death benefit. If you buy insurance on your crazy-expensive new phone, you pay that additional ten dollars a month in case it breaks (or you drop it in the toilet or your kid puts it through the washing machine), but once the time period is up, you're on your own. A term policy has no investment component, and you don't get any of your money back. I think of it as terminate or terminal life insurance, and it is often sold in ten-, twenty-, and thirty-year policies.

When you're in your twenties and thirties, the premiums for a term policy of $250,000 worth of coverage (for a generally healthy person) are as low as $20 or $25 a month. This equals about one latte a week. As you get older (or if you or your family has health issues), the premiums get higher because, well, you are more likely to die during the term of the policy and the insurance company will have to pay the $250,000.

Honestly, this is really just math. You are willing to give them $20 a month (or give up a latte a week) to feel secure that if something happened to you, your spouse, kids, or parents wouldn't be screwed. The insurance companies (and their giant, data-crunching actuarial departments) will take that $20 each month betting that you *won't die*, based on shit-tons of data. If you *should* die, the rest of the people your age who are still alive will keep paying that monthly premium to keep feeling better, more than covering the payout on your individual policy.

WHOLE LIFE Whole life policies combine life insurance coverage (a death benefit) with an investment fund, like a savings account in that it gives you a guaranteed return. This policy builds over your entire life and pays a fixed amount on your death. The rates will never go up, and you can borrow against (a portion of) it later in life. However, whole life policies tend to be more expensive than term insurance, with lower payouts, and like term policies, if you stop paying before the maturity date, you don't get to keep what you've put in so far.

Annuities also blur the lines between investment and insurance. Their big selling point is guaranteed payments you can count on during retirement. You have to put a lump-sum payment down to "buy" the annuity, and there can be a waiting period of a number of years before you can begin receiving the annuity payments. There's a bit of a ruckus about whether these are a good option or not, and I've enjoyed watching Suze Orman get her knickers in a twist about how much she doesn't like variable annuities. I have to agree with her assessment, so do yourself a favor and please research the pros and cons thoroughly if someone is trying to steer you in that direction.

Which one is better? The general consensus among the dozens of financial advisors and insurance professionals I've spoken with is that *insurance is for insuring you against financial catastrophe and investments are for investing and building assets.* Ask yourself what you really need and what your intention is for getting insurance.

OTHER CONSIDERATIONS

Pay Premiums on Time. That seems like an obvious requirement. However, you have to keep an eye out. Over the next ten to thirty years, you are very likely to replace credit or debit card numbers, move, change banks, or do *something* that could prevent payments from arriving on time and lead to cancelation. Most policies allow a short grace period on late payments, but if your policy is canceled due to nonpayment, you have to start all over again and will most likely have to pay a higher premium.

Income Replacement. Life insurance is essentially income replacement—money. Because "time is money," I'd suggest expanding that definition to include all the paid work your household would need to cover expenses moving forward and to operate smoothly for years to come. Specifics will be in the worksheets on the coming pages.

- If your spouse is no longer alive, you'll likely need to hire someone to fill in the gaps for childcare, household chores, repairs, yard work, pet care, cooking, cleaning, etc. So how does one estimate what it costs to replace free labor at home? Well, in 2016 Salary.com estimated that the most common duties performed by a stay-at-home spouse added up to a $48,509 base salary, plus another $94,593 in overtime for a total of $143,102.

- Please take extra care if kids are left with no surviving parents. If you have limited family support, I'd press harder on making sure your kids have financial resources and some additional padding. Right away there could be costs to move to a new home, school, or part of the country. Over time, additional funding would go a long way toward getting them more support—counseling, tutoring, music or sports lessons, clothes, school supplies, college, a car, and housing to get them off to a good start as adults.

Read the Fine Print. There are exclusions in the fine print that can make the policy invalid, meaning that the insurance company will not pay. Exclusions frequently include high-risk activities like mountaineering, scuba diving, hang gliding, and flying a small airplane. There's generally also a suicide exclusion for a certain number of years (usually two) after purchasing the policy. So if you're really into competitive BASE jumping, get a policy that doesn't exclude it.

Hey, Young People! Yes, even if you are just out of school and don't have kids, a house, or debt, a small policy could still be a really good idea. If you die, someone still needs to take time off to come pack up your closets, clean out your apartment, sell your car, and . . . you get the picture. That's *at least* a few thousand dollars in lost wages, and many folks do not have $5,000 or $10,000 that they don't know what to do with burning a hole in their pocket.

Children Under Eighteen. Many parents name their children as beneficiaries for life insurance. Note, however, that life insurance companies won't give payments directly to a minor. The funds have to go into a trust, or legal arrangements must be made for someone to manage the money on the children's behalf. (Learn how to set this up in the Legal section on page 208).

SOCIAL SECURITY

Receiving Survivor Benefits. If you are a widow, a widower, a divorced spouse who was married for ten years or longer, a child eighteen or younger, a disabled child or stepchild, a widow or widower taking care of a surviving child under age sixteen, or a dependent parent of someone who has died (even before they were at retirement age), and if the dead person had earned enough to qualify, you could be eligible for survivor benefits. Note that there are limits on how much income survivors can earn and still qualify for benefits and that your widowed status can be canceled if you remarry. (Apparently we become someone else's financial problem then.)

Same-sex couples: as of 2015 Social Security recognizes same-sex couples' marriages in all states, which makes you eligible for Social Security benefits, Medicare, and Supplemental Security Income (SSI) payments.

Find out more at www.ssa.gov, or call and ask for someone to help explain eligibility requirements and walk you through the process of applying.

HOW MUCH LIFE INSURANCE DO I NEED?

Estimate. One frequently suggested calculation involves adding up your annual income for ten years as a starting point. For example, $50,000 a year would be a $500,000 policy, and $200,000 a year equals a $2 million policy. Another approach is based on tallying up your expenses and spending to project a total amount to cover those needs:

- **Your home:** What would it take to pay off the house or cover your rent for a comfortable period? Plan for that amount or chunk of time.

- **Living expenses:** Calculate you or your family's monthly expenses against how long you or your survivors should be able to focus on healing without having to work.
- **Debt:** How much do you have? Is it in your name, both names, or your partner's name? If it is in both names, your spouse is responsible for it.

How Much Do I Need? Worksheet

INCOME	EXAMPLE	YOU
Annual work income	$50,000	
Additional income from trusts, Social Security, investments, or other sources	0	
Total annual income to be replaced (subtract additional income, as needed)	$50,000	
How many years? **Note:** The total number of years of income replacement needed for a spouse and children depends on each family circumstance. One quick calculation is to multiply your annual income by ten years.	10	
Replacement income needed	$500,000	
EXPENSES	**EXAMPLE**	**YOU**
Funeral and other memorial expenses	$25,000	
Mortgage (if payoff is preferred) or other debt	$250,000	
College tuition for children ($100,000 × 2)	$200,000	
Total expenses	$475,000	
Total needed (income + expenses)	$975,000	
ASSETS	**EXAMPLE**	**YOU**
Savings and investments	$25,000	
Retirement savings	$50,000	
Life insurance and other assets	0	
Total assets	$75,000	
Life insurance needed (total needed – total assets)	$900,000	

NOTE: If the debt was in only your partner's name and you live in one of the ten community-property states, you may still have to pay it (more on this in the Money section).

- **Education:** If you want your kids to go to the best college they can get into, go to college at all, and/or if you are considering private school along the way, you are looking at major expenses. Add them up.
- **Retirement:** Most people are woefully unprepared for this. Consider how well your current savings will cover retirement costs and whether an insurance policy can help fill any gaps.

SHOPPING TIPS

1. Be clear about what you want to solve or accomplish. *What is your primary worry, concern, or goal?*
   - I am purchasing life insurance so (name/s) _____ won't worry about or have to _____ and will have or be able to _____.
2. Calculate how much you need and what you can afford. Use the "How Much Do I Need?" Worksheet above or run the numbers using an online calculator.
3. Shop around. Life insurance is frequently offered through your employer. Bear in mind, though, that your policy is usually valid only while you work there. If you can't or would rather not purchase a policy through your employer, shop via an independent agent (you can find one online) or ask friends for a referral. Your current car- or home-insurance agent might also offer life insurance.
4. Select from term or whole life policy options based on which better meets your needs, and compare at least three policies. Price is important, but pay attention to the terms and read the fine print.

5. Buy from a solid company with a good reputation and good evaluations.

   • The Insurance Information Institute (III) lists five independent agencies that rate and rank insurance companies: A. M. Best, Fitch, Kroll Bond Rating Agency (KBRA), Moody's, and Standard & Poor's.

   • *Consumer Reports* often evaluates insurance agencies, and I'll bet your local library will have a stack of them in the magazine section.

6. Buy now. Insurance almost always gets more expensive as you age. You can cancel it later if and when you decide you no longer need it, but every year you wait, the price goes up.

DISABILITY INSURANCE Life insurance provides financial support when you die; disability insurance protects your income while you are still alive if you are unable to work due to an illness or injury. That happens a lot. According to the Social Security Administration, one out of four of today's twenty-year-olds will be disabled before retirement. Surprisingly, accidents are not the main culprit. The Council for Disability Awareness reports, "Back injuries, cancer, heart disease and other illnesses cause the majority of long-term absences." Disability insurance is more expensive than life insurance, because you're more likely to need it. That's why having an emergency fund to cover expenses for at least six months is important.

People purchase disability insurance policies to retain financial independence for either a shorter period of time (short-term) or for as many years as they need until retirement (long-term). Had José's accident been less severe, any disability insurance coverage would have helped cover his salary until he was able to go back to work. And, if I hadn't been able to work, it would have been our only income.

Short-term disability insurance generally lasts for one to two years and is designed to pay about 60 percent of your regular salary to help cover necessary expenses until you are able to return to work. Like most insurance, the rates vary according to your age, health, occupation, and the policy's coverage amount. To collect benefits, you will need to present documentation, like medical files or a doctor's confirmation. In addition, there is usually a waiting period of 30 to 180 days, depending on the policy.

For example, let's say Brian is an office worker who does not smoke and is in his twenties. Brian will receive a much lower rate than Shannon, a construction worker who smokes and is in her thirties. Shannon is considered more likely to be injured on the job or disabled than Brian because of her increased risk factors, and thus her rates will be higher.

Long-term disability insurance is designed to protect against long-term or permanent income loss—over a dozen years or even decades. Coverage usually begins one or two years after a qualifying disability and is meant to provide additional (or continued) coverage after an emergency savings account or a short-term disability policy has been exhausted. The timeline the policy covers may extend up to retirement age.

VARIATIONS In addition you'll want to consider noncancelable or guaranteed-renewable options. Under a noncancelable policy, the company cannot change your premiums or cancel your coverage as long as you pay your premiums on time. If the policy is guaranteed renewable, you have the right to renew it with the same benefits, but the insurer can increase your premiums, as long as they are increased for all other holders of the same policy.

Social Security's disability assistance. You may qualify for disability assistance through Social Security if you "first worked in jobs covered by Social Security." *Then* you have to qualify by having a medical condition that meets their definition of disability, and you have to have been out of work for a year or more due to disability. If you receive Social Security disability benefits when you reach full retirement age, your benefits will continue.

Find out more at www.ssa.gov, or call and ask for someone to help explain eligibility requirements and walk you through the process of applying.

GETTING DISABILITY COVERAGE Some companies, usually larger ones, provide their employees with group coverage; check with your HR department to find out if you have options and what types of policies are offered, how much coverage they provide, and whether you can "take it with you" (keep the coverage and pay the full premium on your own) if you are no longer an employee.

Groups or associations like AARP, credit unions, or neighborhood associations often offer disability-income benefits for members, because they can buy them as a larger group. You can also shop through an agent or online.

SHOPPING TIPS

1. Be clear about what you want to solve or accomplish. *What is your primary worry, concern, or goal?*
   - Is short-term, long-term, or both the best option for you?
   - Is getting a lower rate worth a longer waiting period before you receive payments? *(If you have a healthy emergency fund, then perhaps yes. If you have no emergency fund, maybe not.)*
   - Would a noncancelable or guaranteed-renewable policy better meet your needs?
   - Are there terms or exclusions you need to look out for?
2. Calculate how much you need and what you can afford. Use the "How Much Do I Need?" Worksheet on page 184, or run the numbers using an online calculator.
   - Balance benefits, premiums, and waiting periods with your emergency savings: if you have enough savings or sick time from work to cover a longer waiting period (90 days instead of 30, or 180 days instead of 90) it can substantially reduce your premiums.

3. Shop around. Disability insurance is sometimes offered through your employer. Bear in mind, though, that your policy is usually valid only while you work there. If you can't or would rather not purchase a policy through your employer, shop via an independent agent (you can find many online), or ask friends for a referral. Your current car- or home-insurance agent might also offer disability insurance or be able to refer you to a good agent.

4. Compare at least three policies. Price is important, but pay attention to the terms, and read the fine print. Use the Quote Comparison Worksheet below.
   - Pay attention to the definition of disability and what types are (and aren't) covered.

5. Buy from a solid company with a good reputation and good evaluations.
   - The Insurance Information Institute (III) lists five independent agencies that rate and rank insurance companies: A. M. Best, Fitch, Kroll Bond Rating Agency (KBRA), Moody's, and Standard & Poor's.
   - *Consumer Reports* often evaluates insurance agencies, and I'll bet your local library will have a stack of them in the magazine section.

6. Buy now. Insurance almost always gets more expensive as you age. You can cancel it later if and when you decide you no longer need it, but every year you wait, the price goes up.

LONG-TERM-CARE INSURANCE Where is grandma going to live? Millions of families are facing that question right now or will be in the next five to ten years. One day, I'm going to be a grandma, or at least grandma-age (fingers crossed), so looking into long-term-care policies, especially given that I'm single, seemed wise. Long-term-care insurance helps cover the very high costs of home health care and assisted-living support as you get older and need more help. Much the same way disability insurance (short- and long-term) provides funds to replace income during your working years, long-term-care insurance is designed to provide additional funds to cover the rapidly rising health-care costs that millions of retired and aging people struggle to pay for.

The cost of an assisted-living or nursing-home facility can quickly exceed $100,000 a year, depending on where you live (costs can vary from state to state). Medicare does not pay for in-home, non-skilled assistance for things like shopping, cleaning, and cooking (called advanced daily living activities) that make up the majority of services needed. And insurance companies, realizing they had not estimated the costs of long-term care high enough, have dramatically increased premiums on long-term-care insurance. These skyrocketing premiums have become exorbitantly expensive and out of reach for many.

Instead, many financial planners advise putting money aside for your long-term-care needs on your own, often referred to as self-funding, as the cost of paying for the care on your own often matches the price of the policy. How do you know if you should buy a policy or even if you can afford one?

First, run some numbers on how likely you are to need long-term care and look at some of the projected costs, then try adding up a high and low estimate. Research collected at LongTermCare.acl.gov shows that most long-term-care costs are for in-home care and that the average wage of a health aide or homeworker is about $20 an hour. At that rate, five hours a day seven days a week is $2,800 a month and $33,600 a year.

Given that most of us will need some additional help as we get older, does saving for those costs on our own, as we do for retirement, make more sense? Some say yes. Insurance companies are also starting to offer hybrid long-term-care policies, which combine a life insurance policy with a benefit to cover the costs of your care while you are alive (rather than just paying out a death benefit). Do your research and talk to a financial advisor (who is not trying to sell you a policy) about your options.

Disability Insurance: Quote Comparison Worksheet

TERMS, DETAILS & BENEFITS	POLICY #1	POLICY #2	POLICY #3
Noncancelable and/or guaranteed renewable?			
How long is the waiting period?			
What is the maximum benefit period?			
What is the maximum monthly benefit?			
If 65 and working full time, can I renew?			
Are injury and sickness covered?			
Is there a rehabilitation benefit?			
Riders available?			
What is the premium (monthly or annual cost)?	$____/mo	$____/mo	$____/mo
Premium waived if/while you are disabled?			

FREE(ISH) INSURANCE After José died, I wanted to buy the most insurance I could afford to protect me and Gabe if anything bad happened again. I also wanted to lower my risk however possible and turn the good-luck dial as far in my favor as possible to make the chance I'd get sick or hurt as small as possible. A grief counselor or therapist might call this "bargaining." I preferred to think of these initiatives as my way of getting "free insurance."

You get better deals on life insurance when you are in good shape, and grief is *great* for weight loss. Losing my appetite and exercising all the time was a fast (not suggesting healthy) way to lose weight. I'm not saying it was good for me, but it sure helped to be at the *actual* weight I'd been listing on my driver's license for the last twenty years when I had the health exam to purchase a new life insurance policy. They take a detailed health survey (you are encouraged to be honest because withholding information can make the policy invalid) and measure your blood pressure, height, and weight, and yes, most companies do a drug test. My height-weight ratio put me in the insurance company's "super-healthy" column, I was still in my thirties (though barely), and I don't have added risk factors or any serious medical issues. So the rates were low.

But the more I thought about it, the more I believed that free insurance is totally a thing. We already do it in a hundred other ways: obeying speed limits, wearing seat belts, getting an annual checkup, working out, eating healthy, flossing, washing our hands, taking vitamins, etc. There are thousands of ways our lives already incorporate these guardrails to decrease risk. We may not always want to do them, but we are encouraged and even incentivized to follow through, and once we work them into the plan, they easily become part of our routine. What else can we do?

Staying healthy is really its own kind of insurance. According to a *British Medical Journal* website article on a Swedish study:

- Living a healthy lifestyle into old age can add five years to women's lives and six years to men's.
- It is well known that lifestyle factors, like being overweight, smoking, and drinking heavily, predict an earlier death among elderly people.
- Of leisure activities, physical activity was most strongly associated with survival.
- The average age at death of participants who regularly swam, walked, or did gymnastics was two years greater than those who did not.
- Being happy can make life richer and "insure" a higher quality of life.
- Money is not necessarily the key to happiness. A 2010 study from Princeton University's Woodrow Wilson School found that, up to $75,000, each boost in income increased participants' happiness. However, bringing home more bacon than that ceased to matter in their overall life satisfaction.
- A Harvard Medical School article on longevity says it is

quite simple "to increase your odds of a longer and more satisfying life span." The top three suggestions are: don't smoke, stay mentally and physically active, and eat a healthy diet.

* The 2018 *World Happiness Report* found that the happiest countries rank high in all six of the variables found to support well-being: income, healthy life expectancy, social support, freedom, trust, and generosity.

Insurance: The Balancing Act

I know it's a bit like rolling the dice, and the price can rise quickly, and you wonder: *What should I spend more money on—disability insurance, an emergency fund, or retirement savings?* There isn't one answer that's right for everyone, but your current situation (assets and liabilities) can shine some light on what you might need most.

* Do you have enough money in your emergency savings account to cover you for a year or so? Then you essentially have your own personal short-term disability insurance without premiums.
* Do you know that everyone in your whole family gets, say, back surgery and has a long healing time but recovers just fine? Maybe short-term disability insurance can cover an extended medical leave, especially if you don't have much in savings to cover such an expense.

My friend Mira, creative genius and strategy consultant, realized she wasn't sure what policies she really needed and wanted to look at the big picture, so we whipped up this quick worksheet. We listed the basic policies and got quotes for the amount of coverage that would make her more feel at ease and that she could afford long-term. We compared online quotes, and it took less than thirty minutes.

Getting Started: Running the Numbers

Remember that this is about covering up your vulnerable spots better than they're covered now. Do not get stuck or overwhelmed by all the disaster scenarios that can run through your mind. Let's try it.

	EXAMPLE	YOU
Medical/Vision	$400	
Dental	0	
Auto	$75	
Homeowner's/Renter's	$20	
Life	$50	
Disability	$200	
Long-term Care	0	
Other: Financial priorities Emergency savings	$100	
Monthly total:	$845	

YOUR INSURANCE: SURVEY

Medical, Dental, Vision
- ❑ I have researched my current policy and am informed about new options or changes that may be in effect.
- ❑ Medical.
- ❑ Dental.
- ❑ Vision.
- ❑ Other health-care or savings options.

Auto, Home, Renter's, Umbrella/Liability
- ❑ I have researched my current policies, compared prices, and am informed about new options or updates I wish to make.
- ❑ Auto.
- ❑ Home or renter's.
- ❑ Umbrella.

Life, Disability, Long-Term Care

❏ I have researched my options and compared plans for me and/or my family.

❏ Completed all steps for life insurance.

❏ Completed all steps for short-term disability insurance.

❏ Completed all steps for long-term disability insurance.

❏ Completed all steps for long-term-care insurance.

❏ Checked optional riders to possibly add to my plan(s).

❏ Looked into other types of insurance specific to me and my life.

❏ Copies of my policies are located here: _____.

3. Money

The best time to plant a tree is twenty years
ago. The second-best time is now.

—ANONYMOUS

We hadn't exactly been living paycheck to paycheck, but we didn't
have "extra" money, for a lot of the regular reasons—getting married, building a career, preparing to have a baby, time off after having a baby, paying for childcare and preschool, buying a new house.
We hadn't saved well along the way. Then, we kinda turned the
family-finances dial from a steady, stable simmer to more of a rolling boil.

The good news is that José and I (like so many couples) had
started the "we have to get smarter" conversations and had already
made a dent in reducing credit card debt and had consolidated
school loans. However, as our careers progressed and we got raises,
our spending easily caught up, or we'd dip into the dwindling savings account.

As long as nothing went wrong, we'd be mostly OK. Well, you
know how well *that* worked. Please take it from me: *hoping for the
best is not a plan.* It still makes me wince.

We'd essentially made a series of decisions that, while not individually bad, collectively added up to living one accident or illness away
from being pretty screwed financially.

Know Your Money

The list of Essentials (page 166) will help you compile in one place the
basic info for each of your financial accounts (checking, savings, insurance, investment, retirement). Now it's time to add two additional
important pieces of information: the type of account and the benefi-

ciary(ies). Knowing whose name is on your money and keeping your beneficiaries updated can keep you protected and help manage risk.

Sitting at the branch manager's desk at your neighborhood credit union removing your husband's name from your life sucks a lot. I was encouraged to leave his name on one of our joint accounts in case any checks or payments came in his name, which happened a few times—so that was good tip. I also needed to close or transition our joint accounts and get my shit together on my money for the future. However, I still *felt* married, and I didn't want to disappear his name from everywhere, either. I had a pile of official estate papers, another pile of our bank statements, a check from the insurance company, random advice from well-intentioned people (invest, save, pay off the house, don't do anything!) bouncing around my head, and a whole lot of questions.

So I looked across the desk at this nice stranger whose job it was to help me (and make the bank money), and I asked, *What should I do?*

If I was your sister, what would you tell me?

If you were me, what would you do?

How you spend your money, where you invest whatever resources you have, and what your priorities are really depends on you and your unique scenario. There is no one right answer, but I quickly learned that almost everyone has to jump through many of the same hoops and deal with a lot of the same bullshit to get to the other side, wherever and whatever that is for you: attending clown school in Prague, starting a small business, moving to (or out of) the country, going back to school, or living debt-free.

Assets and Access: What You Have

You know the accounts that you have, but what *type* of accounts are they? Is the account a single account (in one name only) or a joint account (in your name and that of another person)? If your name is on the account, you have access to it. If your name isn't on the account, you don't (unless you are named as a beneficiary; more on that on page 201). I had to fill out tons of forms, and it was a time-consuming pain in the ass, but I was able to gain access to those funds eventually.

JOINT ACCOUNTS The process of closing or consolidating the dozen joint accounts we had in four different banks was made a little easier because we were legally married, lived in a community-property state, and had listed each other as the beneficiary on everything. Frequently banks will consider the surviving account owner the sole owner once you confirm the death with the legal certificates. This is the same for debt, too.

AARP advises couples to confirm that they are the primary owner of at least one credit card to avoid losing access to credit once a spouse dies. You can also establish a credit account that specifically assures joint owners that when one spouse dies, the remaining one becomes the primary owner. This way you can avoid having your credit card shut down, sometimes without your knowledge or any advance notice, forcing the surviving spouse to reapply and perhaps receive a lower credit limit—just one more thing you can barely muster the energy to do.

INDIVIDUAL ACCOUNTS After slogging through the someone-died forms and mailing numerous copies of the death certificate, our marriage certificate, and the court document proving that I was the administrator of the estate for our joint bank accounts, there were still a few accounts and debts remaining:

- **School Loans:** José had less than $10,000 in school loans, and because he had applied for them before we were married and my name wasn't on them, they were forgiven and "died with him," as some industry folks like to say.
- **Credit Card:** José had applied for a credit card not long before the accident and used it to pay for that very expensive Italian carbon-fiber bicycle. I was the administrator of the

estate (as decided and confirmed via probate court), and Washington is a community-property state (more on these below), so I was personally responsible for paying off the debt and closing that account.

I probably should have pushed back, but when the credit card company sent a letter offering a significantly reduced payoff amount, I just sent them a check. When I think of it now, the financial mega-institution might not have come down too hard on me for the few thousand dollars to pay off the bicycle my husband had just been killed on, but at that moment cutting a check simply meant that I'd make fewer phone calls and spend fewer hours filling out and mailing more death forms. *I just wanted to stop thinking about it.*

I've heard from dozens of other widows who've received numerous high-pressure calls to pay off debt, often debt that they're not even legally responsible for. It happens all the time.

Do: Confirm what types of accounts you have and note them on your Essentials list. Update or consolidate your accounts so you have the access you need and managing your accounts is streamlined.

Don't: Pay anything until you are absolutely certain you have to pay it. If and when the forms get you down, ask for help, or have someone call on your behalf. You will want or need that money, and if you don't, then I am (a) overwhelmingly happy for you and (b) still 100 percent certain it should be in your kid's college fund or your retirement savings. The banks are doing just fine.

Note on Autopayments: Just like the saying "Set it and forget it," you can make sure your important bills, especially the ones that affect your credit, are always paid on time by setting up automatic recurring payments by your bank. Of course, keep a master list of all recurring payments so you don't lose track of where your money is going.

Debt: What You Owe

When it comes to debts and what you are really on the hook to pay back, here are general guidelines you should know about:

BOTH NAMES ON CREDIT CARDS If you jointly request a credit card or apply for debt with your spouse, or if you cosign a loan or line of credit with a parent or child, you are both equally responsible to pay back that debt. There are some important nuances:

- If you're an authorized signer (for example you work for someone and purchase items on their behalf), or if you were added as an additional cardholder (meaning you were given permission to use it but never applied for the credit), you should not be responsible.
- However, if your recently deceased spouse was the primary account holder, the card can be canceled and the account closed even if you want it to remain open.

If the credit card or debt is in the deceased person's name alone, usually the heirs and spouse are not responsible for paying it back. Essentially, if you sign up for the debt, you are responsible for paying it. Period. *Unless* you live in a **community-property state**, which we did, and you do too if you live in Arizona, California, Idaho, Louisiana, Nevada, New Mexico, Texas, Washington, or Wisconsin. Nolo, the first consumer advocacy group to demystify the legal process and provide DIY legal documents, notes that, in addition, "Spouses in Alaska can also declare that certain assets are community property assets."

This is a good news/bad news situation.

- **The good news:** If you don't have a will (which half the country doesn't) all assets during the marriage are considered jointly owned. Assets go to the spouse if they weren't included in a will, had been overlooked, or weren't in the picture when you wrote your wills.

- **The bad news:** So do the debts, at least the debts incurred after you were married.

When someone dies, all their debt doesn't just disappear, and creditors do have the right to seek repayment from the estate of the person who died. It is the responsibility of the executor of the will (see page 211 for a definition of that role) to handle financial issues, including paying off any debts. If creditors or family members call you seeking payments or information about the estate, direct them to the executor (or the administrator designated by probate court), and tell them not to call in the future. In essence, don't pay money or provide financial or personal details to anyone unless and until you are certain the request is valid.

Beneficiaries and Heirs: Who Gets What You Leave Behind?

The beneficiary beats the will. Let's say that again. The beneficiary beats the will. The beneficiary listed on your financial account (as one usually is on financial and investment accounts and insurance policies, if you filled it in) is the one the bank will recognize, even if your will says otherwise.

Take this example to heart: if you've created or updated your (current, legally binding, totally legit) will, but you forgot to update the beneficiary on the 401(k) you set up when you weren't married yet or were married to someone else, at which time you listed your sister as the beneficiary, your sister gets the funds *even if* you've more recently written your (current) spouse into the will to get everything. The bank or financial institution will give the money to the person listed as beneficiary on the account, because *the named beneficiary beats the will.*

Sometimes the family works it out without any issues, but often such an oversight is absolutely devastating. You'd be surprised how many times I've heard something like, "I just can't believe that (insert ex-spouse's name), who is just awful because (insert long list of reasons why they are the most terrible person alive), got the entire life savings—and they'd been divorced for over ten years!"

Do this right now: update your beneficiaries. Most accounts and policies allow you to do this online. It takes five minutes. *Do not wait!*

HEIRS If there is no will, no named beneficiary, and no community-property laws, your state's probate court will decide who the heirs are. The order of heirs is most often spouse and children first; and if there is no surviving spouse or child, then the next closest living relatives are usually parents and siblings, although laws are not identical in every state.

Often, however, the state doesn't know whom to find or where to look. In fact, the National Association of Unclaimed Property Administrators, a nonprofit organization, estimates that more than $33 billion in unclaimed assets is being held by state treasuries and government agencies—not including more billions in US savings and treasury bonds, unclaimed pensions, and income tax refunds that were unredeemed, unclaimed, or returned to the IRS.

If you don't want your money to drift away, it's a good idea to note which accounts (such as your mortgage, auto loan, or credit cards) are scheduled on autopay. You don't want to keep paying for a service you no longer need or miss a payment if the card number expires or the account is closed. The consequences of letting a bill lapse can range from the annoying—cable company might charge a re-sign-up fee—to the disastrous: you could lose health benefits or life insurance due to missed payments.

Whom to Notify

In addition to the first, most important phone calls and notifications to make in the weeks and months following a death, there are some others that aren't urgent but are still important. For example, you should notify Social Security or the Veterans Affairs Office and contact household-utility companies, cell and Internet providers, and the Department of Motor Vehicles (for car titles and registrations) to close accounts or transfer them into your name.

CREDIT-REPORTING AGENCIES Credit-reporting companies track your credit score and provide the rating numbers that determine how good your credit is. Anyone who has had a sucky credit score knows the pain it causes—you can get turned down for a home or car loan, your rental application goes to the bottom of the pile, and at the very least, you have to pay a lot more in interest on credit cards and even in car-insurance premiums.

The executor should notify the three big credit-reporting agencies: Equifax, Experian, and TransUnion. If you have already notified Social Security, the information may have been passed along. The executor should also send a copy of the death certificate to each of them. This can help keep scammers and fraudsters from trying to open new accounts in the dead person's name; identity theft would create yet another pile of paperwork you'd have to deal with.

> **NOTE:** You are entitled to receive one free credit report each year from each of these companies directly, or go to AnnualCredit Report.com. Other third party services or apps track your credit score for free, but that usually means that you have provided personal information to sign up and they will advertise other products to you.

Manage Your Money

My personal goal is to be a very old, smiling woman walking up and down the beach in a too-small bikini with long gray hair and a too-dark tan scaring the children with my flappy elephant skin. I think of this and smile when the automated contribution into my 401(k) happens every month. Putting 20 percent of my annual income toward my financial priorities is a smart tactic, most financial folks agree; it just sounds so boring. But bathing-suit lady? I'll fund the hell out of that.

1. **Have an emergency savings fund.** Some 28 percent of Americans have no emergency savings, and 49 percent have only three months saved (six months is the minimum recommended). General advice is to save enough to cover your expenses for at least six months, and make sure the money is easily accessible (long-term savings or a CD ladder) but not so accessible that you can dip into it on a whim (like your day-to-day checking account).

An emergency fund will help with:

- Loss of income if you lose your job.
- Medical emergencies if you are ill or hurt.
- The unexpected, like travel costs for a family funeral or illness.
- Housing emergencies—the furnace breaks, the roof leaks, etc.
- Transportation—if the car breaks down but is critical for work, you need to be able to pay for repairs.

2. **Fund a retirement savings account.**

- Start early, even if it means paying the minimum on your student loans for a while (look at income-based repayments if you qualify).
- Take 15 percent of your income and save it. Consider a 401(k), a no-load index mutual fund, and a no-load IRA retirement fund.
- If you can't save that much, start with a lower percentage of your income and increase it over time. Some companies will set it up to rise by 1 percent a year.

* Many 401(k) plans offered through a company include matching contributions from the employer—*free* money. Get the full percentage match they offer.

TIP: Think you can't save for retirement? Siphon off a few percentage points of your income automatically each month and see if you miss it. If you don't, siphon another percentage point the next month. Then another.

3. Lower debt.

* Pay down the highest interest rate first.
* Pay more than the minimum balance.
* Check your credit rating. Are there any errors? Is your credit rating being lowered by your debt or payment history? Keep your credit balance (utilization) around 20 to 30 percent of your total credit limit, and follow up to get any errors removed from your credit history.

4. Cover risks.

* Buying and/or updating insurance? Where are your holes and financial weak spots?
* Needs vary, depending on your life scenario, situation, and priorities.
  * No emergency savings and high expenses? Perhaps you need disability insurance.
  * Health issues with no retirement savings? Look into long-term-care insurance.
  * Growing family with young kids and a mortgage? Some, or maybe more, life insurance.

How to Live Within Your Means

Everyone will tell you to find the joy of living within your means, but we all know people who struggle to make ends meet or live well outside that limit. If you think about it, the right thing is to live *below* your means.

After conversations with dozens of personal-finance experts and everyday good savers and budgeters, here's the "best of" advice that I've remembered:

1. Spend less than you make. Period. Being mindful can go a long way toward changing your habits for the better.
2. Make and follow a budget. Many free online tools can easily track spending and send you spending updates. Review your spending. Track your habits for a month or even just a week, and see where it all really goes. Go through your monthly bills to find and eliminate excess regular expenses. You might be surprised by how much you spend—and on what!
3. Reduce interest rates on credit cards. Call and ask; shop around.
4. Plan ahead. Save up for birthday or holiday presents, plan meals, and buy groceries for the whole week.
5. Pay yourself first. Set up autopayments to saving accounts for an emergency fund, retirement, vacation, college, and so on—to make sure you don't spend your savings money before you save it.
6. Spend less on little things. Bring lunch to work, and take public transportation.
7. Shop smart. Compare prices first, buy things on sale, and ask for a discount.
8. Value what you have. Take care of your stuff and maintain it so it lasts longer. If possible, fix the thing instead of buying a new one.

YOUR MONEY: STATUS

Budget

- ❏ I have completed a budget and track monthly actual costs to my budget (income and expenses).
- ❏ I have considered my personal values and the areas where my spending and saving do (and don't) line up.

Savings

- ❏ I have _____weeks/months of expenses saved in case of accident or emergency in an emergency fund located

  _____.

- ❏ I have a short-term savings plan and put away _____ percent of my income each month toward financial priorities.
- ❏ I have a long-term savings plan and/or retirement plan where _____ percent of my income goes each month.

Planning

- ❏ I have reviewed my financial situation and, if necessary, discussed it with those closest to me.
- ❏ I have thought over and written down my financial goals.
- ❏ I have researched tools, advice, resources, etc., to learn skills in the areas where I'm less confident about meeting my goals.
- ❏ I have a plan in place to make steps toward my financial goals.

CHECK IT OUT: The Budget Spreadsheet is available online at chanelreynolds.com.

4. Legal

Among the questions I hear most frequently are: What is the difference between a will and a living will? Is that the same thing as a trust? Do I need a lawyer? What happens if I don't have a will?

Most of us don't really know about this stuff—and that is perfectly reasonable. I don't know much about building a patio deck in my backyard, nor could I tell you how to knit *anything* even if my life depended on it, but when I need to, I can read a book, do an online search, or even hire someone to do these things for me. No biggie.

Yes, there are countless edge cases and what-if scenarios that estate attorneys will mention as reasons you should *never, not ever,* do it on your own. I won't argue with their law degrees. However, I will point out that insinuating that I can't understand enough about basic estate planning to gather the information, know what I'm signing, and perhaps save myself an hour or two of your impressive bill rate is not the best way to convince me to hand you a fistful of my hard-earned dollars. So to any attorneys reading this who are already thinking, *Wait! But, well, actually, sometimes, it depends on, and except . . .* Yes, I know, thank you, but just chill out. Most of us need to start with the basics.

Estate Planning 101

Estate planning sounds like something land barons do. Most of us are not land barons, but everyone needs to complete a few basic legal documents, whether you own a home or have kids or not. I would say single, broke, young adults should do this, too, because if *you* don't take care of your estate—and yes, you do have one, even if you think you don't—someone else will. Your parents, your sister from Virginia who's in medical school and doesn't have time to come dig through your crap, or maybe a family member you don't like at all—someone will have access to all your banking records, search through all your emails, pack up your socks and underwear, and get all the apps and music you've paid for over the years. Maybe you've spent hundreds and hundreds of hours building up your *Fortnite* resources or leveling up your *World of Warcraft* avatar. I mean, holy hell, you don't want just *anyone* playing your level seventy-two elven-dwarf-knight-warrior or whatever, do you? In any case, you can make it a pretty easy process if you get organized *before*.

Estate-Planning Documents: Wills, Living Wills, and Powers of Attorney

There were three documents sitting in my inbox that we had drafted with a lawyer months before but never gotten around to signing, even though our son was already in preschool by the time we'd started. These are the documents included in all standard estate plans. I call them the Big Three, and in them are roughly a dozen things everybody needs to document, no matter how much or little you own.

1. Will (Last Will and Testament)
2. Power of attorney (POA)
3. Living will (advance care directive)

HOW DO I GET AN ESTATE PLAN? The three most common ways to complete an estate plan are:

1. Hiring an estate-planning attorney ($500 to $3,000 and up)
2. Using an online template or fill-in-the-blanks product ($50–$300)
3. Doing it yourself

DO I NEED A LAWYER? Some situations have more complex legal needs and may benefit from, or need, an experienced professional's assistance. Perhaps you anticipate that someone might contest your will due to unfortunate (or batshit crazy) family dynamics, so you want your documents bombproof and watertight. That's when the attorneys say you should *really* hire an attorney, and in truth, there's a pretty good list of "Oh, yeah" details that you *want* to get right to avoid some very avoidable "Oh, fuck" moments. The American Bar Association (ABA) lists these items in their Family Legal Guide as common scenarios that should trigger a call to an expert:

- Owning a vacation home or other property in a state other than that of your primary residence.
- You and your partner are not legally married.
- Divorce or custody disagreements.
- Remarrying and blended families, especially those with children.
- Concern about federal Estate and Gift Taxes (In 2017 you needed to have an estate valued at over $5 million (combined property and assets) before Estate Tax would have applied. In 2018, you were allowed to pass on an estate in excess of $11 million without paying federal Estate Taxes.)
- A strong preference that someone get (or doesn't get) access to be with you at the hospital (some have rules allowing family-only visitors) might require legal steps in addition to your living will.

Everyone's situation is different, and my take is that, if you *do* have the ability or resources to hire a lawyer and make it easy on yourself, then awesome. They will do the heavy lifting and nudge you along to get it done. However, most people need only some basic estate planning in place to document things such as guardianship instructions. In that case, a template may serve all your needs for a fraction of the cost. I suggest that you just get it done the best and quickest way you can. Almost everyone agrees that having a will that's only 95 percent perfect is better than having no will at all.

1. WILL (LAST WILL AND TESTAMENT) Making a will is critical for everyone. Not having a will is, frankly, not an option, or at least it's a pretty bad one.

Wills 101. A will is a state-specific, legally binding document that states your wishes and instructions for who gets what after you die, with specifics regarding guardianship of children and pets and ownership of financial assets and family heirlooms.

WHAT TO PLAN IN YOUR WILL

- **Assets and property:** what property and assets are included.
- **Beneficiaries:** who inherits your property and assets and when.
- **Custodian/Trustee:** if a minor inherits property, an adult custodian is named to manage money on their behalf in a trust account.
- **Executor:** someone to manage your will and close your estate. An executor is also called an administrator or personal representative.
- **Guardianship:** who takes care of your kid(s) and pet(s).
- **Money and debt:** instructions on finances, distribution of money, and paying debts.
- **Additional instructions** for funeral or burial, if arrangements are already planned.
- **Gifts** to individuals or charities.

Dying Without a Will. You do not want to die without a will. I had no idea what that meant and couldn't even concentrate on what probate was (it's the judicial process that manages wills and estates), much less go to the courthouse and figure it out. A few weeks after the accident, I called the lawyer who had drafted our wills, to ask him if they would help and what I needed to do. He confirmed that, while having our unsigned wills to reference was nice, legally speaking, they weren't worth the paper they were (not actually) printed on. However, our state is a community-property state (again only nine are), which meant that our combined assets went to me as the legal spouse. Of course, if we'd finalized our wills I'm sure things would have been easier, but our situation was pretty cut-and-dried, so there weren't any curveballs. Still, because we did not have a valid will it cost several thousand dollars in time, documents, and fees.

At the hospital and funeral, at least a dozen people approached me to offer condolences but then launched into how they didn't have *their* wills done, either, and could find themselves in the very same shitty situation I was in. They did this when they walked with me to take a short bathroom break, get a very terrible and scalding-hot coffee, or stood with me literally right over José's body in the ICU. So I started taking mental notes to share with them how much worse, longer, and more expensive probate was than sucking it up and taking the few hours to just get the damn documents done while you're still above ground. Here you go:

Each state's laws decide what happens to your kids, pets, money, and other stuff if you die without a will. Dying without a will is called dying intestate, and you do not want this. Period. Just like speed limits or the legal status of marijuana, laws can vary widely from state to state; each state determines what is legally sound and binding, who receives your assets, and how probate works, including how long it takes (sometimes years) and how much of your estate is taken for fees and taxes—the national average is over 5 percent of what your estate is worth.

Let's say it again a little louder: if you die without a legally binding will, what happens is *completely up to the state*. If you don't agree with all your state's laws while you are alive, chances are good that you wouldn't agree with the way it'll handle your money, property, or kids once you're gone. In addition, not having a will can introduce questions and disagreements about what you *would* have wanted. During a hard emotional time, we all struggle; family relationships can get ugly, especially when folks argue about money. Bad things can happen.

Consider what you are leaving behind. An epic family court battle? A loving memorial? You can decide.

COMMON MISTAKES TO AVOID

1. Biggest mistake? Not doing one at all.
2. Thinking you don't really need one, because you don't have that much stuff or you don't care what happens "because I'll be dead," so it's not that big a deal.
3. Half-assing it. If you do cut-and-paste from someone else's document, use a template from a different state, provide incomplete or inaccurate information, don't have the will signed properly (typically two witnesses are required), or even use an inexperienced or sloppy lawyer, those mistakes can invalidate your will and make it unusable.
4. Rushing. Take care to remember all the important things. Include your business (restaurant, company, etc.) in the will, provide for pets, and include specific instructions about how heirs should share, own, or sell property or items of different sentimental or financial value.
5. Not specifying how and when money and other assets are distributed. Many financial planners recommend periodic payments instead of a lump-sum payout. Especially for young adults who haven't managed budgets, you can space out the payments and earmark a portion for housing or education. This type of specificity and oversight is often used when a beneficiary struggles with addiction, lives with a disability, or suffers from ill health.
6. Not updating your will. Many things can change; you may have more children, divorce, or remarry, and people can get left out (or stay in) by accident.

7. Not updating the beneficiaries on your financial and invest-ment accounts so they're current and consistent with what is planned (or assumed) in your will can have terrible conse-quences.
8. Getting stuck on guardians. It is hard to ask people to be guardians, and sometimes parents disagree, so the will doesn't get finalized.

WHEN SHOULD I UPDATE MY WILL?

1. Anytime you want. You can update it every week if you feel like it.
2. When things change. For example:

Marriage, divorce, or remarriage
Purchase of a home or other property
Inheritance of property or other assets (especially in a different state)
Having your first, or more, children
Whenever guardians of children or the executor of the will needs to be changed
When children become adults, go to college, move away
When you create or purchase a business
When state or federal laws change

3. Every five years or so. Review your documents every few years to confirm that they are still accurate. Often small revisions or additions are helpful.

Picking the Executor. Being the executor of a will is a significant role that requires lots of attention to detail, forms and follow-ups with banks and insurance providers, and some solid project management skills. It took me dozens, more likely hundreds, of hours of making phone calls and filling out forms—and that was just the administrative work. Handling one insurance claim or disputing charges for an X-ray can eat up a full day. Being an executor is no small job.

Ask someone you know who is very good at this type of work and choose a second person as a backup (you can specify that the executor of your will be paid with funds from the estate), or hire someone to do the job (some banks offer this service). It's common to pick one's spouse, which is not a bad idea in any way, but it could be that your spouse isn't a good fit for this role. Moreover, spouses tend to have enough on their plate dealing with their grief. The good news is, you don't *have* to sign them up to take on this job.

Conditions or Provisions of Guardianship. Do you have specific requests or terms for custody? For example, if you grant guardianship to a married couple and then they divorce, what is your preference for whom your child or children should live with while they are still minors? Or would time be split between the two custodians? Do you have other wishes or conditions, like your children remaining in the same state, spending summers with grandparents, or going to a specific school?

Temporary Guardianship. Do you want to name a *temporary guardian*? If the person or persons you have named in your will live out of state or happen to be out of town or for some reason can't immediately get to your children, there could be confusion about where the kids should stay temporarily. You can name a friend, babysitter, or neighbor as a temporary guardian to watch the kids for a few days or weeks (up to you) as a backup.

Pets. Many people forget to include pets in a will, and immediate family members may not know what to do. You can make it easier on your pets and feel more confident that they'll be well cared for if you leave specific instructions in your will for legal guardianship of them and then, if able, specify an amount of money to go to that person to help cover pet-care costs. The ASPCA estimates that pet costs can be about $1,000 a year if you consider food, shots, and basic care plus a few extras, like grooming, pet sitters, toys, and treats—not to mention those unexpected emergency trips to the vet.

You must name a *person*, not the animal, as the beneficiary. There are some years-long, million-dollar court battles on this very topic, so be warned that some courts will not award money to anyone under eighteen, and *none* will cut your Fluffy or Fido a check, no matter how smart you know they are.

Signing and Notarizing. The standard procedure to make a will legally binding is to sign it in the presence of two witnesses and include their signatures to validate it. In most states, it does not need to be notarized to be legally binding. However, it is common practice and highly recommended to have your legal documents notarized as an additional safeguard.

Where Do I Find a Notary Public? Your bank or credit union is a good place to start. Someone there should be able to notarize your will free of charge. Insurance and real estate agencies, some public libraries, and most government offices have a notary public available. You can also find notary public practices in your local business listings; many will offer a mobile notary service for an additional fee and travel to your office or home.

Can I Handwrite My Will? Yes, if you can believe it, a handwritten will (called a holographic will) is still allowable in about half of the states. There are a few things to note:

- The whole will needs to be in the person's handwriting.
- Those serving in the military, especially in combat, are considered special cases for whom a handwritten will is more permissible and binding.

Where Do I Put My Will? If the original is not with your attorney, you should keep it in a safe location with your other important documents. Also make sure to give a copy to the person(s) you named as the executor and/or power of attorney, and let them know where the original is stored. You may want to inform one or two others named in your will, for example the guardians, to ensure that your A-Team of people are informed and able to execute it if need be.

Trusts. Trust templates are often offered as adjuncts to a will by online legal services or an attorney. Here's a quick rundown of each type, should you want to find out more.

Trust Basics. Trusts are often set up and incorporated within a will, as they are an effective method for deferring or minimizing Estate Taxes, avoiding probate, and getting your assets more quickly and inexpensively into the hands of whom you are leaving them. In many cases they are required when the beneficiaries you name in your will are minors. Trusts are not necessarily beneficial solely for wealthy people or to avoid Estate Taxes, but whether or not you need or should have a trust depends on the state you live in and other circumstances. Many states such as California have mandatory probate fees that can be very costly, thus having a living trust can help you avoid expensive probates.

Depending on when the trust becomes effective, it is either

Living: immediately effective, or
Testamentary: effective after you die.

You can also set one up that you can later change, or one that you cannot.

Revocable: you can still control the trust while you are alive.
Irrevocable: you give away your rights to the assets when the trust is set up, and can't change anything.

You name people in your trust.

Beneficiaries: recipients of the assets you named and included.
Trustee: the person who manages the trust (yourself or others).

Trust Issues. Many people have found the process easier than they thought, but there are additional steps to set one up. You have to set one up ahead of time and move the assets into the trust so they are technically no longer owned by you but rather by the trust, because you have transferred ownership. You can set it up so you can move assets in and out of the trust or cancel (revoke) it.

2. POWER OF ATTORNEY (POA) In addition to drafting your will, you also need to create a power-of-attorney (POA) document that names specific people to whom you grant permission to take care of important matters on your behalf, like financial and medical decisions while you are alive. Once you have died, a POA is revoked and no longer has any legal authority, and a will becomes effective only after you've passed away.

Power of Attorney 101. A power-of-attorney (POA) document allows you to name people for different roles (executive, financial, medical, digital). You can name someone (in fact I've named several people) in your POA document to handle financial stuff, like college funds and any insurance money, and someone else to manage guardianship and kid-related things, like camp, school, and doctor appointments. It is strongly suggested that you name a backup person for each role in case your first choice is no longer able to manage those responsibilities. Here are the most common POA roles:

> *Executive—manages the whole will.*
> *Medical—makes medical choices on your behalf.*
> *Financial—manages all or some of the finances (if monetary tasks are too much for an executive or you prefer different people for each role).*
> *Digital—access to your online and social media accounts.*

Executive POA. The executive POA is the one who takes the lead in making big decisions on your behalf, the one responsible for making sure that your directions, wishes, and instructions are followed as well as possible and that everyone on the team does a good job. If you don't include different people to serve specific roles in the POA document, then the executive POA will make all the decisions.

> **NOTE:** An executive POA is not the same as the executor of a will. Remember, a will doesn't take effect until after you have died. An executor handles only the instructions contained in a will. An executive POA makes decisions while you are alive, as well as other decisions that are not specified beforehand.

Medical POA. This is not the same as a living will, which is the third document in the Big Three described in the next section. The medical POA document is meant to cover a situation in which you cannot advocate for yourself, communicate about your medical preferences, or provide consent, *other than* an end-of-life decision—in other words, for a person who is not close to death but incapacitated while hurt or ill. For example, medical POAs are often of great help when people have Alzheimer's and can no longer manage their medical care independently or live on their own safely but likely have years to live.

However, young and middle-aged adults need this backup too. If I was recovering from surgery or an accident and was still regaining my speech but was unable to communicate clearly or reliably, my friend Erin (acting as my POA) would say, "Can you please turn off the twenty-four-hour Zeppelin-only radio station? Chanel is more of a Bowie fan." Or, "Yes, as Chanel's medical POA, I approve proceeding with the additional surgery to be the world's second bionic woman."

> **REMEMBER!** Designating a POA or medical POA is not the same as having completed your living will.

Financial POA. Some people are better than others at navigating paperwork and contracts and also have the patience and experience to do so. You can name a specific person to manage the financial accounts or include additional people to provide oversight. For example, you can ask an accountant friend to provide an annual review as an extra set of eyes to help manage banks accounts, or you can leave instructions for the executive POA to hire a professional to manage the bookkeeping, file the taxes, and review statements to be certain everything is running smoothly.

Digital POA. As mentioned, be sure to specify a *digital* power of attorney and/or add specific language granting your executive POA all access and permissions to your online accounts and digital assets for extra legal protection should any problems arise.

> **NOTE:** For more information, review the digital assets part of the Essentials section on page 174.

3. LIVING WILL (ADVANCE HEALTH-CARE DIRECTIVE) A living will is a state-specific, legally binding document that records your end-of-life wishes about the types of medical care you do or do not want if you are unable to speak for yourself. I prefer the term living will, but this document may go by many other names, including health-care directive, advance directive, advance care directive, declaration, or directive to physicians, depending on the state, hospital, or end-of-life group, but under any name it defines your end-of-life wishes, and the point is to be very, very *direct* about what you want and don't want in *advance*.

A living will communicates your wishes should you be in a terminally ill, noncommunicative state and your preferences for the medical care you do and don't want. It frees your loved ones from the potentially unbearable burden of wondering, on top of grieving, if they're doing "the right thing" with your medical care. Your living will designates the plan of action for the end of your life, based on your beliefs, values, and most personal wishes, and ensures that your plan gets implemented without guessing or disagreements. If things are not as black and white as they were in our situation, you can say,

"I know what this person's line is. I know when we're getting close to it."

These were the questions that kept me up at night and poked at me as I walked the halls and took quick glances at the faces of patients in the other rooms, the eyes of the families who sat with them, and the many visitor chairs that remained empty. *How do we know what to do?*

Living Wills 101. Your mantra must be "Do it in *advance*, and be very *direct*." When you leave clear definitions and instructions, not just general concepts, you make it easier for everyone involved because they will know exactly what your wishes are.

Of course, you can't provide specific guidelines for every medical nuance or possibility, but even so, the document can provide details about what you do and don't want. You can make it easier to navigate the end-of-life territory on your behalf when you provide mile markers to identify what lines you don't want to cross when you get there. It's like directing people to a new place they've never been: "Take the turn right after the red barn," or "You'll know you've gone too far if you get to the bridge." In the same way, a living will can reassure those around you that you have indeed "passed the bridge" and gone too far or for too long. "Oh, we've passed it, we're no longer in the neighborhood where the kind of quality of life he/she described is possible." Clear and direct language helps calm fears and remove doubt that one is doing the right thing. It's a matter of *following* instructions, not guessing what they would have been and being left to worry or wonder. In our situation the choice was very clear; yours may not be.

Years later, I was still thinking about this, so I called Darrell, the Palliative Care director from Harborview who sat in the room with me, to ask him what makes a good living will good. It also gave me the chance to ask him what I did wrong and what I got right.

Your living will should instruct others what "quality of life" really means to you. Be very, very specific. For example, write, "Do everything possible," or "I never want to be on a ventilator ever again," or "I do not want experimental treatments or medical interventions (including surgery) that will not allow me to return home."

You'll also want what's usually called a health-care advocate. You appoint someone you trust to be your health-care agent (aka an attorney-in-fact for health care, a health-care proxy, or a health-care surrogate, but the terms generally mean the same thing). This is not the same role as the medical power of attorney in your POA, but you can name the same person to do both roles.

The laws that define these are state specific, like the laws for wills, and the form must signed with two adults as witnesses. Notarization is not required but encouraged. People often include, or attach, post-death instructions about organ donation, burial, or cremation, or about other wishes as part of or alongside the living will.

Without a living will, things can get complicated very quickly for a number of reasons, one of them being the fact that medicine is often "not that black and white," as Darrell put it. Without your clear guidance, those trying to do right by you end up "having to come up with goals of care and desires of functionality" themselves—and quite possibly guessing wrong.

YOUR LEGAL DOCUMENTS: SURVEY

Will (Last Will and Testament)
- ❑ Done (reviewed and/or updated in the last year)
- ❑ Drafted (actively in progress)
- ❑ Questionnaire complete
- ❑ Must update ("the old one must be around here somewhere")
- ❑ On my to-do list

Guardianship and Custody
- ❑ Custody of child/children (permanent and perhaps temporary)
- ❑ Conditions or provisions for custody (e.g., should a married couple divorce, must live in the same state, brother can't smoke in the house, etc.)
- ❑ Letter or video with wishes, values, and instructions to guardians

Pets

- ❏ Custody of pet(s)
- ❏ Conditions or provisions for custody (allowed on sofa, walks, etc.)
- ❏ Letter with wishes and instructions to new caretaker/owner

Money, Assets, Stuff

- ❏ Distribution of assets (money, savings, property, jewelry, etc.)
- ❏ How distributed (lump sum, annual payment, when beneficiary graduates)
- ❏ Debt instructions
- ❏ Trust (if established)

Burial, Funeral, Memorial

- ❏ Funeral, burial, or memorial wishes letter (including any pre-planning you have done, arranged, or already paid for)

Power of Attorney (POA)

- ❏ Executive
- ❏ Medical
- ❏ Financial
- ❏ Digital
- ❏ Other:_____

Living Will

- ❏ My health-care advocate (and backup person) is informed of my wishes, and we have discussed my instructions.
- ❏ I have written end-of-life wishes, directives, and instructions.
- ❏ I have defined what quality of life means to me and that definition is included in or with my legally binding living-will document.
- ❏ I have written a letter to my doctor to convey any additional information, wishes, and instructions.
- ❏ I have considered where and how I would like to be cared

for if I am seriously or terminally ill or injured, and I have discussed these wishes with friends and family, with my doctor and/or medical team, and with my medical POA.

- ❑ I have reviewed my options, discussed them, and written my instructions about burial or cremation.
- ❑ I have discussed and written down the type of funeral or memorial service I desire.

Location of Documents

- ❑ My will, POA, and living will are complete, signed and legally binding. Check your state's law, but usually these documents must be signed in front of two witnesses who also sign; they should be notarized even if the law does not require them to be. The originals are located here/with:_____
- ❑ A copy or copies are located here or with (note instructions to access if needed):_____

Practice Makes Progress

Like marriage, parenting, and house remodels, grief doesn't look like you think it will. It is, in fact, an absolute motherfucker. In October, after the kids had been back in school for a few weeks, I had already been seeing Delia once a week for a month or so, I was training for a half marathon, and I had upped the kickboxing sessions to four or five times a week. The intense exercise helped me stay grounded, or at the very least not drink too much, because I could never have done all those squats and crunches being hungover all the time. In kickboxing class, I was getting better at the punching and kicking, and I had just set a record of fifty push-ups in one minute and had to admit I was loving the new body I was living in.

In addition, being legally married in a community-property state made probate *much* easier than it could have been. After I called our attorney, he did most of the legwork to navigate the process through probate court. It only took a few weeks of shuttling papers back and forth for him to confirm that I was the official administrator and beneficiary of the estate. Whether or not there was a case against the driver, or whether, say, the brakes were faulty on the van, was a whole other question.

Even though it made me feel like throwing up, I knew I had to do my due diligence. Was it an unsafe intersection? Was the view obstructed? Was someone at fault? Could the accident have been easily prevented if a few trees had been properly trimmed? The last thing I wanted to do was drag myself or the kids through court or a trial, but what if it wasn't just a terrible, tragic, totally unfair accident?

Our friend Josh did some research and arranged for me to talk to three experienced attorneys in the state. He also suggested and helped arrange for an independent road and transportation expert to survey the accident location; the report confirmed that nothing was remarkable or out of place regarding the location or intersection.

All three lawyers told me there wasn't a case. It *was* just a terrible, tragic, totally unfair accident. The van wasn't owned by some large company with a huge liability insurance policy that might at least have provided some sort of settlement to set aside for the kids' college or to pay off the house. But each suggested I could probably use some help dealing with the driver's insurance and getting them to move at anything other than their usual, glacial pace. There was already over $300,000 in medical charges, and after I paid the annual out-of-pocket maximum of $10,000, there was a lot left over someone had to pay. Thankfully, Josh and a colleague at his firm named Tom, an absolute angel with the patience of Mother Teresa, knew how to navigate medical insurance and saved me from the torture of trying to wrap my head around multistate insurance policies, claims, adjusters, investigations, and ERISA laws; they did almost all of the heavy lifting for me.

I could finally exhale a bit after getting the insurance check. It took about six weeks to come in the mail, but once I had some money in the bank and wasn't living off help from friends and family, I was less panicked. With the mortgage on pause and Gabe's school able to offer some emergency financial aid, money moved off the Urgent ("Oh Shit") list and over to the Important list. Nevertheless, an unsettled feeling always surrounded me. I was relieved to have made progress but was wiped out for a day or two after just one of those numerous legal and insurance phone calls or meetings. I still had a hard time opening the mail, and listening to voicemail was a herculean effort. I often caught myself staring at the wall, unsure what I was in the middle of doing or what I should do next. There was so much wall staring and floor gazing that I began to hate the paint color and the floorboards, so I hired a contractor to paint the walls and update all the trim.

I started to dig through the plastic bins of pictures and wonder about what to do with José's belongings. I left his closet exactly as it had looked before the accident and put the clothes he'd worn to work and the shirt he'd slept in the night before in a plastic bag so they would smell like him a little longer. I scanned his drawer full of socks and underwear and ran out of gas. There was so much stuff. I stared at the wall instead. Months later, my nervous system still felt as if it had been singed in a fire. My skin would hurt one second, but then an hour later I'd be exhilarated and grateful to be alive.

In an attempt to feel less crazy, I would visualize healing energy with every slap of the jump rope during cardio. On the hill repeats, with every footfall I'd imagine my head and my heart reconnecting to make me feel whole again. I repeated *It won't always feel like this* with each breath in thousands of sun salutations. For long minutes at a time, I could feel like a real, regular person. For ten minutes I'd be test-riding my friend Andrew's motorcycle. In another twenty, though, I'd be back on the floor in my closet hyperventilating into sweaters.

If I could keep it together (mostly) for the week in the hospital, why am I starting to feel worse months later? Am I just tired? Of course I'm sad, but is something wrong with me?

I tried to pull it together around Gabe so he wouldn't have to watch his mother fall apart in front of him. On our fifteen-minute car rides to school each morning, I would tell him stories of made-up grand adventures, and his job was to throw me plot-point curveballs, like "then the dragon ate him" or "but it was Opposite Day, so none of that happened." We'd laugh, ride along with big smiles, and I'd sip my latte out of my 8 Limbs Yoga Center commuter mug printed with the motto "Many paths. Follow yours."

Seconds after he skipped through the front gate and hung his Clone Wars backpack on the peg outside the kindergarten door, I'd have to pull the car over because I couldn't drive through the sobbing. I even started wearing a bra and real clothes instead of yoga pants (OK, they were pajamas) because I didn't want the normal, regular-human-looking people on the sidewalk to look inside my car and see a disheveled woman hunched over the steering wheel, making noises like an animal being slowly crushed to death. I was certain I was just one more maniacal side-of-the-road cry away from someone calling the cops on me. I wasn't 100 percent certain I could appear reasonable heave-crying on the sidewalk while wearing knockoff Uggs, unbrushed hair, and untethered breasts in such a nice part of town.

"Feeling all the feelings" was one way I kept telling myself I was going to get through this. I had to *actually go through it.* Even so, in the moments when I could catch my breath I'd wonder what was wrong with me. I wasn't sure what the "regular" version of despairing grief was supposed to feel like; I worried I'd gone off the deep end. Knowing that you can't (shouldn't) compare, I still assumed that losing a grandparent or childhood pet isn't exactly the same as removing medical support from your husband when he was in the prime of his life. I wondered, how is a trauma response different from single-parenting stress while grieving? How would I even know how to tell the difference? I didn't feel that I was going insane exactly, but I also slammed back and forth between feeling not like myself at all and more like *me* than I ever had in my life.

People tried to reassure me by saying things like, "Your brain has gray spots on it for a while from the trauma." Some advised me not to "make any big financial decisions for a year." I'd nod in agreement but didn't really know if I believed in those gray spots or should take the advice. Was that just an old wives' tale like starving a cold and feeding a fever? Or is it the other way around? Is there some science to support it? How exactly was I supposed to not be able to trust myself?

I decided to go to the place in Seattle where one goes to be understood, to access endless knowledge, and to be surrounded by wise people with answers to your vague and open-ended searches: the Elliott Bay Book Company. I grabbed a coffee from Zeitgeist, dodging the siren call of the Top Pot doughnut in the display case, and walked the few blocks to the store, past historic brick buildings and saloons from the early logging-boom days. I moved through the shelves, collecting a dozen books about grief, death, loss, and trauma. I sat curled up in a chair with them stacked around me.

Grief and Loss: The Only Way Through Is Through

Most folks know of *The Five Stages of Grief*, by Elizabeth Kübler-Ross. It had been years since I'd read the book, but I felt I was bouncing around among all of the phases and feelings dozens of times a day. I found most of what I thought I knew about grief to be as useful as a newspaper horoscope: interesting and "kinda sounds like me" but not really helpful. I wanted something more instructive.

Even though at least a dozen people told me I should wait to read *The Year of Magical Thinking*, by Joan Didion, "until you're ready," I was apparently feeling bold, so I cracked it open and side-eyed the first few pages, where Didion describes her husband's fatal heart attack.

Her story was enough unlike mine that her experiences didn't seem too close. I even felt reassured to know I wasn't the only one to have ever felt this devastated. However, when she got home from the hospital to the very loud quiet of an empty home and stared at the spot in the room where she'd last seen his body, I slammed the book shut. Lump lodged in throat, I stared hard at a hole in the well-worn and scuffed hardwood floor to try to stop myself from crying.

Too late. Tears fire-hosed out of my face.

So instead of reading it, I decided to just scan pages randomly. A terrible, really awful idea. When she describes seeing others after losing a spouse or child, "how these people looked when I see them unexpectedly . . . how exposed they seemed, how raw," I slammed the book shut again and pushed it away like a dead animal in my driveway. I was exposed. And raw—that scrubbed-hard-with-bristle-brush red-skinned rawness that made me hurt inside when even a soft breeze found me. It was exactly how Tía Marcia had looked at the hospital when she told me I was doing the right thing. And how everyone must see me now.

That was me at the grocery store or in the pickup line after school when I felt everyone's eyes on me. That's why I overheard them all saying, "Ohhhh, that poor woman" to each other behind my back.

I'd spent nearly forty years working very hard to never feel, be, or appear anywhere near raw, ruined, or vulnerable, but now no matter how hard I punched or kicked or ran or drank, I was all of them. Exposed. Fragile. Unstable.

Add stupid to the list, too. Because just what kind of asshole scans Didion, anyway? Apparently, me. I am that asshole, and I didn't want anything to do with that book for a while. And I couldn't help thinking she was still lucky. They'd had time. *They'd had time, lots of time.* Grief and loss aren't things we should compare or rank, weighing whose grief is harder or worse. But we do. It's hard not to. We also don't really know what grief is—but we all sure know it when we see it.

Merriam-Webster's Collegiate Dictionary defines grief as "a deep and poignant distress caused by or as if by bereavement," or "a cause of such suffering," or "an unfortunate outcome . . . mishap . . . trouble," or "annoying or playful criticism." I like the Oxford definition better because it gets to the guts of it with "intense sorrow." Grief is messy, visceral, deep, and harrowing suffering.

The word *loss* in this context has always sounded too sanitized and almost dismissive to me. Loss of a husband, parent, or child is the worst thing that can happen. The loss of your favorite watch? What a big gosh-darn bummer!

As I read through the grief-and-loss stuff, I noticed the word *trauma* sprinkled everywhere but used pretty generally to describe a sudden or untimely death.

However, while grief and trauma can be entirely separate and different experiences, we react similarly to them, so it can be hard to tell which is which. I wanted to pull apart what was a natural grief response that requires mostly time to heal and what was "the trauma," the part that I maybe needed to do something about. What did I have to look out for?

The books ranged from dense and heavily peer-reviewed and footnoted academic studies to collections of inspirational quotes in scripty fonts over pictures of clouds or beaches. I tried to dig into the trauma and PTSD specifics, but I found myself putting those books aside quickly. Clearly, I'd felt the impact of a trauma, but a "disorder" just didn't, you know, sound good at all. I wasn't diving under tables when a van drove by, right?

Grief was a "natural response" and apparently quite debilitating all on its own and has a very real effect on the body. Only half of my brain was working. Knowing that the ship-is-sinking craziness in my head and exhaustion I was feeling were perfectly natural and normal didn't help, though. I still *felt* that I was flying at half-mast. Worse, I learned that grief increases the risk of cancer, cardiac disease, and hypertension.

Now I have to call upon superhero-level executive-functioning skills to parent well and dig myself out of the hole we'd passively and incrementally dug ourselves into? Great. PTSD could take a number and get in line as far as I was concerned. I was already too busy getting my ass kicked by grief.

Then I went to the Kids and Grief sections. I was searching for answers, and I wanted to feel better myself, sure, but I really, really just wanted the kids to be OK. There were a lot of books about losing a pet or grandma but nothing that looked as though it would help me at the family grief group we were all going to attend next week.

The New Normal(ish)

I am not what I'd call a great candidate for group therapy. Connie and I had gotten a few referrals for a grief group for the kids. The place that offered a group session for kids of all ages through a hospice group seemed like a great thing, what we were supposed to do. This was offered at the same time as the parent group session down the hall, so they automatically signed me up.

I agreed to do the support group because I really wanted the kids to be in a group together as siblings. It was especially important because, after years of living among the blended family every other week or weekend schedule, they now lived in different houses full time except for one night a week. Connie and I rotated Friday-night sleepovers. In many ways, Lyric and Gabe understood how each other felt in ways that Connie and I just couldn't, so we wanted them to have a chance to grieve or talk about it *together*. And they'd get to do that with a group of other kids who'd lost a parent, guided by the nicest and most dedicated-looking group of childhood mental-health specialists you could hope for.

The first night, I brought the kids to the room where their session was to take place and went down the hall to my group. Sixteen single parents sat in an awkward circle. Except for the one lady whose husband had died of a heart attack, everyone else's spouse had died of cancer. Even though I knew that we had all lost spouses, that grief is grief, and that we were all here to support each other, I couldn't stop feeling impatient, dismissive, and angry that they all had it *so much easier* than I—and they didn't even appreciate it.

I knew I was being irrational, even unfeeling and cold, but I didn't feel bad about it. I had no capacity for feeling anything other than what I was feeling. I had no capacity for empathy at all. When Karla talked about how it had "happened so fast, eighteen months after the doctor first told us it was all over," I wished I could shoot lasers out of my eyes. A widower brought his new wife along with him to the group. (She, by the way, had been the nurse for his late wife.) When she held his hand as he fondly shared his and his wife's "last vacation together with the kids before she got too sick" story, all I wanted to do was lunge out of the metal folding chair, across the circle of safety, and reunite this guy with his first wife—who seemed to me to be pretty easy to replace.

How about zero warning? No time. No final vacation. No good-byes.

Regular Chanel would have had nothing but kindness and empathy for this woman and her kids. Grieving Chanel would have felt compassion for her. But Traumatized Chanel was seething inside. I knew I should be able to feel bad for him and even happy for them, but I couldn't. My version of raw and exposed might have looked angry, but I was just as fragile. All I could think of was my kids in the other room talking about their dad, how desperately I wanted his death to not ruin their lives, and how scared I was that I'd fuck it up and never feel like a whole person again.

During our break, I neared the kids' room and saw them spread out in the hallway with long pieces of butcher paper, the kind we used to draw on when I was in elementary school. I found Lyric and Gabe coloring in life-sized outlines of their bodies with grape- and cherry-scented markers.

Lyric had used a lot of different colors to draw her shirt and hair but had filled in her knees and thighs on both legs with black. I asked her about the colors she picked, and she replied that the black was "for all the times people lied to me," when everyone said her dad would be OK and he wasn't.

"They all lied," she said.

Gabe had used a variety of colors on his drawing, too, but had blackened his entire heart. My little baby, not even six years old, had drawn himself a black heart that smelled faintly of licorice.

I didn't say a word.

I went back to the adult meeting room and found my seat.

How did I not know they felt this way? What are we not doing that we're supposed to be doing?

We stowed the giant scrolls of paper, rolled up and snapped closed with rubber bands, in the backseat of the car for the ride home. They seemed content goofing off, flicking rubber bands at each other. I worked very hard to make my voice sound as if everything was fine.

"Hey, guys, can I ask you a question about tonight?"

I saw in the rearview mirror that I had their attention.

"It was great to see your art projects tonight. Thanks for showing them to me. Lyric, you used the word *lies* on your body project and said people didn't tell you the truth when your papa was in the hospital."

They both nodded.

"Well, I just wanted to tell you that I don't think anyone would lie to you on purpose. It was really hard to know what was going to happen. Your papa was in the hospital for a whole week, and it was very confusing for a while how big and bad his owie really was, because your papa . . . The doctors tried everything."

They didn't say anything.

I tried not to ramble. "And sometimes when we say 'everything is going to be OK,' it's because we really want it to be, but sometimes we're wrong or we don't have the right information. But I want you to know we wouldn't lie to you on purpose. We just didn't know, but as soon as we did we told you.

"I'm really sorry you felt as if we lied to you, but we wouldn't lie to you, ever, on purpose. And I'm promising you both I won't lie to you."

Silence in the back seat.

Then Gabe piped up. "So, can we get tacos now?"

I turned left toward the restaurant lights instead of right onto the highway twisting across the floating bridge toward home.

My job for the first year after the accident was to help the kids, go to therapy, and read up on grief, trauma, and healing. I was hell-bent on healing, which seemed to involve practicing happiness, gratitude, and mindfulness; I was determined to do everything possible to "fix" things. I tackled these the way someone would approach a short prison sentence or military basic training—something hard to be "gotten through." Hey, I had to start somewhere.

Once a regular routine was established (said everyone), I was supposed to feel relieved, but instead this new normal didn't fit right, as if I were wearing someone else's clothes and living on someone else's schedule.

I did have six hours to myself on school days now. The second-smartest decision I made (next to getting my will updated and buying another, bigger, life insurance policy) was hiring a male nanny. Chase came highly recommended even though he had no childcare experience. When he first came over to meet Gabe, they quickly clicked and went upstairs to play. Chase came down twenty minutes later wrapped up like a mummy, covered head to toe in toilet paper. I figured anyone who was a good sport and would play hard and be silly with my son would be perfect. We'd cover positive discipline approaches and car seats another time. I wanted Gabe to have an adult male buddy in his life.

Even with the routine and Chase, however, I felt more and more like I needed to get the hell out of town. By myself. A temporary jettison to a faraway, sunny place where no one knew anything about me, with a pool, sounded like exactly what I needed. I also felt conspicuously single and widowed in every inch of Seattle, so I wanted to see if I could pass as a regular person. I asked my parents to fly out to Seattle so I could get away. The only problem was that I hadn't been more than twenty minutes away from Gabe since the accident. When

I felt anxious that something could happen to him, I'd have to talk my catastrophic thinking down by repeating to myself dozens of times, *Nothing bad is happening right now, Chanel.* And that was when I was in the next room. This was a put-your-mask-on-first situation. The best way for me to not break wide open was to release a little pressure—a few states away, just to be safe.

I left my parents a twelve-page, single-spaced novella of "critical" instructions about Gabe, including details like, "If he says he wants a 'back-scratchy tornado style,' this means concentric circles about the size of an orange." Then I took off for five days in Palm Springs. A fabulous hotel, pool, sun, and no plans. Totally alone.

A few days later, I woke to a hand sliding over my naked thigh. Clothes, wine, and a few of the neon-painted, dehydrated fish that someone had brought back from a party at the Salton Sea and we'd tossed around like beach balls were strewn around my hotel room.

Oh god, I really hurt myself. Can you still get your stomach pumped the next morning after going on a bender?

The hand slid over my hip.

I went stiff, eyes wide, unsure if I was going to puke or panic.

OK. If I can just lie here for a second, focus only on breathing in and out of my mouth, I'll figure out if I'm having my first anxiety attack or if this is the most hungover I could possibly be without actually dying.

I managed to drag myself to the bathroom, turn on the shower, and sprawl out on the bathroom floor.

OK. Retrace. Great day at Joshua Tree, art show, lovely dinner, then the Halloween drink experiments with the bartender, the Violent Femmes acoustic talent show, late-night champagne next to the poolside fire pit. What was up with those fluorescent fish the guitar player had brought from a party out at the Salton Sea? Does that sound right?

A soft knock at the door.

Oh shit, someone is talking to me.

"Are you OK in there?"

"Yup! Great. Thanks. Just, uh, quick shower."

"Want some company?"

"Nope. All good. Out in a bit," I said.

Think, Chanel. What happened?

I'd said good night to the group, and the knee-bucklingly gorgeous friend of a friend walked me to my room. After stumbling into my room, I tossed my bag and shoes on the floor, and—yup—when I turned back around, his stunning eyes were still smiling at me. He stood at the open door. Holding two drinks in his hands. It had taken me two (very long) seconds to realize what was supposed to happen next. Duh. I considered considering the pros and cons, but I had already taken a half step back while thinking, *Oh, right. Yes! This is the part where people (who haven't been with only one person for fifteen years) have SEX!* I said, "So, are you a vampire and need a formal invitation to come inside?"

The formalities were quickly over. Any nervousness I'd had about what it'd be like to be with someone else after so long vanished. Some things really are just like riding a bike.

Now, hugging the toilet, I was a little pleased with myself. I'd managed to get myself mixed up in some advanced-level debauchery in a town full of retired people and gay men—in the off-season. For a brief time, I'd passed as a regular person, out in the world, living it up like a normal human.

It didn't last.

As wave after wave after wave of nausea rocked me, I whispered to the cool white tiles, "I want my life back. I want my life back."

After what felt like the longest, most gut-churning plane ride in history, I was back in Seattle with enough time to get home from the airport and go trick-or-treating with Gabe. Mom came along, but Dad wasn't feeling well, so he stayed home; she said he caught a cold, had been up most of the night, and wanted to rest before the plane ride home the next day.

The two or three stories we read before bed each night were often the usual suspects, Dr. Seuss's *Hop on Pop* was often in the top three, along with a Clone Wars book, and anything with a dog—

especially a golden retriever—was always a big hit. *Zen Shorts* was making the rounds again, and while we usually whipped through it pretty quickly, we often talked about Stillwater the Panda Bear making friends with the three kids next door. Between chapters were little retellings of old fables. One of my favorites, "The Farmer and the Horse," by an anonymous writer (some say a Taoist), is said to be thousands of years old. It is told many ways but usually close to something like this:

The old farmer lived with his family and worked his crops for many years. One day his prized horse ran away.

Upon hearing the news, his neighbors came to visit. "Such bad luck," they said sympathetically. "Maybe," the farmer replied.

The next morning the horse returned, bringing with it three wild horses.

"How wonderful," the neighbors exclaimed.

"Maybe," replied the old man.

The following day, his son tried to ride one of the untamed horses, was thrown, and broke his leg. The neighbors again came to offer their sympathy, calling the accident a misfortune.

"Maybe," answered the farmer.

The day after, military officials came to the village to draft young men into the army. Seeing that the son's leg was broken, they passed him by. The neighbors congratulated the farmer on how well things had turned out.

"Maybe," said the farmer.

The next morning, after I dropped Gabe off at school, my mom sat in the kitchen looking anxious. No luggage in sight. No to-go cups for coffee being poured. This was not the regular "get there two hours before" airport departure routine.

"Your father is moving slowly," she said.

That wasn't exactly news, because he was always the last one out of the house, but she said he was having trouble getting dressed. She'd mentioned that he had been sick, and I'd heard him coughing, but this was weird.

Mom was clearly nervous and working on keeping it together, but she said he wanted to go home. She was clearly going with this plan, so I stood there wondering whether the daughter should step in or follow their lead.

When I suggested options, the only one seemed to be that I get them to airport so he could on the plane. He was insistent. So we called about finding assistance to get to the gate from the baggage check-in.

It was clear that Dad wanted to get on that damn plane and get home, to his doctor, to his state, and likely not go back into the same ER or ICU his daughter had seen her own husband die in just three months before. He would not be seeing any doctors in Seattle.

The "right thing" to do next wasn't black and white, and I wondered if I would have done something else if the world still hadn't seemed fogged over and if I hadn't still been hungover from Palm Springs.

Maybe.

We didn't know that what seemed like a really bad cold had turned into a serious case of pneumonia and that by the time he landed, they would need to see a doctor right away, as in urgent care. Even though we didn't know it was that bad, shouldn't I have tried to do something else? Perhaps. I had to think about what getting my shit together really meant, especially since I had to do it all over again and all on my own.

I knew I couldn't get my old life back, and while José and I had what I'd call a successful marriage that seemed to be getting better with each year, it most certainly wasn't perfect. However, I had no control over what had happened, and nothing could be undone. What I did next, or now, was one of the few things that I did have any say over. I would have done our whole life over again, but from where I was sitting post-accident, I would have done a few things differently, and not just the wills and life insurance stuff, either. Now I had some hindsight and a whole new rest of my life to try to get right.

My parents had always been there for me to rely on, but now they were getting older, and I would have to step in at some point to help them, whether that point was a week away or over ten years from now. What happened if one of them got sick and needed help? I had a really big mortgage. Gabe was in school now. My job was high-stress project management with clients who demanded last-minute changes meaning frequent late nights.

José and I had often felt that we could barely make it through the day when there were two of us. Now I had *more* responsibilities, I was *more* vulnerable than I had been, and had *less* help. Could I figure out a way to pull all that off? All alone?

Maybe.

As it turns out, getting my shit together was getting to be a bigger deal than just figuring out what I'd done wrong in the past so I could avoid the same set of mistakes all over again. Did I have a whole new set of what-ifs and oh-shit scenarios to think through? Yes, perhaps I really did.

Drink, Fuck, Run

Now that the universe had blown a whistle into the middle of my life and called a do-over, what did I want my life to look like? Traveling around the world for a year or leaving my life for the Pacific Coast Trail weren't options for a single mom, but I still felt there was some magical combination of things I could do to fix myself and come out the other end of my grief, but I hadn't nailed the recipe yet. Perhaps the missing ingredient I sought was the old-school kind of fun—staying out late drinking, dancing, and making out with people on the dance floor.

So my plan to feel better for the rest of this year was to let myself do whatever helped me feel alive, as long as Gabe's and Lyric's well-being were always the priority and their health and safety were never compromised. My rule was any adult activities would have to help me have fun in my life but not avoid dealing with my life. Heroin was clearly out; extra workouts and going out were way in. Since I couldn't have my old life back, I would insist on prioritizing fun and more pleasure while forging ahead into this new one.

After Gabe was born and I was trying to get back in shape, I could barely manage one push-up. Now, when the annual Seattle Marathon rolled around on Thanksgiving weekend, I did pull-ups. In fact, one day Chase teased that I was starting to look like one of the women on *American Gladiators*, which got Gabe laughing. He ran around the house with mock Incredible Hulk arms, pretending to make a snack or do laundry and saying, "Mama is hulking out!" It was true, and I felt great. The last fifteen pounds of baby weight was gone, and I looked amazing. This was also around the time the cougar thing was hitting a popularity peak, and I'll say that was very, very helpful. I was forty and in the best shape of my life. Feeling strong and healthy and sexy helped balance out the crushing sorrow and loneliness.

"Feeling all the feelings" might be what I had to do, but it still didn't feel very good. I didn't like it when the phone rang, or there were changes to plans, or there was a surprise I had to deal with immediately. When I was running (or kicking or punching), I imagined that every breath or step was helping me rewire my broken heart and brain and be a whole person again, because otherwise I worried I'd end up day-drinking at a bar. I wasn't good at feeling bad, scared, or sad, but when a feeling came it pulled me wherever its current dictated; I had no choice but to just let it. Oh, and I bought a Ducati motorcycle. Was it a smart choice? Certainly not. Did I do it anyway? Absolutely.

These were the kinds of decisions I looked forward to talking through with Delia at my weekly counseling session. If Jamie Lee Curtis had an edgier sister who used to party a lot in college but has since found enlightenment, it would be Delia.

"So, how do you know I'm not depressed?" I asked.

"Well, weren't you just telling me about your holiday plans?"

"Yes. We're going to Mexico to reset for the holidays, and I signed us all up for surf lessons and found a great house right by the beach."

"And how are you feeling about the trip?"

"I'm actually looking forward to getting away. Holidays have always been stressful with all these rules about who to see on which day and lists of who wanted what present. I'm excited to have it be easy and someplace sunny, maybe start a new tradition."

"Tell me more about new traditions."

As I talked about redefining holidays, taking more vacations, and making sure we traveled and how great it would be for the kids, I also knew that was exactly what I wanted and thought it would be great for *me*.

"What's self-care and what's just plain selfish? How do I know this is just the grief talking, that I'm not depressed, that something isn't wrong with me?"

"Your grief is deep, but you and José had a loving, supportive, and positive relationship. You don't have a history of depression, and even if you did, the feeling of depression that is tied to your terrible loss and appropriate grief is not the same as complicated grief, being clinically depressed, or suffering from depression."

I took that in and let it simmer.

"Chanel, let me put it this way. Depressed people usually don't make exciting plans for the future."

As the clock ticked closer to the one-year marker, I needed to be as far away from my old life as possible. I felt stuck, half still untangling from my "before" life while the other half was trying to warp speed into the future. A part of me realized that I was racing forward to get past all the "firsts," as though there would be some kind of emotional finish line I could break through. I thought getting through to the other side of the first year would offer relief, or a pass, or something that would change so it would get easier.

How does one mark the one-year anniversary of a death? And how could we balance it with love and respect for José but also acknowledge that we were the ones still here, still alive? It wasn't exactly what I would have planned to honor José's death, but if I was going to be heartbroken, I might as well do it while surfing in the sun in Sayulita. I packed our bathing suits and as many beach toys as I could find and got Gabe and me out of Seattle a week before the anniversary.

Gabe and I had arrived in Sayulita, a cute beach town in Mexico, a few days ago. We were staying with my expat friend Lori; her partner, Beto; and their young son. We'd met earlier that year over Christmas break on a surfing trip. Her partner was a great surfer and helped Gabe and Lyric stand up on the board in no time, so we started calling him "the surf whisperer." I was taking them out to dinner at a sushi place closer to Puerto Vallarta when they mentioned that a friend of theirs remembered us from the beach and wanted to meet me. That night. For a drink. And Lori and Beto would watch Gabe for me.

"Beto, seriously, going out on a *date* on the first anniversary of my husband's death isn't exactly what I was thinking."

Beto teased me. "Ahhh, *Cha-nell*, we're already having dinner and he wants to meet at nine, so no worry it's a 'date,' because it's a tie-up."

"Tie-up?"

"You know, you are hitching?"

"Getting hitched is slang for getting married," I said, even more confused.

"Ahh, how you say, you . . ."

"A hookup, Beto. It's called a hookup," laughed Lori.

"Yeaa-ah!" Beto pulled out his most charming smile, which is rather epic. "Hookup. It's not a date. *Sí*? So *es* no problem."

I half-argued for another minute, mostly for show. I realized that I really could use a good, uh, distraction.

"OK, Lori. I'll meet him, for an hour."

She smirked back, clearly unconvinced.

Beto was already on the phone. "Ahhhhh . . . *¿Qué onda? Jajaja. Síííí.*"

With Gabe safely tucked into bed for the night at Lori and Beto's house, I made my way to the town plaza. It was steam-room muggy, and I was killing it in my tropics-sized sundress (read: teensy). Meeting someone for a date felt spontaneous and thrilling, but what happened next wasn't a big surprise.

"*¿Dónde vas a vivir?*" he asked in a whisper.

I'd dozed off. My half-open eyes looked at the mango tree visible through the open window.

Where am I going to live? I'd mentioned perhaps moving. Good question.

I didn't answer.

Early morning light filtered into the room. I had about two hours to sneak back into the house before everyone woke up.

"*Te gusta Mexico, sí?*" he asked with a sly smile.

"*Pues, aquí puedo ir a surfear cada día.*"

In Mexico, I could surf each day and have more nights like the previous one. At the little beach past the cemetery, he'd held me perfectly, my hair tangled in his hands, and kissed so deeply I felt turned inside out. It was still early in the rainy season, but the mud was already ankle deep in places on the unpaved roads, so he bent down on one knee and insisted he carry me on his back until the paved road began. One hand gripped my sandals and the other wound tight around his neck.

I could get used to this. Why not stay in Mexico? Gabe could go to the international school and become fluent in Spanish.

The prospects were: go home and figure out how to reverse-engineer my life, or stay in bed with a man with soft, massage-strong hands, who smells of the jungle, the wet taste of it sinking into my skin. Right then, Mexico was an easy win. But it also felt too much like pulling the ripcord on my life when I was still inside a perfectly good plane. As the fan whirred a barely there breeze on my skin and I was fed perfectly ripe mango in bed and . . . well, perfect moments like that don't come often. That's what vacations and getting away are for, but how much of my "real" life could look more like an "ideal" one?

José had said frequently, "You don't have to do anything you don't want to do." Which he often did while I was talking about projects that were driving me crazy or obligations that I felt too tired or over-committed to meet. Those words would get my face bunched up in that overfunctioning you-don't-get-it way as I explained that I *had* to show up for the preschool fundraising meeting and *had* to take on that stressful client because we needed the money. Maybe he'd been more right than I'd realized. What would it look like *if I didn't do anything I didn't want to do?*

Walking up the steep hill back to the house, I took in the panoramic morning view of the whole bay coming to life. It felt like my brain was having a spinout, like the one on the grass a year ago at the hospital before the sprinklers came on and I met with Darrell and really talked about quality of life and what that means at the end of life. But when you think about it, we're really all on a quality-of-life plan right now; some people's are just much longer than others'. How much of my old life is dead and gone and never coming back? What are the things I don't want back? How would I write a midlife quality-of-life plan?

> *How alive can I be?*
> *How much better can I get?*
> *What is most important to me?*
> *What is unacceptable?*
> *How do I describe being able to meaningfully engage in the world?*
> *How do I define my quality of life now?*
> *What does home look like now?*
> *What does Gabe need most?*

One year and a day after I'd removed medical support, I was now packing suitcases with sandy swimsuits and a dozen Mexican wrestling luchador outfits and stuffing Gabe's backpack with as many Playmobils and comic books as possible, to keep him entertained on the flight back to Seattle. We'd go home to the house I hated to sell but didn't want to live in and couldn't afford anyway. It was home but also the very *expensive* remains of my former life. I'd allocated a year to heal and reset, and time was up. The life insurance money I'd allocated to fund a year off from work was gone too.

Even if I didn't have all of the answers a year later, at least I did have some good days. The bad days weren't as frequent, so perhaps I had learned a few things. I'd certainly made some discoveries: (1) grief sex is totally a thing, and (2) never underestimate the power of a man with soft eyes and strong hands.

I'd also discovered that José wasn't the one who never replaced the toilet paper or the only one who left dirty dishes in the sink. It wasn't because he didn't vacuum thoroughly enough that there was always dog hair everywhere. It turns out that he hadn't been shrinking my clothes in the dryer; I'd gained weight. It wasn't on him that we'd not saved well enough. We'd both signed up for stretching ourselves financially on a new house and still ate out just as often.

The motorcycle wasn't smart, sure, but I didn't ride it in the city much (where you're most likely to get hit by a car), and I wore protective gear, so I argued that I was mitigating risk and also having something that was just for me even though it didn't make sense. Saving every extra scrap of money I had and putting it into savings was the right thing to do. Maybe dumping every cent I had into paying down the mortgage was smarter and safer—or just one more bad financial choice. I didn't know, but I didn't want to pretend that "doing the right thing" meant that nothing bad would ever happen again.

The housing-market crash meant listing the house for less than we'd paid, but my options were a financial slow-bleed by a very high mortgage for years and years till the market recovered, or brace for a sucker punch hard enough to get the wind knocked out of me and just get it over with. We had been living one accident or illness away from total catastrophe, and I never wanted to be so vulnerable ever again. At the same time, if my whole life can go away at any minute, I want to enjoy it and do things, not play it safe. I had been choosing sanity over security, because every way I did the math, it didn't seem that I could afford both.

However, adding any more risk to our family's financial security sounded unconscionable: I was all Gabe had. But if *everything* can all go away at any minute and there is risk everywhere, even if you try to do "everything right," there are no guarantees that anything will work out or go as you hoped or planned. How do you carve out a life where you aren't afraid to really be alive? How do you raise a kid to feel safe in such an unsafe world? I needed to make some decisions or at least get us one step closer to what was next, even if I didn't know what that was.

Missed Connections

It was some sort of dinner gathering, a wedding reception maybe. Sitting at a round table halfway across the room, he's smiling at me.

I smile back as I make my way past happy greetings and warm hellos from everyone to reach him. The quick hugs and "excuse me just a minute" distractions slow me down. He moves to stand as I near.

As I put my arms around him, in the half second before we touch.

Do our bodies remember each other?

I sink into him.

We fit.

At first like sand locked into place but then like when light fills a room.

with no spaces in between.

The pull from behind comes and I melt away.

I don't open my eyes to hold on.

Until each piece of light fades.

PART III Always

The most difficult times for many of us
are the ones we give ourselves.

—PEMA CHÖDRÖN, *WHEN THINGS FALL APART:*
HEART ADVICE FOR DIFFICULT TIMES

The Overview Effect

When astronauts return from space, they often report a strange feeling they can't shake—a euphoria or an awakening—from being able to see differently what had always been there. NASA astronaut Ron Garan described the Earth he saw from space as a "stunning, fragile oasis," yet he was consumed by sadness and "hit in the gut with an undeniable, sobering contradiction." Author Frank White called this phenomenon the "overview effect." Observing from a great distance, or as Joni Mitchell sings, "from both sides now," Garan recognized that a "little paper-thin layer is all that protects every living thing on Earth from death."

As I rounded my journey through the dark side of grief, my view of the world was similarly transformed. It was beautiful. So much bigger than me. And terrifying. We are all so very, very small, I realized. That's why any sort of convenient, binary, bright-side, silver-linings saying ("making something good out of something bad," "beauty from pain," or "the gifts of loss") made me cringe. I'd changed. Everything had changed. As Buddhist teacher Jack Kornfield has written, "Our hearts can grow strong at the broken places." It might be simple, but it certainly isn't easy.

I'd done as good a job as I knew how of slowly getting my life back together while still keeping the plane in the air. But now that the emergency seemed to have passed, it felt as though really getting my

shit together meant that I needed to land the plane, not just keep circling the landing strip. That felt much, much harder.

*Where do we go? Where should I land? What if I land too soon or
in the wrong place? How do I know?*

"Edit, edit, edit," said my real estate agent, Brad, walking through
the house. "This is what I say to everyone. Just clean everything out."

*Fine. I want to get rid of most of it anyway. Whatever it takes to
get out of this house.*

"We'll put some art over here." He pointed to the big wall opposite
the sliding glass doors that lead to the side garden.

"And we'll have to box all this up," he said, indicating the heaps of
toys and plastic crates of LEGOs.

While jotting down staging notes, I wondered if I was doing the
right thing.

I had thought that getting through the first year would change something, that I'd know what the future looked like and feel better. But the
future was still murky, and I didn't feel better. I felt *different*. The gravity wouldn't pull me as low for as long as it did in those first months,
but in other ways I felt more alone and left behind than when I was
just merely trying to make it through the day. I wouldn't say life settled
down so much as it eventually began to spread out. I would joke that
after the lasagnas stopped coming was when I really could have used
the lasagnas. The grief was less acute but also more *cumulative*.

Saying I was in denial of José's death seemed, well, dumb. There
were moments in those first weeks when for a slice of a second I
thought I saw him out of the corner of my eye or had a flash of an
urge to tell him something funny someone said at his funeral. But
I *knew* he was dead. I saw his body and cashed the life insurance
check. He hadn't come home in well over a year now. Was I in such
denial that I couldn't see how I'd become trapped in a death-denial-
anger-bargaining loop that had me second-guessing every decision?
Werner Herzog's voice played in an almost continual track in my
head, questioning each financial choice or life plan with existential
musings: *Maybe yes the house must go but perhaps no if you're now*

just too sad to know what is best. Only you can know but how can
you know is the larger question.

How was I supposed to know? So I made a pact with the Erins
and asked them to let me know when my ruminating was making
already hard decisions even more difficult or when I just wasn't thinking clearly. They didn't love the motorcycle and were skeptical about
the guy I was starting to date, but both agreed that the house was a
huge financial burden. Selling it, even at a double-digit loss because of
the housing market crash, and moving to a smaller, more affordable
house sounded like a reasonable plan.

It helped a lot to hear them say that, but I still worried that I was
being impulsive, irrational, and dumb about the future. What if the
housing market cycled back sooner than expected? What if my desire
to get the hell away from that house was making me act irrationally?
But losing money, even a substantial amount, seemed far easier to
stomach than what we'd been through in the last year or so. Really,
what was an additional financial loss when I'd already lost pretty
much everything?

I'd sell the house, even if it felt scary, because trying to do the safe
thing didn't bring any guarantees, either.

I also asked the Erins to alert me, and someone else, like my mom
or Delia, if I was finally going off the deep end.

They said I wasn't.

Or hadn't.

Or hadn't yet?

Upstairs in the office, Brad was wrapping up. "The house looks great.
Just add some flowers and get rid of the extra furniture we talked
about, and, well, all of the stuff that seems . . . too personal."

"Sure," I agreed.

He walked closer. "Like the family pictures. We want to make the
house look like it could be anyone's home."

"Do we leave some photos to make it look more . . . homey?" I
asked.

"Well, maybe a few. But all of the José pictures? There are just so many. He's in every room. It's like he's following you around the house."

"I left all the pictures to make it seem more natural for the kids. That he's still their dad." It was important to me that José didn't get disappeared from our lives as if he'd never been there.

"It's just for when it goes on the market," Brad reassured me.

"No, I know." I sighed, even though I totally got it. "Whatever I need to do to sell the house, I'll do it, Brad. It feels like I'm living among the remains of my former life. I have to get out of here."

The house was on the market for weeks with marginal interest. The holidays were approaching, a notoriously slow time to sell, when I got a "see if they bite" number. I bit. It was the only offer I'd gotten, and I was tired of drifting in limbo.

Sanity or Security

As I walked into the far-too-large two-car garage, I realized I had already let the house go a long time ago. I surveyed all the things stacked along the walls that we'd worked to buy so that we could buy more shelves to put it all on. Why did we have four different types of garden hoses, a once-used bread maker, the old baby jogger, and boxes and boxes of stuff from an old life that I couldn't have anymore?

I vowed to never again let my life slip into cruise control. To never be the person with seven shovels I didn't use living a too-tight life in a not-right house. We'd wanted this new home more than we really needed it. The old house had been big enough, and the mortgage had been less than half of this one. As much as we talked about how less is more and prioritized vacations over stuff, we still had a lot of crap. Take-out dinners and treat-yourself treats had slid into busy, bored, and habitual spending. We'd fallen into the American dream Ponzi scheme of getting, buying, having more. Too much.

So I announced on Facebook that I was moving and the Big Give-away was about to begin. I had tons of stuff that I didn't need and others would likely use and want. They could have it for free on the unlikely condition that one day I could ask for it back if I needed it again. I assumed I wouldn't, but just in case a year or two later I needed a lawnmower or giant Crock-Pot, I wouldn't have to spend money on something I'd just given away. I posted a bunch of pictures, someone said, "Me, please!" and then came to get it. I loaded up friends' cars and watched loads of our wedding presents and garage-sale finds drive away with happy new owners. Matt and Holly got the articulated ladder; Connie and Jake got the leather armchair; Sarah got all the gardening tools; Paul and Wendy got the electric lawn-mower.

Years later I have a (now private) album of photos I can look at if I want to know who got the pressure cooker, but I haven't once wanted or needed any of it back.

It took months to sell the house but only a week to get rid of so much stuff. I stood in a completely empty garage. I gave it all away. Even the shelves that used to hold everything were packed in a truck headed down the alley to be used for a friend's new consignment-and-collectibles store. José and I thought the new house and nicer stuff would make us happier. It didn't.

I raised my coffee mug in salute and appreciated a not-un-comfortable feeling of surrender that felt more like letting go than giving up or giving in. Like the end of a deep exhale when you are out of air but you realize that, even though you're empty, you can pause, hold, and wait for another second or two. I was relieved. I felt there was more room for me—but damn, I always thought I'd figure out how to make bread in that bread machine.

Perhaps trying to make one choice at a time, to the best of my abil-ity, was as good as it was going to get.

Did I want to sell the house? *Yes.*

Did I have some apprehension that I might regret it in the fu-ture? *Yes.*

Should I let doubt and possible future regret stop me from moving forward the best way I know how, with the information I have right now? *No! God, no.*

I looked around the house that I had to vacate in forty days. José and I had always talked about moving to the San Francisco Bay area or somewhere warmer once Lyric was out of high school. I figured I *could* move now, but moving to a new city where I didn't have as large a support network and where Gabe and Lyric wouldn't see each other nearly as much sounded like a bad idea. Gabe was already very upset about selling the house, and "more sun in the winter" wasn't a good reason to drag him away from everyone and every place he knew. So we would stay close and ride out the storm. I planned to rent a smaller house, closer to Gabe's school, with three bedrooms so Lyric would have a room. And a fenced-in yard for the dog. Dressing for weather instead of yelling at the rain was a choice, too.

What Would Cher Do?

After the first year and into the second and third, I was better able to see how the grief worked when it hit. The month and a half from my birthday to our wedding day to the anniversary of his death was always a tricky stretch, oddly much more so than Thanksgiving or even Christmas. I still flinched when the phone rang, and if I didn't know who was calling, I didn't pick up. I never listened to voicemail. When the mailbox filled up with dozens and dozens of messages, I just deleted them all.

All those books about changing your life, midlife crisis, being happier or less *fill-in-the blank* didn't seem as fluffy and scornworthy as they did that first year or two. My earlier attitude—a sour, eye-rolling "How hard can it be to get 'happier' when your spouse isn't dead and you're just . . . bored? Boo-fucking-hoo!"—softened dramatically, even if it didn't vanish entirely.

Even though I wouldn't say I had PTSD, I started to practice saying "trauma-impacted" out loud. Despite my best efforts to be a "regular" compassionate person again, there were moments, over drinks with friends or lunch with coworkers, when someone would share a hard story and I'd felt nothing. Part of me was sympathetic and acknowledged that we all have our struggles and said, "Sure, that must be hard for you." The Buddhist in me had to work overtime, resolutely and patiently ignoring the Bootstrapper, who sometimes wanted to yell that people really needed to suck it up and get on with it. *It's not like you're the one bleeding in the middle of the road. Sheesh!*

Taking a mixed-martial-arts approach to my mental health meant that I had to do some sucking up, as laundry and groceries needed doing and buying, as well as another round of counseling with Delia and nurturing my spiritual side. I listened to audiobooks, started writing, and went to a meditation retreat—and more and more often when the bad times hit, I knew I could ride it out until the moment passed, which was kind of the point anyway. But sometimes the present moment sucked a whole lot, and I just wasn't interested in feeling every sucky second of it, so I'd have to try to imagine sitting down and talking to these spiritual leaders in person.

I envisioned walking through the dusty paths of Deer Park Monastery with Thích Nhất Hạnh and asking him for advice. Sometimes he'd smile, then bow, and say something like, "My dear, you already have the answers you seek inside you." And I'd smile back and say, "Yes. Yes, Thầy, I do. Thank you."

Sometimes when I'd want to know how I could be happy and feel better, he'd only walk slowly along, so slowly, and point at clouds. Eventually, he'd stop in front of an old palm tree and say to no one in particular, "This tree looks as though it suffers and is dying, but when you look deeply, you see the new green leaves at the top. Because this tree knows there will be dry seasons, it has strong, deep roots to find water for nourishment and create new growth."

Which was lovely, but if I wasn't feeling particularly leafy up top or deep-rooted below, I'd say, "OK, nice tree metaphor, but come on. It's easy for you to sit around and contemplate tea leaves and the breeze all day—and take forever to walk just two city blocks, by the way—but how's that going to actually help?" One doesn't simply walk into a monastery and kick back for a chat with a world-renowned peace activist and then call him a stupid monk, but my imagination didn't seem to care.

Other times, I'd set the timer for five teensy minutes to meditate, take a seat, then get up to get the dog out of the room, because all seventy pounds of her wanted to be in my lap anytime I got near the floor. I'd name feelings that interrupted my breathe-in-two-three-four and out-two-three-four mindfulness practice: *impatient, impatient, tired, tired, tired, hungry, hungry, hungry, oh crap, I have to send that email to . . . oh whoops, OK, distracted, distracted, distracted, and . . . in-breath. And out-breath. In. Out. Oh, angry, yep, angry, angry, super angry, ANGRY, ANGRY.*

Meditation is called a practice because it *takes* a lot of practice. Dr. Bessel van der Kolk, a leader in the trauma field, has said, "Practice makes progress." It was hard to stick with, but at least my five-minute baby meditating was trying something. As Pema Chödrön teaches, acknowledging how shitty you feel and what fertile ground for awareness it offers you is far more productive than running away from the truth—but man, such fertile ground really stinks.

We humans can be quite good at surviving and thriving despite overwhelmingly hard things. Shit goes wrong. Way wrong—but the sun will rise tomorrow. That outlook helped me to have some perspective, but it didn't tell me what I should do. In fact, knowing superhuman resilience had enabled people to climb Everest helped me in *zero possible ways* when Gabe's teacher called (again) to discuss the fact he was talking back and unable to focus in class. In those intense situations, I'd wonder, *What would Ruth Bader Ginsburg or Oprah or Maxine Waters do right now?* Or, really desperate, I'd call in the big guns: *What would Cher do?*

Cher had very helpful advice. If the moment called for taking up space, getting on with the show, or getting loud and swearing to be heard, she'd say something like, "You know, sweetie, sometimes you just gotta say 'Fuck it' and throw something."

Any criticism of the kids tripped my hypervigilance alarms. I struggled to manage a stressful, full-time job, but the kids were expected to behave and perform at school like all the other kids who weren't experiencing a loss and working through trauma? At some meetings with Gabe's teachers, I would pinch a little half-moon in the soft skin webbing between my pointer finger and thumb under the table and focus on nodding, smiling, and thanking them for their time and feedback. At others, I had to call bullshit on uninformed opinions from folks whose hearts may have been in the right place but who didn't have any training or experience with grief and trauma, not to mention childhood grief and trauma.

Didn't they know to never call a mom who'd recently experienced a traumatic, unexpected death and start a conversation with, "Something happened at school today"? I'd assume my kid was hurt or dead. The "something" they were referring to was the fact that the way Gabe talked about his father's death was making people uncomfortable.

Cher was not impressed by these phone calls. In fact, Cher was dressing up, Oscars style, for a well-informed fight. Cher did not care that in the Pacific Northwest we are expected to have passive-aggressive, mild-mannered, soft-spoken disagreements. I raised my voice and was asked a few times to lower it because other people could hear us. Cher didn't care who could hear us.

Cher always comes prepared, so before a meeting at the school I'd spend ten minutes googling "childhood grief and trauma" in the parking lot in case there were any new, specific studies or advice to quote. "Actually," I'd say, "research on childhood grief suggests that talking about his dad is a normal and positive way to normalize his loss and doesn't mean he is depressed or trying to scare the other children."

The response was usually, "We appreciate what you've gone through, but other kids or parents are uncomfortable."

That word again. *Uncomfortable*?

"My kid has a father, a father who loved him, and just because his father happens to be dead doesn't mean he doesn't get to talk about him. Not talking about what actually happened, or pretending that death isn't a real thing, is not healthy. If Gabe asks me in a worried voice what happens if I die and I say, 'Oh, don't worry, honey, I'm not going to die,' that's not helpful. It's not true. And he knows it. He is asking to be reassured that he will be safe and loved and wants to know whom he will live with."

The real issue wasn't that Gabe talked about his dad or felt sad sometimes but that healing and resilience are supposed to look a certain way. We were supposed to be graceful, gracious, and strong in the face of loss, because that's the response to grief that people feel comfortable being around. When it gets messy, loud, unfamiliar, or too personal? Not so much.

Guide:
What Makes a Difference

When death bombs a big hole into the middle of you and your whole family, you will feel like you're operating in a half-oxygen atmosphere for quite some time—weeks, absolutely; months, most certainly; years, most likely. It takes a long, long time. It took me about four years to feel mostly like myself again (and not just me-doing-OK-after-my-husband's-death). If some of the most common advice for what you should do after a death sounds most relevant in the immediate aftermath, let me assure you, it remains relevant for a long time afterward and will continue to help you take care of yourself or others.

When life goes sideways for the people we love, we're not always sure what to do, say, or suggest that will actually be useful. Everyone is different, and there is no one right thing, but trying is always appreciated, and helping makes a difference. It makes a *big* difference.

How to Help Yourself

Self-Care

This is the advice I wish I could have given myself.

1. Put your oxygen mask on first. Adrenaline can keep you going for a little while, but then it's gone. This is a marathon, an ultra-marathon, not a sprint.
2. Assign captains. Organize the shit out of the important stuff and ask one person to captain each category (childcare, housework, financial donations, food and meal help, etc.). Everything else? Meh.
3. Ask for help. Asking for help can save you hours in a day and get projects done that you'd never have time for. Ask!
4. Accept offers of help. Letting people help you will make them feel better. They want to and you need it. Say yes.
5. Eat, sleep, sweat. Sleep enough. Eat enough. Move your body. Every day. Consider this your job. Period. That is all.

How to Help Others

Friendship Amnesty

Your friend will not be a good friend for a while. You will still be friends, of course, but getting through the day and keeping your head above water does not leave a lot of room for reaching out, remembering birthdays, writing down lunch plans, returning voicemails in a timely manner—all that stuff. Or, depending on whether it's a good day or a bad day, her usual behavior could just be inconsistent; she may flake on you half the time. This is normal and should be expected. Do not take it personally. And please, keep showing up for your friend. She needs you. So remember you can:

- Reset your expectations.
- Find support elsewhere.
- Be patient.

Pitch In

Offer to take on as much of the day-to-day stuff as you can. Be mindful about not invading anyone's space or taking over the household, but even in good weeks I was behind on shopping, laundry, errands, and cleaning. It made a huge difference in the first weeks (and months) after José died that friends and family helped keep my fridge stocked and laundry done. Huge. When you do offer help, keep these three things in mind:

Be proactive.

> *Do: Organize in easy-to-manage individual chunks.*
> *Avoid: Making assumptions or taking control of the house.*

Be as specific as you can.

> *Do: "I'd love to swing by before work and walk the dogs."*
> *Avoid: "Can I help with the dogs at all?"*

Anticipate recurring needs.

> *Do: "I know school is starting soon. I'm already on the way*
> *to work in the morning, so can I drop off your kids for the*
> *first few weeks?"*
> *Avoid: "Do you need some help with the kids' school stuff?"*

Keep offering.

Grief, loss, and healing do not look like a Lifetime channel movie. It takes longer than you think and will not look the way you thought it might. After a few months, the offers (and lasagnas) stop coming, but for years your friend will appreciate a "thinking of you" note on a birthday or anniversary. Here are thirty things you can offer or help organize in the days, weeks, or years after:

Do the laundry.	Create a dog-walking schedule.
Clean the house.	Take care of the yard or plants.
Organize and mail thank-you cards.	Take care of pets.
Deliver regular, scheduled meals.	Gather and sort mail.
Create a food-delivery schedule.	Take walks or hikes outside, in nature.
Take kids to movies or a park.	Pay bills or insurance, or give budget help.
Schedule and take walks together.	Do homework with kids.
Arrange or offer home-repair work.	Babysit kids.
Get your friend out of the house.	Look for counselors and resources.
Schedule exercise time.	Suggest researching grief resources.
Arrange and pay for wellness support, like a massage, a spa day, or bodywork.	Help gather and organize documents.
Set up a fund to raise money.	Research legal questions.
Pay for an exercise or movement class.	Give little gifts or comfort items.
Show up and listen.	Give toys, puzzles, art projects for kids.
Remember the death anniversary, and send a note or a story.	Keep showing up, gently check in as time goes on. Grief does not end.

What to Say

There is no perfect thing to say. Therefore you can't come up with it, so take the pressure off of yourself. Even if you find some magical combination of words that helps your bereaved friend laugh or smile for a moment, there is literally nothing you can do to take away the grief or somehow carry even a part of it. But you can be there. That helps a lot. You can help make a grieving person's life easier and less tiring. And by being specific, you'll make it easier to accept your help. For example, you could ask:

Why don't you call me when you get home tonight?
May I shop (cook, drive to or attend appointments, take notes)?
Are there any friends or family members you'd like me to call?
Are there any other phone calls I can make for you?
If it's OK with you, I'd love to . . . ?

What *Not* to Say

Knowing what to say is tricky. I've gotten it wrong myself, really wrong. I've also witnessed others get it way, wayyyy wrong. Here is some tried-and-true advice for not saying something you'll regret, and to avoid feeling like an asshole, please avoid these:

"At Least . . ."

If anything you are saying to a grieving person starts with the words "at least," you should probably not say it. Seriously, don't say:

"At least . . . you had a few years together."
"At least . . . Gabe wasn't still an infant when he died."
"At least . . . you weren't there."
"At least . . . he/she died doing something they loved."

Several well-intentioned people said these statements to me at one time or another and they *did not help*. Ever. When a friend said, "At least José died doing something he loved," I replied, "That's a nice thought . . . but I don't really remember *getting run over by a van* being at the top of José's favorites list!" She felt awful, horrified, and embarrassed. I felt awful, irritated, and mean. And the friendship never really recovered.

Platitudes

"Everything happens for a reason."
"She was too good for this world."
"His work here is done."

You might believe this to be true, and it may help *you* feel less afraid, but no one has ever told me that any attempt to make them feel better with a thin layer of nice-sounding sentiments made it hurt any less. Even if you share a common faith, the general advice is to stay in the present moment, acknowledge that the person is hurting, and avoid clichés that could make someone feel that their grief is being mini-mized or dismissed.

Comparing

I understand that you're trying to reach out and relate, and I believe you deeply loved and grieved for your grandmother, but I wasn't able to give a shit about what flowers you picked for her funeral, nor did I have *any* capacity to care about your feelings. I have grieved over pets, grandparents, distant relatives, and even strangers. Those feel-ings are real, but the right time to share those stories is not with some-one newly grieving or anyone you are trying to comfort.

"I Don't Know How You Feel, But . . ."

" . . . when my grandmother/cat/friend/Prince died, I . . ."

Stop talking after, "I'm so sorry. I don't know how you feel." That is enough. I grew up in Minneapolis, and I can assure you, no one loved

Prince more than I, but still, I would never say that to his family. Please don't say it either.

"I Know Exactly How You Feel . . ."

Nope. No, you don't.

Help for the Helpers

If you do say something you aren't sure about, you can say so: "I'm here to support you however I can, but I'm not always sure what the best thing is to say to be helpful."

If you know you got it wrong, try, "I think that came out wrong. I'm sorry if that was upsetting."

Or, don't "say" anything at all. Just offer to be present: "How about I come over and make some tea and keep you company?"

In *It's OK That You're Not OK*, psychologist Megan Devine offers a few very important pieces of advice that I've seldom found in other books or articles on how to help and what to say during times of grief. She and I lost our partners in the same week of the same year, so yeah, she knows what she's talking about professionally and, I'm sorry to say, also personally. According to Devine:

Grief belongs to the griever. You have a supporting role, not the central role, in your friend's grief. You may believe you would do things differently if it had happened to you. We hope you do not get the chance to find out.

Stay present and state the truth. Stay present with your friend, even when the present is full of pain. Stick with the truth: This hurts. I love you. I'm here.

Do not try to fix the unfixable. Your friend's loss cannot be fixed or repaired or solved. The pain itself cannot be made better.

Tackle projects together. Depending on the circumstance, there may be difficult tasks that need tending—things like casket shopping, mortuary visits, the packing and sorting of rooms or houses. Offer your assistance and follow through with your offers.

I quote this line all the time, "Some things cannot be fixed. They must be carried."

Message in a Bottle

After selling the house, we settled into the rental and stayed for a few years. I freelanced part-time as a project manager and walked Gabe to school every day. I'd been jotting down notes from phone calls, advice from lawyers, and tips from the financial folks and having occasional late-night wine-fueled writing sessions to get down all of my thoughts. To remember. Those early notebook scribbles and Post-it notes are ugly and angry and still painful to look at now, but I'd left behind me a pretty good trail of bread crumbs in answered questions and done to-do lists that I hoped might help someone else find a better path when lost in such dark and scary woods.

I couldn't shake the idea that I should do something with all the information and advice I'd collected. It would have made a very, very big difference for me when the shit hit the fan. I had been thinking of creating a website and from the very beginning knew it could be named only one thing, the words I said in the hospital while standing over his bed: Get Your Shit Together.

My friend Laura agreed to look at what I'd put together so far and share her thoughts on the advice and checklists. I knew her many years of experience working with trauma would be invaluable. When we met, she said the content all looked helpful, especially if it was my true experience and what I wish I would have done. But she didn't want to talk about the site as much as why I was so hell-bent on launching it. Did I understand how steep and slippery the slope of this mission to help others might be and where the desire to do this was coming from? she asked. Yikes. Good questions. We went for a walk.

She talked about "trauma mastery," which involves revisiting or mentally re-creating situations like the traumatic incident in hopes of experiencing a different outcome. Completing such an exercise does not mean you're anywhere near actually mastering trauma or getting over it, but revisiting it can help your healing process. In fact, those who study and treat PTSD often work by helping people reenact the trauma by telling the story. Sometimes remembering loved ones, sharing stories, and talking about what happened can help people move through the aftermath.

Then she asked, "Why would I even want to go there?"

I told her that I had no interest in reliving the trauma but felt compelled to keep looking at it to figure out what I should have done differently. The accident being totally out of my control was the sort of mind-fuck message that flashed in neon: *Control is merely an illusion! You control nothing, you foolish, mortal, puny human!*

However, the double-trauma sucker punch—the knowledge that I had screwed up some of the things I *could* have controlled, such as legal stuff, insurance, and money—made a very hard time even harder. Control is perhaps merely an illusion, *except for all the things you can control!*

As for why I wanted to do this, I didn't have a good answer. I'd known Laura for more than a decade, and she knew more about trauma than anyone. She could easily call bullshit on my half-assed thinking. So that was the question I had to chew on—and answer—as we walked our big, not perfectly behaved dogs around the two-and-a-half-mile Seward Park loop I'd circled hundreds of times before.

I ran that loop when I was getting in shape so I'd have a better chance of getting pregnant. The day we found out we were pregnant, after years of trying and fertility treatments, José and I walked that loop and smiled at each other and touched my belly and talked about baby names. I slow-jogged that loop years later pushing a jogging stroller, trying to lose the baby weight. After the accident, I crushed that fucking loop for breakfast as one of the legs in a much longer training run with headphones screaming out a steady eight-minute-mile beat while I sobbed, somehow without stopping. *That* loop. And now, here, I was within sight of the spot on the road where he was hit, where he bled, where a crowd gathered around him. This is where I have to answer the question, *Why am I doing this? What is this for? What can I hope to accomplish?*

Of course, saying "I can't not," sounded definitely like a mental-health red flag. And it wasn't quite true, either.

As Laura and I turned the bend past the pottery studio, near the small beach that in the summer had the lifeguards with the white noses and megaphones and the swim test you had to pass before you could go past the rope to the raft, the loop ended at the small parking lot. On one side, the slow-grade hill leaned up toward the neighborhoods. On the other, just a half mile away, stretched one of the largest standing old-growth forests within the city limits, filled with nighttime owl prowl walks, coyote sightings, and trees so old they have names like "The Old Man." Gabe took a summer wilderness awareness camp there and learned that the antidote to stinging nettles is to place the underside of a few fern leaves on your skin to sooth the pain and burning. The plants often grow close to each other.

I couldn't control or stop José's accident, but we could have taken a few steps to make it easier on the other when one of us died. We can't stop experiencing trauma or grief. The heartbreak and emotional suffering that go with them is just part of life. This suffering is hard, if not impossible, to avoid. But the additional hardship and pain that come with the tactical and logistical problems, that suffering, is optional. And that was what I wanted to do—remove as much optional suffering as I could from my life and the lives of others. And that was really it.

Toward the end of our walk, Laura asked, "You still working out? Meditating?"

I said I wasn't working out like that first year but I was still running and going to yoga three or four times a week.

"Good," she said. "And if you're not meditating every day anymore, you should start."

I agreed. Thinking about meditating wasn't the same as actually doing it.

"If you're going to do this, then the best thing you can do is really take care of yourself. Whatever you're doing now, double it."

My friend Deborah designed the site, with a cute logo of someone giving a "Hey you" shout. After the headline, Get Your Shit Together, came the lead-in question: "Sometimes bad things happen. Do you have a plan?" My coworker and friend Jibran did the development. Dozens of friends looked it over and made suggestions. I uploaded the final downloadable checklists in late December 2013 and launched the site in early January. I hoped that, once the website was live and I got this information off my chest, life might steady out a bit. In a hastily written Facebook post, I announced the site to friends and family.

Friends and family, when I ask you now to please Get Your Shit Together, it is a most heartfelt invitation. I have been working on this for some time, and am pushing this early, iterative, imperfect project out into the world, for you.

When José was killed I was far more vulnerable than I should have been, and a few very basic things would have saved me a mountain of unnecessary suffering when it was already hard enough to just get dressed in the morning. I collected these core items, streamlined them to make sense to me, and want you to have them so you can better protect yourself, family, and community.

Get it done. It's easy. Holler at me for help, questions, or comments. The project will change over time and I'd love to hear from you what works or is actually helpful.

Xoxo

It was a thank-you to everyone who had stepped in and held me up, showed up, delivered food, donated money, helped with childcare, gave their time, and showered me with love. And in the spirit of a giveaway or ceremony where you put things you no longer want or need into the flames of a giant bonfire, I believed that helping people would be a way for me to let go.

Letters from Everywhere

Usually, a message in a bottle is meant for a faraway love, to track currents, or to send off final words to the world from a sinking ship. The Get Your Shit Together website was really my "what I wish I would have done" message sent out in a modern-day bottle on the Internet. I didn't realize how many other people had messages of their own they needed someone to hear.

Within twenty-four hours, my post had been shared out so far that my inbox was overrun with notes and questions from friends and total strangers, which is probably why I missed the email from Ron Lieber at the *New York Times*. He dug up my phone number and called me at seven a.m. the next morning. Before the week was out, the website server almost crashed because my story was the most read and shared article throughout the weekend. Answering emails and talking to more press and retelling and reliving the story quickly became an emotional roller coaster. All of a sudden, I felt a huge amount of pressure to make the website successful and professional, though my story and the advice I shared was so, so personal. And then there were all the letters. Oh my god. The letters.

The same experience I had at the hospital was coming in loud and clear from everywhere. No one was immune. It wasn't just my story; it was everyone's story. Or it would be someday if we don't get better at actually getting our shit together. I read every single one and I started writing everyone back, for about a week.

I had no idea how to help the woman whose husband had a stroke or whose daughter was in a coma. I thought about those women and their children for days and spent time researching online what they could do so I could write back a very thoughtful and helpful letter. I wrote some back with long letters of suggestions, drafted incomplete emails to others, and then just didn't. Then I felt shitty. Then I felt guilty for feeling shitty and still not writing them or the hundreds of other people who really could have used some help.

And then, after a week or two, there was just not enough oxygen in the room anymore. I'd read these letters, type half a response, and have to take a nap because I was so exhausted.

I had hoped that the website would be of help, and it was. It had struck a chord—a lot of people out there were in a world of hurt, just like me a few years before, and they didn't know what to do. And now I feared I might not be able to really help any of them.

Where's the Bear?

While I'm certain I wouldn't have made it past the first year without all the help from so many people, it was the Erins whom I would seek out when I doubted or worried about myself the most. We'd chat at dinner parties, on backpacking trips, between cake and presents at our kids' birthday parties, or after yoga class. Especially after yoga. We had our yoga mats huddled together one morning after a weekend class when I asked them, trying to be casual, "So, how can you self-assess if you have PTSD or when you're over a trauma?" Both are well-trained professionals and neither reacted but I knew them well enough to see a nearly invisible flash of raised eyebrows in each other's direction as they settled in to more comfortable positions. Uh-oh.

"There are psychiatric tools that we could talk about, but to better answer your question I'd love to hear more about what you're looking for," said Erin the Counselor.

"Yeah, I'm so curious about all of the press you've gotten. Catch us up. What's going on, *chica*?" asked Erin the Social Worker.

They were both smiling at me. Damn. *OK, here we go.*

"What if doing hard, rewarding work just feels too hard sometimes? Or what if this project is the opposite of helpful and I'm just dragging my dead husband around with me wherever I go? Now I've got a lot of other people's trauma being delivered to my inbox and they're in the same shitty, terrible spot I was a few years ago. The swirl of it all makes me want to crawl under the bed with a bottle of wine," I admitted.

I had known that launching the Get Your Shit Together project was going to be hard, and it felt hard, but it was bewildering in a new way. I felt knocked sideways all over again. And I was doubting myself.

They were nodding, listening. I looked at their reflection in the full wall of mirrors, still humid from class. The hot yoga studio was named, appropriately, Breathe.

"In the first year or two after José's death, how did you guys know I was really OK? How do I know if I'm OK now?" I asked.

I asked them to keep their answers simple and really basic. Like I don't need to know quantum physics to know how warp speed works in *Star Trek*. So we played the "Where Is the Bear" game. For example, if a big scary bear is in front of you, do you:

Fight the bear?

Freeze up and hope the bear ignores you?

Run away from the bear?

ERIN THE COUNSELOR: Well, feeling like you want crawl under the bed is one thing. So my question is what do you do? Do you crawl under your bed? Or open the wine?

ME: Well, no, because I can't get under the bed very far with the vacuum and it's really gross under there, but I will go lie down and take a nap. Or, yeah, sometimes I have a big, as in huge, glass of wine after Gabe goes to sleep.

ERIN THE SOCIAL WORKER: One of the things about trauma or a traumatic event is we react, we get triggered. Like a fight or if someone at work yells at you, we get triggered, and those fight-or-flight responses kick in. Those responses have been hardwired over thousands of years because they can be helpful. They help us get away from danger, right?

ERIN THE COUNSELOR: But when the response is bigger or longer than it needs to be in that situation, if the intensity of a reaction stayed the same years later as it was, let's say, for you that first week in the hospital, then there is an "intensity and duration" piece of the trauma, or trauma response, or PTSD, that gets stuck or can't emotionally regulate or calm down.

ME: There were days when I didn't want to get out of bed.

ERIN THE SOCIAL WORKER: Of course there were times you didn't want to get out of bed, and some days you still may not feel like it, but years later are you still not getting out of bed for days or weeks at a time? That's when we'd look at that response as impacting day-to-day life. That's the duration piece.

ME: But what about the letters? I just stare at them and try to write back but only jot down a line or two and then give up. I don't know if that's freezing up or running away. I always thought I was more of a fighter.

ERIN THE COUNSELOR: But that's the difference. We all have our "stuff" and react differently to the things that scare us. It's not about not reacting; we react. You know I'm a crier. Erin's a fighter for sure, but sometimes she doesn't like conflict, so there's some flight in there, too. You're a fighter, but what you're saying now sounds different.

ME: Yeah. Is it flight if I'm just getting flooded and not responding? Or is that more like a freeze? If I'm going numb like folks in the ER who've seen so much trauma they can't even care anymore?

ERIN THE COUNSELOR: Freeze is the scared bunny rabbit or deer in the headlights who is paralyzed. You can't move; you can't run or fight. Like when you're on a sinking ship or you are being held down by an attacker. Freezing up can be a way to protect yourself, to disappear or detach from the bad or scary thing that is happening.

ME: Yeesh. No, I just feel so tired, like depleted and out-of-batteries kind of tired, where my eyes get heavy and I just can't look at the computer for one more second.

ERIN THE COUNSELOR: OK, so you notice that, where you feel it in your body, right? So, when you read those letters—which, by the way, you can do just once a week on a schedule after a yoga class, or we could get someone else to reply to them with some words of encouragement from you, and we'll pull together some resources, OK?—but when you get a new email from someone in your inbox, what happens next? Where's the bear?

ME: I know there's no bear in front of me, but I remember what it was like to feel truly fucked, vulnerable, and lost. I remember what it was like when the bear was sitting on top of me.

ERIN THE COUNSELOR: So, sweetie, where's the bear now?

ME: It's at that other poor woman's house, dragging her around by the neck. I don't feel afraid or anxious that something will happen to me or my family, even though I know it could—just sad. You guys, it's just so heartbreaking. I remember when that woman was me.

ERIN THE SOCIAL WORKER: Absolutely. After what you have been through, you know there are bears in the woods. It sucks. And that's why what you're doing, why you're doing it, is hard.

Erin was right. At the hospital I certainly approached the threat head-on by asserting myself with the doctors. At least I made friends with the bear, which I suppose is a type of fight response. I thought I was a mostly a fighter, but I was fleeing, too.

Flight seemed easy enough to identify, at first. The moment I sprang from my chair in the family meeting at the hospital after hearing the word *unrecoverable* over and over was about as flight-mode as it gets. Sitting there, I could hear my blood pulsing through my ears and a buried-alive feeling flash-flood up my chest. I recall trying to breathe in through my nose and out my mouth and staring hard into one specific square inch of low-loop Berber at my feet. I was barely able to ask if there was anything new to say before I sprinted down the hall. Literally, I fled.

Running out of a hospital room is one type of fleeing. Reckless behavior, like drinking, was a more serious type of running away. Did my motorcycle count? I didn't really ride it anymore, so I let that one slide.

We'd been in the yoga studio for long enough that the instructor wasn't rushing us out but had started mopping the floor before the next class. The Erins are very good at listening and had noticed that I'd gotten quiet. They held my gaze longer and looked at me a little sideways. They were very comfortable waiting. Damn.

"Yeah, it's a lot, isn't it?" I said.

By then the response I'd been using for years—I'm doing just fine thank you very much for asking—felt less like a defense and more like calling it how I was. And I suppose it was progress that I could cry in the car on the way to the gym and still make it to class or sneak into an open conference room if I felt a sob coming on at work. I hit the snooze button a few times, sure, but I did get up. I still looked forward to making exciting plans for the future.

What they heard was that my grief and the impact of the trauma, as much as it still sucked years later, was not getting in the way of day-to-day life. I didn't always get Gabe to school on time, but being on time most of the time, with a packed lunch, was better than many other people can swing it even on good days. And though I joked about having "mental health moments" with the Erins, I was, in fact, having a therapy session with them even if I didn't know it at the time. Encouraging me to "notice that" and asking me "What happens next?" are foundational elements of trauma therapy. Realizing that I could still feel sadness and grief without it meaning that I was somehow broken was a relief. I'd even started answering people who would ask, "So, do you feel better now?" with "Well, it gets different."

What I wanted to do with Get Your Shit Together—and still could do—was double down on what I set out to accomplish in the first place. Tell my story, the whole good-bad-and-ugly story, and continue to remove as much optional suffering from my life and the lives of others as I could.

Do I know bears are out there? Yes.

And they are scary.

One day there will probably be one right in front of me again, perhaps even standing on top of me.

Today, so far, is not that day.

Some days I may still hear them roaring out in those woods.

Nevertheless, I decide what I do next.

Guide:
What Matters Most

The main thing is to keep the main thing the main thing.

—STEPHEN COVEY

When I lost my husband, not only was he gone, but the life we had, the plans and dreams, the whole idea of what I thought the future was going to look like—all that was gone, too. If there were a band called the Four Horsemen, Death would certainly be the lead singer, but Diagnosis, Disability, Divorce, or some other Disaster could be the other riders, and they can kick up a lot of dust and knock everything in your life sideways—and the future you imagined or planned right along with it. In that terrible moment, you can lose your security and financial stability. In the worst-case scenario, you could lose everything.

Once I had a little more energy, or capacity, after "getting through" the first year, I found that getting through the day or week is one thing, but planning the rest of your future? That was when a whole new kind of emotional rubber hit the road. I hoped this would be the first and only time I'd have to learn these lessons. I challenged myself to build a new life I could be proud of and to let honesty and clarity be the gentle current that guided me.

Life Do-Over: Resetting the Future

Talk about It

What is "it"? It is whatever it is. Whatever is bothering you. Whatever is taking up space in your mind and heart. Yes. Talk about it. You have to. We have to. I spoke with chef and social curator Michael Hebb, author of *Let's Talk About Death (over Dinner)*. As we talked about "talking about it," he explained why his dinners evolved from food-focused to conversation-focused: "I saw that we could really heal each other through conversation." Remember, he advises, it doesn't have to be an awkward, heavy conversation; perhaps think of it "in the same way that we would courtship."

- Approach such a conversation the way you would with someone you wanted to befriend or date, and then "apply the same creativity." Try to look forward to, and be excited about, talking about it. Approach the conversation with the same enthusiasm and preparation you would if it were a job interview or a parent-teacher conference—not *deadly* serious, but you still have to "show up" and engage.
- If people bristle or are unwilling to talk, try starting with or redirecting the conversation "by bringing up something that you both share in common." Perhaps like talking with our kids about driving or sex, "It's rare that it is in one conversation that we cover all aspects." Pause briefly, or take a longer break, and try again later.
- We don't get to be in control of how others respond. They may shut down or even refuse to "go there," but initiating and trying to have the conversation can still be meaningful. The more "we are able to express ourselves, the more our life resembles the life we want to live and the more our culture

is a culture of well-being." Taking the steps to bring up the conversation can be considered a personal victory, even if it doesn't go the way you hoped. Even that helps move the collective conversation forward.

Leave Traces

There is a video of my late husband doing a work presentation; I get to watch him talk for a whole hour. I get to see him make gestures that are so familiar but are gone now. Because of this video, his kids will be able to hear his voice whenever they wish to. This is a gift.

So, for all you camera-shy folks out there, remember that someday your kids, family, partner, spouse, and friends will want pictures of you. It would be great to have video of you talking or telling a story. Try to leave some things along the way so people can feel close to you, listen to your favorite music, smell you, wear your clothes, hear your voice, or look at pictures of the both of you together. It can be incredibly comforting. *And there's nothing morbid about it.*

- Take a few minutes to record a few videos of yourself, or of you with someone you love, telling a few of your favorite jokes or recalling a memory. Save it somewhere easy to find later, or go ahead and share it now.
- Get a journal or find a fill-in-the-blanks legacy book like Anne Phyfe Palmer's *This Life of Mine* and just jot down stories as they come to you.
- Find a box or large glass container to put some of your most cherished pictures and trinkets, maybe shells from that special trip years ago. Remove those boxes of photos hiding in the closets and display some for others to appreciate. I have a gallon-size glass jar with José's old watch, a lock of Gabe's hair, some pictures of me from high school with very Bon Jovi–era hair, mixed in with sea glass and a Princess Leia

LEGO action figure Gabe gave me years ago because, he said, "She looks like you, Mama."

Be a Better Friend

If it were not for my amazing friends and community of support, I would not have made it through the aftermath of José's death. As you are writing or updating your will, you will have to ask yourself who will carry out your wishes, care for your children, advocate for you medically, or pull the plug on you as you wish them to. If you are at a loss for whom to name, get out there and tighten up your friends and family relationships. Find some better friends. Start being a better friend. This is everything. Friendship and community mean everything.

It can be hard to know where to start, but if you're at a loss, you might try some of these ideas:

- Have a dinner party or barbecue. Make a special toast thanking your friends for being part of your life. Then have more of them. Rotate hosts. Start a "What if"–themed conversation.
  - If you don't like hosting, send an email invitation to someone, or a big group, to go to a concert or see a show when you come across an event that looks like fun.
- Be more proactive and keep in better touch. Nurture friendships with a few more "Hey, thought of you" messages.
  - If you are good at dates and planning in advance, remember birthdays and anniversaries, and send a card with a handwritten note.
  - Send a note about a book or a link to an article and say, "I'd love to hear your thoughts on this."

Finish the Unfinished

Bearing witness to regret and remorse is devastating. Watching people realize that it's too late to make up for lost time or say the unsaid brings me to my knees. You don't get a do-over once someone is gone. Unfinished business and things left unsaid can't be done or fixed then. Clean up your messes. Even if your outstretched olive branch is ignored, you will feel better knowing you pushed aside your pride and tried. Unless you'd prefer to jump, baby-step your way into this.

- Return your neighbor's rake. Return those library books.
- Send a card to someone you've lost touch with.
- Clear the air over a previous dispute with a coworker.

Tell the Truth

Do not one day find yourself having missed out on something because you were too busy being angry, too invested in being done wrong by someone, or too shy to speak your mind, to say how you feel, or to admit you were wrong. Don't be afraid to live your life exactly as you would like to live it. Be brave. Be mindful. Be honest and vulnerable even if it feels hard and scary. It's far easier than lugging your doubts and fears along with you.

Show Gratitude

If I had known in advance that I'd get only nine married years with José and five years with him and our son, I would still do it all over again. I became a better person through our marriage, and I am grateful to have had the years together that we did.

Gratitude overwhelmed me in the moment when José died, and that is the feeling I work hard to conjure and remember during any awful moment. Gratitude is powerful medicine. Research shows that expressing gratitude improves your mental and emotional well-being and increases your overall happiness. Cultivating and nurturing these feelings has long-lasting and positive effects on your life. Better yet, happiness and gratitude are not tied to income. Many of the happiest people have few financial resources but an abundance of family and community support.

Showing support for others can be as easy as a phone call or dropping something off on the way home, just taking an extra ten or twenty minutes to add a little joy or relief to someone's day. Practicing gratitude, even in little ways, is a good habit to have. Gratitude adds up, and those small gestures become a much larger, positive influence in the world. It's also a great self-care practice. Practice gratitude by appreciating the big and little things whenever you can.

A good night's sleep	Morning coffee
Seeing the sun rise	A good joke
A really good hug	Taking a walk
A sunny day	Friends
Being outside	A really good book
Dancing like no one can see you	Singing loud in the car or shower
Exercise	A favorite pair of jeans
A handwritten note in the mail	Finding money in the laundry
A clean bathroom	A beautifully cooked meal
Vacations (and staycations)	Old friends
Music	Good health
Money in the bank	Weekends
Making your own choices	Being able to say no
Saying Yes!	Kindness from others
Art	A warm, safe home
Family	Great sex
Learning from mistakes	Being honest
Trying something new	Comfort food
Access to medicine	Schools for your children
A neighborhood park	Volunteering
Fresh fruit and vegetables	Good conversation
Being alive	Speaking your truth
Laughter	Deep breaths
Saying thank you	Saying I love you

Life Do-Over:
The Ultimate What-If Game

Once the basic, more immediate plans are in place and you've got a better idea of how to handle the essentials if (or when) the shit hits the fan, you get to the less paper-heavy part and enter the softer side of your to-do list. Now it's time to take a closer look at where your vulnerable spots might be and shore them up.

The What-If List: Upping the Odds and Stacking Your Deck

You are probably quite good at playing a version of the What-If Game already. It goes something like this: late-night worry about something bad happening followed by a merry-go-round of fears about what else would happen if that bad thing happened. Frequently, we run a catastrophe loop about events not in our direct control (global economic collapse, rising sea levels, poverty) or even lose sleep (yep, me, my hand is raised) about ones that will probably *never* happen (zombie apocalypse, aliens take over).

When it comes to situations that might actually happen, it is tempting not to think about them and simply hope for the best. But those are the very circumstances that are most likely to barge through our lives and leave a mess. We *can* plan for them. My version of the What-If Game includes a final round: identifying what you can do to minimize the mess.

First, let's get some perspective about the big life sandbox we're playing in. There are four main categories of statistically possible life wrecking balls that we can plan for. Warning: the statistics are bleak and sobering. We are really vulnerable—more than we realize.

1. **Diagnosis.** About 1.7 million new cancer cases are expected to be diagnosed in the United States in 2018, according to the American Cancer Society.

- According to a *Chicago Tribune* article, "Cancer patients are more than twice as likely as those without the disease to declare bankruptcy."
2. **Disability.** One in four Americans will be disabled during their adult life.
3. **Divorce.** About half of all marriages end in divorce, according to the American Psychological Association.
   - After divorce, women's financial standing often declines, while men's remains stable.
4. **Disaster.** Because so many Americans live paycheck-to-paycheck, any additional stress or distress, such as a natural disaster or an accident, can lead to financial ruin.

These four may not kill you (at least not right away), but they can cause long-term financial, legal, and emotional problems. As a single parent, I freak at the thought of not being able to take care of my son.

Now, take a breath, and let's play.

What if I can't work?

- First, I have six months of emergency savings.
- Then, I can cash out my backup emergency stock.
- Then, if I cannot return to work, I have to:
  - Claim disability (60 percent of current income).
  - Dramatically lower expenses by moving.

Takeaway: it is an immense relief to me that I have the answers to these gut-wrenching worries figured out and written down.

NOTE: I did not have an emergency fund or disability insurance until after José died. Currently, only 25 percent of adults living in the US have three months of expenses saved in case of an emergency.

OK, take another deep breath. It's your turn. Pick one: diagnosis, disability, divorce, or disaster.

What if _____happened?

1. Well, first _____.
2. Next, I/we would _____.
3. After that I/we would have to: _____
   _____.
4. Or, if necessary, I/we could _____
   _____.

Now, where are the weak spots and what (if anything) can you do to strengthen them?

Additional Challenges for Women

For women, the struggles are more formidable, the risks are higher, the margin for error is smaller, and the cushion we have to land on is thinner. It's not fair, but that's reality. Knowing the challenges that I faced helped me to feel marginally better than pretending they don't (currently) exist.

After the age of sixty-five, women are almost twice as likely as men to live in poverty. Women of color are even more likely to live in poverty in their old age.

- Women make less income and receive lower salaries.
  - The gender pay gap meant that I would make 20 percent less than a man working in the same position. For every dollar a Caucasian male makes, a Caucasian woman receives eighty cents; an African American woman, sixty-two cents; and a Latina, fifty-four cents. I had to assume I'd be working harder and longer than a man to save enough for retirement.

- Women do more of the caregiving work.
  - Women do the majority of the caregiving for children, parents, and other family members and often choose part-time work or lower-paying jobs with flexible hours to accommodate these commitments. Consequently, they earn less money over time than if they had worked steadily full-time.

- Women have less money to save for retirement.
  - Women are able to contribute less money to their retirement savings because of a lifetime of lower wages. On average, a woman has over $300,000 less in her retirement savings than a man of the same age.

A Small Series of Losses

After a few years doing a pretty good job of putting my life back together again, I thought I had a pretty good understanding of loss. Secretly, I believed I'd nailed it in the loss department, gotten the life-experience version of a PhD in grief and loss, and I could move on. Nope.

Which made it especially horrifying the day my son came home from school with Chase and wouldn't even look at me or speak to me. Chase had to pull me aside and explain what had happened. I had screwed up. Really, really fucked up.

Gabe's cheetah presentation had been that day. And I'd missed it. When it was his turn to present his papier-mâché cheetah and painted diorama and tell the class how fast the cheetah could run, he said to me, with a quivering chin and teary eyes, "I kept looking at the door for you to come." He was the only kid with *no* parents present.

"Papa would have come," he said.

I was less than a mile away staring at my laptop, I didn't show up, and I couldn't use being dead as an excuse.

Chase took Gabe to the park to try to cheer him up, leaving me a few hours to do *something*. My son was sad and felt abandoned, so now I had to fix it. I raced out the door, picked up and dropped off Lyric at an appointment, and because I had no other ideas, sped to the closest pet store hoping to find a cat or a dog I could buy. They didn't have dogs, and all the cats were at an adoption event. *Fuck! No cats!* Fish didn't do anything for me, and Lyric had had a few birds and hamsters when she was little, and they all died, so I couldn't get something that was going to just die the next day. Snakes and lizards, nope. Turtles, not very cuddly. *Shit.* As I paced up and down the aisles like a teenager on prom night trying to find condoms, I finally stopped, albeit reluctantly, in front of the guinea pigs.

They were bigger than hamsters and apparently could be friendly and social. I had a friend growing up who really loved her guinea pigs. Mostly, I was in a pinch. I had only twenty minutes until I had to pick up Lyric and head home. I considered going to a cash machine and cruising by a dog park in case someone didn't want a dog anymore and needed some cash—but too risky, I decided. Maybe a little suspicious, too.

Two hundred bucks later, I had the reddish-brown, furry thing in a cardboard travel box and a shopping cart full of wood shavings, food, toys, chewy sticks, a water dripper-feeder, one of those circular treadmills, a plastic ball to take a spin around the house, and a build-it-yourself Habitrail bendy tube so he—no, she?—could wander outside her new fish tank–type home. Ten minutes later, Lyric and I were screaming in the parking lot, running from car door to car door and frantically looking inside the car; the guinea pig had bolted. Lyric couldn't resist opening the carrier to hold her—just for a minute—but when the animal pooped on Lyric's hand, she accidentally dropped her (lightly) onto her lap. Freedom! That guinea pig was not easy to find and put back in the box, but we did it.

"This isn't a good sign," Lyric commented.

She was right.

We met Gabe at home.

"Ta-da!" I said enthusiastically, revealing our new family member.

Gabe stared back at me. After a long pause, he said, "You missed my presentation so you got me a hamster? To make up for it?"

"It's a guinea pig," I replied. "And yes, kiddo, I feel terrible I missed the presentation and was hoping it would be a nice way to say I'm sorry and have another pet in the house. What should we name her?" I asked.

He squinted sideways at the furry thing burrowing in the woodchips we'd put into the habitat home and after a second or two said, "No" and walked down the hall to his room. Chase and Lyric shrugged, but I could tell what they were thinking: *This was a terrible idea, and now you're stuck with this big-eyed guinea pig.*

"Aw, she's kinda cute," Chase said. "You know guinea pigs are just big rodents, right?"

I'd been doing everything possible to mitigate any additional loss in Gabe's life, to normalize his dad's death, to heal the pain, and to be the best kick-ass, shows-up, everything's-fine, helps-others, does-it-all single mom in the world, and it had blown up in my face.

So, at the otolaryngologist's office (don't worry, I had to look up the word too), I told the hearing specialist that more and more frequently I couldn't hear things. Way too often, I'd found myself saying "What?" to my blank-faced son or popping my head up quickly with a pasted-on smile to appease the annoyed person who had to repeat themselves—again—and probably was thinking I'm a bitch for ignoring them.

Sitting in the soundproof, padded, and slightly claustrophobic audio booth with wires going into uncomfortable earplugs, I thought about something my counselor Delia had said: "Divorce or the death of a spouse from a long illness is a devastating loss, but those can be experienced as a series of small losses over time. Your loss happened all at once."

After I'd listened to a series of hums, pings, beats, whirls, chirps, and repeated some words, the technician returned. She paused and took an extra intake of breath before speaking. Clearly, she carried bad news.

"Just tell me," I said bravely, channeling Cher.

"Yes, you have significant hearing loss," she said. "Surprising for someone so young but well in the range for hearing assistance." She kept talking but the only words I could hear kicking around in my head were "a series of small losses."

Had my hearing faded so slowly that I didn't even notice the signs along the way?

While it sucked to learn that my suspicions were correct, I couldn't do anything about a genetic hearing issue. However, I'd had some practice looking at uncomfortable things, especially uncomfortable losses, head-on. So what did I really have to lose?

The immediate and catastrophic loss we'd lived through as a family was all-encompassing; like the Big Bang, it made everything explode out in every direction. A few years later, there was enough space to see the pieces that make up our little universe. All those little stars added up to a really big thing.

I don't get to choose how bad my hearing is, but how well I listen *is* my choice.

And what happens next is absolutely up to me.

I had been missing out on my life, as it was happening. I'd allowed myself to become so overwhelmed that I'd gotten the date wrong for the cheetah presentation.

I should have gone to his room and talked to Gabe about how terrible that must have been to feel abandoned, about how his dad would have absolutely been there (if I had reminded him, but Gabe didn't need to know that). Instead, I had messed up. I ran out the door—*fled* would be the word—and frantically bought him a guinea pig he never wanted.

Be present. Show up. Pay attention.

The doctor stared at me from her chair. She'd just started her soft, well-practiced speech about taking the time to think about next steps when I interrupted her. I was missing out on my life and had allowed this to happen.

"How soon until I can get fitted for hearing aids? I want to know what I've been missing."

All those moments, all the little day-to-day things, the casual words that may be the last ones you get, eyes smiling back at you from the audience—those are the big things.

OK, I hear you, Universe. Got it!

Can I stop learning this lesson now?

Departure

I am back on Vashon.

It's early, but light is already blasting through the bedroom windows.

I hear a noise from the kitchen and crawl out of bed.

José is making coffee.

He'd always make me coffee in the morning. He was the earlier riser.

But today was the fourth anniversary of his death.

The accident day, not the death-day. I keep them separate.

And who's the blonde sitting at the table?

He isn't looking me in the eye.

Oh, for fuck's sake . . .

He's holding printouts of divorce papers: two sets.

Of course, he adds while sitting down, he wants custody half the time.

His girlfriend whispers in the close-low-voice only lovers do and reminds him, no kids next weekend because—they're going on a trip.

"So, wait a minute, you come back now, after being dead all these years . . ."

Out the big windows, I notice how still the bay is.

Wow, it's going to be a great day to go paddleboarding.

"And you want . . . to divorce me?" I say.

There is silence except for the rustling of papers and the sound of a pen's pressure on the table as he scrawls his signature on the bottom of each page.

"*Hey,*" I say, looking at my empty hands and the two steaming cups in front of them, "where's my coffee?"

Jump

We took The Street to the park and to Lyric's house all the time, which must be why I'd never told Gabe where the accident happened. The kids hadn't asked. I would tell them the truth if they ever did (I did promise), but for years I'd been driving us back and forth over the spot without their realizing it.

Immediately after the accident, I approached driving that section of road as if it were hot coals I had to walk over. I had to gear up for it, brace myself in case it hurt. It took three years for those feelings to diminish and play as background music. I didn't worry the same way—well, not as *hard*, anyway—but as my own ritual, I still held my breath when we drove by.

When we got to the four-year anniversary of José's death, I realized that it wouldn't be too long before Gabe would have been alive longer without his dad than with him. Time was adding up.

And just like that, one morning while driving home with Gabe, I realized we'd passed the spot. It was a half mile back. And I had missed it. I jumped in my seat and snapped my head up, eyes searching behind us in the rearview mirror . . . *Oh shit! I missed it!*

Gabe's happy chatter about making pizza while watching *Lord of the Rings* froze midsentence during Gandalf's big "You shall not pass" scene. He stared at me through the mirror, eyes asking, *What happened?*

"Nothing, baby. Sorry if I scared you. I thought I saw something," I said.

"What was it?" he asked.

For the first time in four years, I'd driven by the spot, too busy living my actual life to hold my breath and wait for the past to yank me backward.

The next day, we packed up snacks, towels, and our bathing suits and headed for the lake. A huge, tipped-over cedar tree, leaning at about fifteen degrees, marks a favorite swimming spot. The tree's roots barely hold it to the soil and its branches skim the water. It looks as if it's levitating. Through the plush evergreen branches, I saw Gabe's gleaming face, his long hair in dripping ringlets.

"Mom! Jump!"

He'd already jumped off the tree and into the water twice, but I was still perched at the top, getting more frozen by the minute.

The twentysomethings in a nearby boat yelled up to me. "It only gets worse the longer you wait."

"You don't have to be afraid, Mom! Just juuuuuuump!"

I didn't exactly leap, but I exhaled and let go of the tree.

My hair sailed behind me, arms stretched up over my head.

Splash!

A moment of perfect underwater calm before I kicked up.

I heard my son cheering as my smile broke the surface, facing the sun.

Afterword:
Finding Shore

Do I have my shit together now? Yep. I do. Have I gotten everything right? Maybe.

At first, getting my shit together was driven by my fear that I'd screwed up the past. Now, if I die before my son is an adult, there is a very clear, Gabe-approved plan, with backup plans and lots of additional support and very few loose ends, if any. Everything that needs finding is findable, guardianship is clear, and money will be available to him. College savings is started, and my life insurance policy would cover the rest. Videos have been prerecorded. For a single parent predisposed to catastrophic thinking, I sleep very soundly at night.

The hand-painted wooden sign hanging from a tree near the pond at Deer Park Monastery that said, "breathe, you are alive" served as my go-to mantra. It was a reminder, or proof. When I was forty, I sat down in an old leather chair in a strip-mall storefront on Oahu with a picture of it in my hand. "Ready to start?" the tattooist asked. I replied, "Absolutely, it already started a while ago." She just shrugged, and in about an hour, I was inked for the first time.

After a year or two trying to work through, past, with, or in the grief, the daily hill-by-hill grind felt mostly behind me, yet waves of grief could still wipe me out. When a particularly fierce set snuck up behind me, I was, once again, flat on my ass like it was day one. The second tattoo, a great wave on my shoulder, was my reminder that these waves are much, much bigger than me, or any of us. The waves come whether you struggle against them, surf them, or get pummeled underneath them. You can get mad at the ocean all day long, but, ready or not, another set will come. It's just the way it goes.

An extension of the wave down my arm, closer to my elbow, where a fish dives down toward deeper and hopefully calmer waters, was the third tattoo. But even though life seemed quieter and a few more years had passed, I did not feel calm. I often felt stuck. I came to understand the phases of my grief, of the trauma, through the images—totems, really—that I chose to tattoo on my arm. It appears I'm quite literally wearing my heart on my sleeve.

Being in the sun is my happy place, so I decided to add a blazing sun on the inside of my arm, under the wave and across from the fish diving down to the still waters. Having that fourth tattoo on the inside of my arm meant I could have the sun with me always, especially when I needed it most. After an hour or so, Jesse the tattooist asked if I needed a break. When the needle slid upward to make the tips of the sun, it felt like white fire.

"You OK?" she asked. "You're not usually a crier."

"The soft spots really do hurt the most." I squeaked out a smile. "I'll live. Keep going."

The nerve endings on your arm are nothing compared to the giant soft spots in our family's hearts for the pets. If you have been distracted for the last few pages, wondering, *What happened to the guinea pig?* She was adopted by a very grateful kindergarten teacher who really wanted a pet for her classroom but didn't have the budget. She seemed to know everything about guinea pigs and promised to take good care of her. The couch-peeing cats were half-feral rescues who, after a year, insisted on remaining wild. Sadly, the skittish one ran away, and the mouser moved to Orcas Island to become a well-fed barn cat. Our sweet girl, Hannah, the golden retriever, whom José and I considered our first child until we had a child, died at the very respectable old age of fourteen. She was snuggled and hand-fed cheeseburgers and fancy vanilla cupcakes from Cupcake Royale by the kids on her last night with us.

Do I know what getting my shit together really means? Maybe.

There is no kung fu finish, but the movements get smoother, like tai chi. There are no silver bullets or guarantees.

It's knowing there are bears out there somewhere but going outside and doing things anyway. On good days, you love harder and open wider, because if it can all go away at any minute, you don't want to miss an inch of it today.

Asking the questions and then letting them go.

Doing the work and then allowing yourself to rest.

Being present to the cheers and critics in your head and then ignoring them.

Being brave enough to define quality of life at the end, absolutely, but being even braver to put a stake in the ground for your quality of life now, for you, right now, today. This second.

It's listening to the soft voice inside you that has been there all along.

Is there a happy ending to this story?

Perhaps.

The Guidebook

This guidebook is designed to be used as a stand-alone exercise, but it also makes a great companion to the Before and After, parts 1 and 2 of this book. The Start Where You Are section identifies and names your personal priority items, and The Big List helps you keep tabs on your progress and track the items left to do. In case you want to organize your own Big Giveaway, there are a few

Start Where You Are

1) THE THREE SITUATIONS THAT WORRY ME MOST:	CAN I REDUCE MY WORRY? Y/N
1.	
2.	
3.	
2) THE TOP THREE THINGS THAT HAVE BEEN ON MY TO-DO LIST FOREVER:	CAN I DO THEM? Y/N
1.	
2.	
3.	
3) THREE ITEMS THAT WILL BE A RELIEF TO GET DONE OR FINISH:	WHAT IS THE FIRST STEP?
1.	
2.	
3.	

tips for setting one up, and I've included a short list of my go-to books, websites, and tools that have helped me get (and keep) my shit together.

These items, plus a few bonus checklists and an annual budget tracker, are available to view, use, or download on www.chanel reynolds.com.

THE GET-YOUR-SHIT-TOGETHER BIG CHECKLIST

Legal
- ❏ My will, living will, power-of-attorney document, and any other health- or funeral-related documents are completed, stored safely, and have been shared with a few trusted people.

Will
- ❏ My will is current, legally binding, and complete.

Living Will
- ❏ My living will is current, legally binding, and complete.

Power of Attorney
- ❏ My medical power of attorney (and backup person) is informed of my wishes and we have discussed my instructions. I have also designated a power of attorney for these additional categories of tasks:
- ❏ Power of attorney: Executive
- ❏ Power of attorney: Financial
- ❏ Power of attorney: Digital
- ❏ Power of attorney: Medical
- ❏ Power of attorney: (other) _____

Money
- ❏ I have thought over and written down my financial goals.
- ❏ I have considered my personal values and my spending and saving.

❑ I have researched tools, advice, and resources to manage my money.

Budget

❑ I have completed a budget, and I track my monthly actual costs to my budget (income and expenses).
❑ I have a plan in place to take steps toward my financial goals.

Savings and Planning

❑ I have _____ weeks/months saved in case of an emergency.
❑ I have a short-term savings plan and put away _____ percent of my income each month toward financial priorities.
❑ I have a long-term savings plan and/or retirement plan into which _____ percent of my income goes each month.
❑ I have reviewed my financial situation and, if necessary, discussed this with those closest to me.

TIP: Follow Suze Orman's advice and "pay yourself first." Auto-deduct a portion of your paycheck into a savings account and track your money with an online tool.

Details

Create a list of your important details and add/edit/delete as you need to, based on your life. PIN numbers, email accounts, and banking information can be easily lost.

❑ I have listed my personal details in case of emergency or if someone needs to retrieve it.
❑ A copy of my details list is located:_____
_____.
❑ I have given access to:_____.

TIP: It's a good idea to update your personal details a few times each year. Consider using an online password manager to update passwords and keep track of new accounts.

Insurance

☐ I have researched my options, and if something happens, if I get ill or can't work, these policies will cover the vulnerable spots:
- Life insurance
- Disability insurance
- Health-care insurance
- Other insurance

REMEMBER! The best time to plant a tree is twenty years ago. The second-best time is now.

Legacy

☐ I have discussed and shared my plans, wishes, and feelings with those I care about.

☐ I have thought about my relationships and how I want to move forward to resolve any unfinished business.

☐ I have reached out to people I have been meaning to (or needing to).

☐ I have deeply considered how my life lines up with my values and priorities, how I am spending my energy, and what I want to do different to have the life that is meaningful and important to me.

Your Own Big Giveaway

Try organizing your own giveaway. You can even do a mini-version at a gathering or dinner party. Ask people to bring something they may love but don't use or wear and are ready to give away. You can suggest a theme, like "for the kitchen," "awesome coats," or "something you cherished that no longer serves you." At the end, everyone gets to leave with something new that I'll bet they'll like and use more than what they brought from home. Or follow or modify the suggestions below:

- Make a list or snap pictures of the items you want to give away. No need to stage-manage the photos. Shoot the items wherever they are, such as in your garage, basement, closet, or storage.
- Send the written list and/or photos with a short description of each item to friends and family via email or social media. Be sure to ask, "Who wants it?"
- Whoever replies first wins. In my giveaway conducted through Facebook, the first person to say, "Me!" in the comments section of the item's picture got it. All they had to do was come and get it.
- Confirm a day and time when folks can come get the stuff, like "anytime Saturday between 10:00 a.m. and 2:00 p.m." (If you share your giveaway list with the general public, be sure to protect your address, phone number, and other personal information.)

Acknowledgments

I am rarely at a loss for words, but this book is the cumulative effort of, and belongs to, so many people—the support for the Get Your Shit Together project and the encouragement I've received for this book is, well, almost overwhelming. My heartfelt thanks to early editorial meditations with Amy Hertz, book-doula focus on the proposal by Shannon O'Neill, and word-whisperer editorial support from Julia Pastore. Endless appreciation to the team at Harper for bringing it into the world: Sarah Murphy, Hannah Robinson, and Karen Rinaldi. My deepest gratitude to my agent, Susan Ginsburg, for believing a book was in me and having the wise words, patience, and solid advice to make it real.

The first Get Your Shit Together website would not have been possible without the help of many, especially Carrie Vincent, Deborah Ro, and Jibran Bisharat. To my partners who helped launch GYST.com, you have been great teachers to me.

My monthly writing group saw nearly every first, terrible draft and (still) encouraged me to continue. Thank you, Gail Hudson, for your generous and always impeccable advice; Laurie Riepe, Jennifer Kakutani, and Liz Stevens for your amazing feedback; and Anne Phyfe Palmer for creating the space for our work to thrive.

Deepest gratitude for the friendship and guidance of Erin Galvin and Erin Brower—let's be clear, so many things would suck without you.

To my parents, AB and Larry Reynolds, for your unwavering love, support, and faith in me (even in high school). I am very lucky to have you as parents. Connie Weiss-Dwyer and Michael Dwyer, it is an honor to coparent and copilot with you; thanks for being the best people to "blended family" with.

I grew up and into an adult with José. Our friendship and marriage made me a better person. I can't be more grateful for the love we had and that I see every day in the kids. Damn, we all sure still miss you.

Lyric, being a parent to you is the highest honor possible. Love you, chica.

Gabriel, you've taught me everything worth knowing, and being your mom is the best thing I've ever done—thank you for being you. Every single day.

Thank you.

Notes

Introduction

6   Over half of the adults in the US don't have a will: Jeffrey M. Jones, "Majority in U.S. Do Not Have a Will," Gallup, May 18, 2016, https://news .gallup.com/poll/191651/majority-not.aspx.

6   Seven out of ten have not written down their end-of-life wishes: Michelle Andrews, "Many Avoid End-of-Life Care Planning, Study Finds," NPR.org, Aug. 2, 2017, https://www.npr.org/sections/health-shots/2017/08/02 /540669492/many-avoid-end-of-life-care-planning-study-finds.

6   Out of all the twenty-year-olds today, over one in four will become disabled before retirement: "Chances of Disability," Council for Disability Awareness, http://disabilitycanhappen.org/overview.

6   About 40 percent of adults in America can't cover a $400 emergency: Anna Bahney, "40% of Americans Can't Cover a $400 Emergency Expense," CNN Money, May 22, 2018, https://money.cnn.com/2018/05/22/pf/emergency -expenses-household-finances/index.html.

Guide: After Death

133   Or that cremating him released: Bill Briggs, "When You're Dying for a Lower Carbon Footprint," NBCNews, Jan. 18, 2011, http://www.nbcnews .com/id/41003238/ns/business-going_green/t/when-youre-dying-lower-car bon-footprint/#.Wx7KHVMvyMI.

135   old-fashioned death industry of $20 billion in annual revenue: Perianne Boring, "Death of the Death Care Industry and Eternal Life Online," Forbes, Apr. 25, 2014, https://www.forbes.com/sites/perianneboring/2014/04/25/the -death-of-the-death-care-industry-and-eternal-life-online/#70cc291c1c1a.

135   only a handful of states *require* you to use commercial funeral home

services: Josh Slocum and Lee Webster, "Quick Guide to Home Funerals by State," National Home Funeral Alliance (NHFA), https://www.homefuneral alliance.org/state-requirements.html.

Guide: The Tangled Web We Leave

163   A 2018 Bankrate survey showed that 65 percent of Americans save little: Emmie Martin, "65% of Americans Save Little or Nothing—and Half Could End Up Struggling in Retirement," CNBC.com, Mar. 15, 2018, https://www .cnbc.com/2018/03/15/bankrate-65-percent-of-americans-save-little-or-noth ing.html.

165   2016 Intel Security survey . . . forget a password at least once a week: Brad Jones, "Intel Hates Passwords, Even on World Password Day," *Digital Trends*, May 5, 2016, https://www.digitaltrends.com/computing/intel-world -password-day-true-key-app.

183   Social Security: Receiving Survivor Benefits: "Benefits Planner: Survivors—If You Are the Survivor," Social Security Administration, https:// www.ssa.gov/planners/survivors/ifyou.html.

183   Same-sex couples: Social Security Administration, *What Same-Sex Couples Need to Know,* Jan. 2017, https://www.ssa.gov/pubs/EN-05-10014.pdf.

186   one out of four of today's twenty-year-olds will be disabled before retirement: "The Faces and Facts of Disability: Facts," Social Security Administration, https://www.ssa.gov/disabilityfacts/facts.html.

186   The Council for Disability Awareness reports: "Chances of Disability."

187   You may qualify for disability assistance: "Benefits Planner: Disability— How You Qualify," Social Security Administration, https://www.ssa.gov /planners/disability/qualify.html.

187   If you receive Social Security disability benefits: "Benefits Planner: Retirement," Social Security Administration, https://www.ssa.gov/planners/re tire/retirechart.html.

190   The cost of an assisted-living or nursing-home facility: "Costs of Care," Long Term Care, https://longtermcare.acl.gov/costs-how-to-pay/costs-of-care .html.

190   Medicare does not pay for in-home, nonskilled assistance: "Medicare, Medicaid & More," Long Term Care, https://longtermcare.acl.gov/medicare -medicaid-more/index.html.

190   How do you know if you should buy a policy?: "Should You Buy Long-Term Care Insurance, or Invest and 'Self-Insure,'" *The Motley Fool*, June 1, 2018, https://www.fool.com/amp/investing/2018/06/01/should-you-buy-long -term-care-insurance-or-invest.aspx.

192   According to a *British Medical Journal* website article: Karen Feldscher,

"Five Healthy Habits to Live By," *Harvard Gazette*, Apr. 30, 2018, https://news.harvard.edu/gazette/story/2018/04/5-healthy-habits-may-increase-life-expectancy-by-decade-or-more.

192   A 2010 study from Princeton University's Woodrow Wilson School: "Two WWS [Angus Deaton and Daniel Kahneman] Professors Release New Study, 'Income's Influence on Happiness,'" Princeton University, Sept. 6, 2010, http://wws.princeton.edu/news-and-events/news/item/two-wws-profes sors-release-new-study-income%E2%80%99s-influence-happiness.

193   A Harvard Medical School article on longevity: "Tips for a Longer Life," Harvard Health Publishing, Harvard Medical School, https://www.health.harvard.edu/healthbeat/tips-for-a-longer-life.

193   The 2018 *World Happiness Report*: UN Sustainable Development Solutions Network, John F. Helliwell, Richard Layard, and Jeffrey D. Sachs, eds., "Executive Summary," *World Happiness Report 2018* (New York: Sustainable Development Solutions Network, 2018), https://s3.amazonaws.com/hap piness-report/2018/ES-WHR.pdf.

198   AARP advises couples to confirm: George Mannes, "What Happens to a Credit Account When Your Spouse Dies," AARP, Feb. 16, 2018, www.aarp.org/money/credit-loans-debt/info-2018/debt-after-death.html.

200   When it comes to debts: Trisha Sherven, "Debt After Death: 10 Things You Need to Know," Credit.com, Nov. 10, 2016, http://blog.credit.com/2016/11/debt-after-death-10-things-you-need-to-know-162406.

200   Nolo, the first consumer advocacy group to demystify the legal process: Cara O'Neill, "Do I Have to Pay My Late Spouse's Debts If I Live in a Community Property State," Nolo, https://www.nolo.com/legal-encyclopedia/do-i -pay-late-spouses-debts-i-live-community-property-state.html.

204   Take 15 percent of your income and save it: O'Neill, "Do I Have to Pay My Late Spouse's Debts?"

210   common scenarios that should trigger a call to an expert: https://www.americanbar.org/content/dam/aba/migrated/publiced/practical/books/family _legal_guide/chapter_16.authcheckdam.pdf.

210   Concern about federal Estate and Gift Taxes: "Frequently Asked Questions on Estate Taxes," Internal Revenue Service, www.irs.gov/businesses /small-businesses-self-employed/frequently-asked-questions-on-estate-taxes.

212   the national average is over 5 percent of what your estate is worth: "Why Avoid Probate?," Nolo, https://www.nolo.com/legal-encyclopedia/why-avoid -probate-29861.html.

216   Can I handwrite my will?: Edward A. Haman, "Holographic Will: Is a Handwritten Will Valid," LegalZoom, https://www.legalzoom.com/articles /holographic-will-is-a-handwritten-will-valid.

The Overview Effect

255   NASA astronaut Ron Garan: Ron Garan, *The Orbital Perspective: Lessons in Seeing the Big Picture from a Journey of 71 Million Miles* (Oakland, CA: Berrett-Koehler, 2015), 4.

Guide: What Matters Most

291   expressing gratitude improves your mental and emotional well-being: Harvey B. Simon, "Giving Thanks Can Make You Happier," Harvard Health Publishing, Harvard Medical School, https://www.health.harvard.edu/health beat/giving-thanks-can-make-you-happier; Jamie Ducharme, "7 Surprising Health Benefits of Gratitude," *Time*, Nov. 20, 2017, http://time.com/5026174 /health-benefits-of-gratitude.

293   About 1.7 million new cancer cases: "Cancer Facts & Figures 2018," American Cancer Society, https://www.cancer.org/research/cancer-facts-sta tistics/all-cancer-facts-figures/cancer-facts-figures-2018.html.

294   "Cancer patients are more than twice as likely . . . to declare bankruptcy": Tom Murphy, "Cancer Patients Are Twice as Likely to Declare Bankruptcy," *Chicago Tribune*, May 22, 2018, http://www.chicagotribune.com /news/nationworld/ct-cancer-treatment-debt-20180522-story.html.

294   One in four Americans will be disabled during their adult life: "The Faces and Facts of Disability: Facts."

294   About half of all marriages end in divorce: "Marriage & Divorce," American Psychological Association, http://www.apa.org/topics/divorce.

294   After divorce, women's financial standing often declines: Darlena Cunha, "The Divorce Gap," *Atlantic*, Apr. 28, 2016, https://www.theatlantic .com/business/archive/2016/04/the-divorce-gap/480333.

294   Because so many Americans live paycheck-to-paycheck: Martin, "Only 39% of Americans."

294   only 25 percent . . . have three months of expenses saved: Martin, "Only 39% of Americans."

296   After the age of sixty-five, women are almost twice as likely as men to live in poverty: Adam Ellington, Associated Press, "Women More Likely Than Men to Face Poverty during Retirement," PBS NewsHour, July 10, 2016, https://www.pbs.org/newshour/economy/women-more-likely-than-men-to -face-poverty-during-retirement.

296   Women of color are even more likely to live in poverty in their old age: Jasmine Tucker and Caitlin Lowell, "National Snapshot: Poverty Among Women & Families, 2015," National Women's Law Center, Sept. 14, 2016, https://nwlc.org/resources/national-snapshot-poverty-among-women-fami lies-2015.

296 The gender pay gap: Kaitlin Mulhere, "Women Need One More Degree Than Men to Earn the Same Average Salary," *Money*, Feb. 27, 2018, http://time.com/money/5176517/gender-pay-gap-college-degrees; Nikki Graf, Anna Brown, and Eileen Patten, "The Narrowing, but Persistent, Gender Gap in Pay," Pew Research Center, Apr. 9, 2018, http://www.pewresearch.org/fact-tank/2018/04/09/gender-pay-gap-facts.

296 a Caucasian woman receives eighty cents: "Pay Equity & Discrimination," Institute for Women's Policy Research, https://iwpr.org/issue/employment-education-economic-change/pay-equity-discrimination.

296 Women do the majority of the caregiving: "Women and Caregiving: Facts and Figures," Family Caregiver Alliance, Dec. 31, 2003, https://www.caregiver.org/women-and-caregiving-facts-and-figures.

296 with flexible hours to accommodate these commitments: "Mothers, More Than Fathers, Experience Career Interruptions," Pew Research Center, Apr. 3, 2017, http://www.pewresearch.org/fact-tank/2018/04/09/gender-pay-gap-facts/ft_17-03-31_genderpaygap_career.

296 On average, a woman has over $300,000 less: "Women and Caregiving," Family Caregiver Alliance.

Index

About the Author

CHANEL REYNOLDS is the founder of the internationally praised website Get Your Shit Together (getyourshittogether.org), inspiring and motivating millions of people worldwide with the kick in the pants they need to prepare for life's curveballs. She also cofounded GYST, was the founding managing director of Worldchanging, and has used her digital expertise consulting for clients such as Nike, Samsung, Microsoft, and Starbucks. She has been featured by the *New York Times,* NPR, and *CBS This Morning*, and she speaks widely at events. She lives in Seattle and spends her free time cooking, practicing yoga, hiking, and adventuring with her family, often staying up late just because she can.

Find her at chanelreynolds.com